MORE COLLEGE
FAITH

Edited by

RONALD ALAN KNOTT

Worthy Books
Berrien Springs, Michigan

Edited by Ronald Alan Knott

Cover art and book design by:
Dale Chapman, Moxie Design
moxie@wwics.com
Typeset in Galliard 11/13

Copyright © 1997
Ronald Alan Knott
Worthy Books
Bethany Communications
6670 Steeplechase Lane
Berrien Springs, Michigan 49103
616-473-3760

Printed in the United States of America
All Rights Reserved

Wide distribution of this book to students in Seventh-day Adventist secondary schools, colleges and universities has been made possible, in part, by grants from the offices of Education and Youth Ministries of the North American Division of Seventh-day Adventists in Silver Spring, Maryland.

Scriptural personal pronoun references to God have been uniformly capitalized, regardless of the usage in the version cited. Unless otherwise indicated, Scripture references in this book are from the King James Version. Other versions used:

The Amplified Bible
The Bible: A New Translation by James Moffatt (Moffatt)
The Clear Word
The Living Bible
The Message
The Modern Language Bible
New American Standard Bible (NASB)
New International Version (NIV)
New King James Version (NKJV)
New Revised Standard Version (NRSV)
Revised Standard Version (RSV)

ISBN 0-9661838-1-9

CONTENTS

THE FIRST FOREWORD

Are stories as important as our values, beliefs and even theology? A growing number of both secular and religious thought leaders now argue that our personal stories are one of the most crucial elements determining who we are and who we become. Our stories provide a framework, a window, through which we interpret every event and aspect of our lives.

John Bolt, a prominent Christian educator, writes, "Stories give us an identity, a selfhood. We are our stories. . . . One's personal . . . story is crucially determinative of how one thinks."[1] From theologians such as Dr. Richard Rice (a contributor to this book) at La Sierra University who calls for narrative theology, to psychiatrist Dr. Robert Coles at Harvard University, who teaches classes in narrative in such areas as medicine, education, government, law, business and design, we are being implored to pay more attention to stories in order to give meaning to our personal lives.

Nobel Prize winner Elie Wiesel wrote, "God made man because He loves stories."[2] If Wiesel is right, *More College Faith* will make God very happy.

In this book, readers will discover how events, which became stories, influenced many Adventist teachers and leaders. Here we'll find first-rate inspiration and encouragement as we compare our stories with their stories. We each may wonder how the story of our life will turn out. With our faith centered on Jesus Christ, we'll discover that we too will have a productive and service-centered story, whether from our college experience or from our lives after formal education.

More College Faith belongs on the reading table of every Adventist who's ever been to college. And it belongs in the survival kit of every Adventist young adult—right beside the jar of peanut butter, the extra cash and the reminder to call home.

The North American Division Office of Education is pleased to help make possible this book for college, university and academy students in Adventist schools. It is our hope that the stories we each are now creating will be inspired and enriched by these stories told by others.

Richard C. Osborn
Vice President for Education
North American Division of Seventh-day Adventists
Silver Spring, Maryland

---

[1] John Bolt, *The Christian and the Christian Story* (Grand Rapids: Christian Schools International, 1993), pp. 57, 177. Bolt is professor of systematic theology at Calvin Theological Seminary.

[2] Ibid., 158.

THE SECOND FOREWORD

My school journey was not always easy. Throughout my childhood I experienced various traumatizing moments that led to deep feelings of insecurity. Many times, people told me I wasn't "American." Because of my distinctly Latino accent in speech, kids often told me—sometimes violently: "Go back where you came from." This confused me because I was born and raised in the United States.

When I attended school in Mexico for one year, I was told pointedly that I was absolutely not Mexican, because I was "born up there (in the United States)." The shock of not being claimed by either country while each took it for granted that I knew who I was, almost destroyed me. I found that discrimination is not a debate, it is an experience that tears at your very soul.

School was where most of this occurred in my childhood. Whether I was a "chocolate covered raisin," a "burrito," a "nigger," a "taco," a "spic," or a "wet back" in the United States, or a "pocho," a "gringo," a "rico," or a "del otro lado" in Mexico, school hurt. I now know that school can make the longest and deepest impression that stays with us all of our lives.

But this is why Adventist education is so special to me. When I first began at Pacific Union College my grades were at their lowest ever. My cumulative GPA after my freshman year was 1.7. When my advisor asked me, at age 19, why I was getting such low grades, I calmly responded that it was because "I am Mexican." That moment was to change my life forever because it was then that I learned, through Dr. David Taylor, that I could train my brain just like everybody else.

Throughout my experience at PUC and then La Sierra and Loma Linda Universities, I discovered my personal identity in God and life, and also the powerful opportunities available to me to serve the world around me in the name of Christ. Education became the key to empowering my life out of the deep chasm of my experience.

In this book you'll read stories about how God revealed Himself, His will and His love to people during their own times as students in higher education. Most of these stories took place when the writers were part of an Adventist college or university campus. That's where thousands of people—just like you and me— have faced life's challenges and found the Christian premise for meaningful success. As you read their experiences you'll find that God can take any human and build a life that makes the world a better place.

Adventist higher education offers students an incredible opportunity to learn far beyond mere quality information through books. My college experience taught me about life itself. I still remember after graduation services at La Sierra and Loma Linda thinking, "I came here to get a degree and I ended up getting an education." Adventist education didn't simply help me, it saved my life.

José Vincente Rojas
Director of Youth Ministries
North American Division of Seventh-day Adventists
Silver Spring, Maryland

PREFACE

When *College Faith*, the predecessor of this volume, was published in 1995, several people of an editorial mind asked me if there had been any plan or system to the order of the stories as they appeared in the book. It was a fair question. To the casual observer, the organizational plan was far from obvious. It was intended that way. The same is true for this book, except that this time, I'll break down and make an explanation.

From the beginning, I have thought of these books as a written record of a series of old-fashioned Adventist testimony meetings. These valuable spiritual exercises occur so rarely now in institutional Adventism that I felt called to do my part by hosting a series myself in book form. Both *College Faith* and *More College Faith* represent a series of 15 "meetings" (chapters) of ten testimonies each.

In organizing these "meetings," I've managed to resist the powerful editorial temptation to group testimonies for narrative effect. Life, and testimony meetings, don't necessarily order their events into tidy packages that exude literary charm. The Holy Spirit works in ways that, to us, may sometimes seem random or disconnected. He often does so in testimony meetings. So, in this volume, the story about praying for rain is not neatly juxtaposed with the story about praying for sunshine. General Conference President Robert Folkenberg's exciting story of God's answer to prayer during his courtship of Anita is not placed opposite Former General Conference President Neal Wilson's revealing account of how he met his life-long companion Elinor. And Morris Venden's moving tribute to former religion teacher and seminary dean Thomas Blincoe is not matched with Roger Bothwell's story about the same man.

Rather, each meeting has been organized to provide what I believe is a meaningful variety of testimonies covering a wide range of issues faced by any Christian college student in any age: academic struggles, financial crises, satisfying or frustrating personal relationships, opportunities to witness, and, ultimately, the call to follow Jesus.

More College Faith has been, to a great extent, a family project. So I owe a great debt of gratitude to members of my immediate family who have borne extra responsibility and put in long hours in a variety of work to make this book possible. These begin with my darling wife Esther, who has been a constant support, helper, adviser, proofreader and patient spouse during a long and sometimes tedious venture. Esther's parents, Ramnarine and Alice Ramharacksingh gave scores of hours of grandparenting attention to our three-year-old daughter Olivia while I was preoccupied on this project and Esther was engaged in her professional ministry as a pastor at Pioneer Memorial Church. Ram and Alice ran our household during these times and made sure we got satisfying, regular and nutritious meals. Ram brushed up on his computer word processing skills developed during production of *College Faith,* and entered scores of stories on computer for this volume. My own parents, David and Rose Marie Knott, opened their schedule—and their house—to Olivia and me for more than two weeks when I needed to get away for some focused editing time. My sisters-in-law, Mary Knott and Debby Knott, provided data management and editorial help at critical times. And my brother Bill Knott, associate editor of the *Adventist Review,* was a constant source of good counsel on matters of considerable philosophical and editorial complexity.

Others outside my family helped make this a better book. These include Joyce Jones, Lynn Sauls and Deanna Wisbey, who read all or portions of the manuscript and made important suggestions. Dale Chapman of Moxie Design in Walla Walla, Washington, created what I think is an outstanding cover and book design. Dick Osborn and José Rojas of the North American Division offices of Education and Youth Ministries provided initial financial and moral support that made the project feasible.

Finally, and most importantly, I owe everything to the writers of this book. They opened their hearts to share a personal testimony of faith for the benefit of the larger church family. What rich benefits that family will receive when each of us fulfills our obligation to do the same.

Ronald Alan Knott
Berrien Springs, Michigan
November 1997

Come and hear,
all ye that fear God,
and I will declare
what He hath done
for my soul.

Psalm 66:16

Our confession of His faithfulness is Heaven's chosen agency for revealing Christ to the world. . . . That which will be most effectual is the testimony of our own experience. We are witnesses for God as we reveal in ourselves the working of a power that is divine. Every individual has a life distinct from all others, and an experience differing essentially from theirs. God desires that our praise shall ascend to Him, marked by our own individuality. These precious acknowledgments to the praise of the glory of His grace, when supported by a Christ-like life, have an irresistible power that works for the salvation of souls.

Ellen G. White, The Desire of Ages, *p.347*

THE FIRST MEETING

Jim Boyle

Daniel Madrid

Susan M. Fenton Willoughby

Gerald W. Coy

Robert J. Walker

Karen Benn-Marshall

Larry D. Marsh

Thambi Thomas

Sallie Alger

Richard Barron

Come and hear, all ye that fear God,
and I will declare what He hath done for my soul.

Psalm 66:16

SUMMER JOB FIASCO By Jim Boyle

In the spring of my junior year at Southern Missionary College (now Southern Adventist University), my friend Jerry and I decided to get a summer job in the logging camps of Washington state. We'd heard our classmates tell stories of adventure, excitement and big money working in the rugged logging camps of the Northwest. As the school year wound down, I made my plans and started dreaming about earning all my senior-year expenses working as a modern-day Paul Bunyan.

Our excitement was so strong that we ignored the counsel of our residence-hall dean, who cautioned us not to go unless we had job commitments. Neither did we listen to our parents, who wanted us to stay closer to home where summer jobs were always available. The school year ended, and we departed our sheltered campus for the unknown world of adventure.

We caught a ride west with a teacher who was driving to Washington to attend graduate school. It all seemed so perfect as he dropped us off just outside Walla Walla, Washington. We began hitch-hiking across the rugged and beautiful country side, heading toward the Olympic Peninsula where we were sure exciting, well-paying jobs awaited us.

When we arrived in Forks, the last town before entering the wilderness of the logging territory, we were shocked to learn that most jobs in the logging business were found in the larger towns much farther south. Still undaunted and sure that God had something for us, we caught a ride into the logging territory.

For two wearying weeks, we wandered from camp to camp without success and realized what a mistake we'd made. Defeated, we headed home.

Mercifully, God watched over us as we caught ride after ride from state to state. Finally, in Denver, Colorado, our money ran out. We were stranded and realized we needed help. We called our parents and asked them to wire us money for the bus fare home.

What embarrassment and what loss we felt. We had wasted precious time that could've been used in earning money for our senior year. Why hadn't God helped us find the perfect job in Washington? What had gone wrong? Why hadn't our faith and courage been rewarded? With all of those thoughts swirling around in my head, I began to search for the rare remaining summer job. An elder in my home church who owned a business had mercy on me and gave me a job.

A few days later, the youth of my church began planning for an evangelistic meeting. I was asked to coordinate the meeting and to be a speaker. We made arrangements for music and gathered names of people who should be invited.

The meetings were a wonderful blessing to all of us. Many former church members came to the meetings and made renewed commitments to Jesus. One adult was baptized. Two of my friends who were also speakers made commitments to attend college and both became ministers.

What started out as a complete disaster became one of my best summers. I learned, from this painful yet ultimately rewarding experience, that my plans are not always God's plans.

For as the heavens are higher than the earth, so are My ways higher than your ways, and My thoughts than your thoughts. Isaiah 55:9 RSV

Jim Boyle is president of Adventist Health Mid-America in Shawnee Mission, Kansas.

THE COMEBACK *By Daniel Madrid*

I was a freshman at Atlantic Union College and was feeling lonely when I received the phone call. The decision I made that night not only had grave short-term implications but offered me a life-long lesson.

Only three of us from the same academy decided to attend AUC that year. One was my high-school sweetheart. I had no male friends with me except for my married brother, four years older than I. Because of my Spanish surname, the dean had assigned me a Spanish-speaking roommate. Unfortunately, I had lost the ability to speak in my parents' native tongue, and my roommate spoke no English. We didn't say much to each other that semester, but we were cordial. I hadn't made many new friends and my grades were slipping.

This fateful night, I'd been awakened from a deep sleep by a phone call from my girlfriend. She wanted to see me. It was late, our minds were not alert and we made a wrong decision. We planned a rendezvous and met, but an efficient security system soon exposed our misdeeds. We returned to our dorms with our heads bowed in shame.

I tried to deny the gravity of the situation. I reasoned that our infraction wasn't really so terrible. It was all quite innocent. The next day, the dean of students invited me to his office. He told me that I would receive the maximum penalty for our infraction. I would not be allowed to return to the college the next semester. I was aghast. I told my older brother who, in turn, contacted other individuals of influence. We even contacted a personal friend of the dean to appeal for leniency, but to no avail. I had to face the consequences alone.

"It's not fair," I screamed to myself. "I'm not a bad person. I'm a decent guy. I follow the rules, except for this one time. It was a mistake. I'm really sorry. What am I going to tell my parents?" I prayed earnestly that if it was God's will, He'd rescue me.

The next semester was not a happy one. I attended a state college and kept my social life to a minimum. I had failed—failed my parents, my friends, my siblings. I was humbled.

However, through prayer and soul searching, there started to grow in me a desire to prove myself worthy and not wallow in my guilt or self-pity. I determined not to be defeated. The Lord lifted my burden of misery and gave me the confidence to make something of myself.

I served my time and returned to Atlantic Union College in the summer, rededicated. The following school year, I was elected to the Student Association and then re-elected. I worked closely with the dean of students and the dean of men as a resident assistant. I received academic honors.

Three years later at graduation, the dean of men drew me aside and told me of his pride in seeing the metamorphosis of a struggling freshman into an ambitious and Christ-filled senior.

No discipline seems pleasant at the time, but painful. Later on, however, it produces a harvest of righteousness and peace for those who have been trained by it. Hebrews 12:11 NIV

Daniel Madrid is assistant professor of business administration and economics at Pacific Union College in Angwin, California.

A BREEZE FOR A BELIEVER *By Susan M. Fenton Willoughby*

The school year had ended and summer had just begun. My husband and I, with our one-year-old son, were living in married student housing at Atlantic Union College. We were both students; so when our semester grades arrived in one envelope addressed to both of us, I opened it, although he was not at home.

We'd had the same teacher for one course, so we had often reviewed for examinations together and compared grades, which were usually about the same. For two working people with a young child, B's were good grades. This time, however, the final grade for the course showed his as a B- and mine as a C+. A C+ for me meant no Dean's List, and probably no graduate-school admissions. I knew it had to be a mistake.

I quickly met with the teacher and pointed out the mistake. He was very understanding of my concern, but showed me that there was a zero entered in his grade book for a particular test on which I was sure I had made 100 percent. I remembered my grade very well, I told him, because my husband had gotten 94 percent (still an A) on that same test.

"If you can produce the examination with that grade on it," he told me, "I will change the grade. However," he continued, "I've never had to do that in all my years of teaching."

The ball was now in my court. And believe it or not, I found every exam for that course *except* the one I needed to find. Our apartment was so small that everything had to be well organized and kept in its place, so finding that test shouldn't have been a problem. After looking everywhere, I called on my babysitter for help. We prayed as we searched but found no missing exam.

Now I was desperate. The grade was no longer important. My reputation for honesty was at stake. We stopped searching, knelt and prayed earnestly for help. Then we went through all my class papers again very carefully, and still found nothing.

As we knelt to pray a second time, a breeze rushed through an open window, scattering my loose papers all over the room. In a moment I'll never forget, I saw that the papers had separated just enough to reveal that my missing exam and my husband's exam had adhered so closely together that they seemed as one.

In my distress I called upon the Lord; . . . from His temple He heard my voice, and my cry to Him reached His ears. Psalm 18:6 RSV

Susan M. Fenton Willoughby is professor of sociology and social work at Atlantic Union College in South Lancaster, Massachusetts.

FRATERNAL RESPECT *By Gerald W. Coy*

D uring my graduate work at the University of Northern Iowa, the Lord gave me many opportunities to let my light shine gently.

One of these occurred during the final semester of my residency on campus. One Friday afternoon, I found a letter in my campus mailbox from my department chair, nominating me to become a member of *Epsilon Pi Tau,* the honorary professional fraternity for education in technology. Several of my fellow graduate students were among those nominated, along with some teachers.

The letter explained all the procedures one needed to follow to be inducted into this national organization. Nominees could participate in the induction ceremony either at the national convention or at a formally designated meeting of a regional chapter. I soon learned that either opportunity occurred only once a year, and always on Saturday.

In my reply to the chair, I wrote that I was honored to be considered for induction into such a fraternity, but due to my religious beliefs about Sabbath observance, I would be unable to accept his invitation.

Following the induction ceremony for other candidates that year, several asked me why I had been overlooked. I explained that it was my choice not to participate in the ceremony and gave my reasons.

One afternoon, about four months later, I was asked to meet with the department chair. Present with him were the officers of the regional chapter of *Epsilon Pi Tau.* They informed me that they respected my religious beliefs and were concerned that I wouldn't be able to join them. Therefore, they had requested special permission from the national office to have a special induction service, not on Sabbath, so I could be part of their fraternity.

Let your light so shine before men, that they may see your good works, and glorify your Father which is in heaven. Matthew 5:16

Gerald W. Coy is associate dean of the College of Technology at Andrews University in Berrien Springs, Michigan.

THE CATCH *By Robert J. Walker*

M y normal position was left field. But on this day the coach, with some grumbling from me, decided to put me in right field where nothing ever happened.

As a freshman on a baseball scholarship at East Mississippi Junior College, my life-long dream of becoming a major leaguer was only a few years away. But there was a catch. The summer before, I had become a member of the Seventh-day Adventist Church.

As the umpire yelled, "Play ball!" a little voice said to me, "It's 11 a.m. and it's the Sabbath. You should be in church."

I was startled. I said to myself, "You shouldn't be thinking like that. Concentrate on the game!"

By the top of the seventh inning, we were winning by two runs. There were two outs and the bases were loaded. A routine pop fly floated directly my way in right field.

"I got it! I got It! I got it!" I yelled at the top of my lungs. And then, incredibly, unbelievably, the unthinkable happened.

As I frantically searched the ground for the dropped ball, runners cleared the bases. The batter who hit the pop fly that was catchable by any little leaguer was now standing on third base with a big, happy grin on his face.

Moments later, with me in the dugout and a replacement in right field, the coach, with a few choice curses, demanded that I turn in my uniform immediately and kicked me off the team.

The hurt and embarrassment was indescribable, and being the only black person on the team didn't help either. How could I go back home and tell everyone I got kicked off the baseball team.

The team lost both games that day and with it any chance to be in the junior college state tournament. But I felt that I had lost much more. Baseball was more to me than just a childhood dream. It was my *life*.

For the remainder of the weekend I stayed in my dorm room and cried like a baby.

"Why, God? Why? I don't understand. Baseball is what brought me to college. Baseball is what took me away from my poor home life. Why Lord? Why did You allow me to miss that simple catch?"

In desperation, I opened my Bible to find comfort. The first chapter I came to was Exodus 20. I read the first three verses and found my answer. Instantly I realized I had made baseball my god. I was using God only to make me a better baseball player.

A week later, the coach asked me to return to the team, but my heart was no longer in it. Something else was now number one in my life.

Although I still remember the event as if it were only yesterday, I thank God for the miracle that happened to me in right field as a college freshman 20 years ago. Even today, I still enjoy baseball. But now it's just a game.

And God spake all these words, saying, I am the Lord thy God, which have brought thee out of the land of Egypt, out of the house of bondage. Thou shalt have no other gods before Me. Exodus 20:1-3

Robert J. Walker is associate professor of education at Oakwood College in Huntsville, Alabama.

THE TOUGH PROFESSOR
AND THE EASIER WAY *By Karen Benn-Marshall*

As my sophomore year approached, and general chemistry loomed, I had to make a decision. There were two chemistry professors from whom I could take the course. Both were considered difficult, but one more so than the other. I planned to take the course from the one with the easier reputation. By happenstance, I told my mother about my dilemma and she suggested that I make it a matter of prayer.

Prayer? I thought. How could the Lord direct me about which professor I should choose? My mother has always been a woman of great faith and prayer, so I agreed. We prayed together, as we often did, asking for God's guidance.

But I was still unsure how, and even if, God would reveal Himself to me. After prayer, I got up to go. But Mom held me back. She held out two slips of paper. Each slip had the name of one chemistry professor on it. She asked me to select one. I was a bit surprised and doubtful about this exercise, but I did as she asked.

I opened the slip of paper and found I had selected the more difficult professor, and the one whom I was sure the Lord was leading me not to choose. Is this really how God rewarded faith? I wondered. My mother responded as though she could read my mind. "God will not fail you if you just trust Him," she said.

Trust Him? How could I trust Him? I thought. Everyone I know who has had this professor has complained. The majority of the class fails. What should I do?

After a struggle, I decided that I would believe that the Lord had worked through my mother's humble efforts to help me choose. I enrolled in the course with the tough professor. At the end of the first quarter, my grade was an A. I couldn't believe it. I was happy with my grade but was unhappy and impatient with my progress. So, against my mother's wishes and my better judgment, I enrolled in the other professor's chemistry course. I rationalized that this was reasonable. After all, I had only asked God for advice for the first quarter.

With my new professor, I struggled through that second quarter as I had never struggled before. At the end, my grade was a C and I was unhappy with both my grade and my progress. *Why Lord?* I asked. *You know I tried my best.*

But of course I knew the answer to that question. I had asked God to intervene in my life and He had. He had shown me the way to go and I followed, for awhile. But then I thought I knew best. Against His prompting I went my own way.

I had to learn the hard way what it really means to trust the Lord completely.

Trust in the Lord with all thine heart; and lean not unto thine own understanding. Proverbs 3:5

Karen Benn-Marshall is assistant professor of allied health at Oakwood College in Huntsville, Alabama.

THE DESIRES OF YOUR HEART *by Larry D. Marsh*

"Why don't we pray for the desires of our heart?" asked my forever-the-optimist wife. It was May again. In a few weeks, I would be moving my family north from our comfortable academy home to Andrews University, where I could begin my third summer of graduate school.

But moving my family for the summer was a major problem. Where would we live? Our first summer we had sub-rented a large home with another family of six. Less than ideal. The second summer we rented a small apartment. But here we were, a couple of weeks from registration and still we had no housing.

"Look at this article I just read," my wife continued. "It says we should pray, specifically asking God for even our heart's desires." Together we reread the familiar text in Psalm 37, and then, with a note pad in hand, answered the question, "If we could handpick our summer home, what would we want?" In a short time we made our list of five desires: 1) affordable; 2) rural location; 3) a garden; 4) a freezer; 5) a musical keyboard instrument.

So we prayed. Though discouraged and almost desperate about our lack of housing, we still continued to pray. Each time we would remind the Lord, "If it is pleasing to You, it would sure be great if our home could also include. . . ."

Four days before summer school registration, the new manager of one our academy industries casually mentioned to me how he would certainly like his family to spend the summer with him. However, they owned a newly built home near Andrews University that they hadn't been able to sell. So his family had remained behind, because they were uncomfortable leaving the house vacant since it was somewhat isolated out in the country.

So here is how the Lord answered our prayer: 1) we switched homes for the summer, with no additional rent for us; 2) the house was off the road, surrounded by trees with no neighbors in sight; 3) the garden was already planted, with fruit trees, a strawberry bed and even a greenhouse; 4) the freezer, 3/4 empty, was available for our use; and 5) we could enjoy the beautiful console organ that came with the house.

Delight thyself also in the Lord; and He shall give thee the desires of thine heart. Psalm 37:4

Larry D. Marsh is principal of Upper Columbia Academy in Spangle, Washington.

HE KNOWS THE PATH YOU MUST TAKE *By Thambi Thomas*

While I was out of college for a few months recuperating from a near fatal attack of appendicitis, war broke out between India and Pakistan. The Indian government was recruiting pilots for the Indian Air Force as non-commissioned officers, offering an attractive salary and benefit package.

I had been fascinated with airplanes as a child and still had a longing to fly. Now the timing seemed perfect. The opportunity was before me.

Much against my father's will, and with reluctant acceptance from others in my family, I applied for a place in the Air Force program. Within days, I was asked to go for my initial screening and testing over a period of three days. The other young men and I in the screening were treated as if we were already officers in the Air Force, and I loved it. About a third of us were selected to go on to the next round of testing. My excitement started to mount, tempered only by my father's disappointment about the direction in which I was headed.

As a Seventh-day Adventist minister of the gospel, my father had been instrumental in bringing hundreds to Jesus through baptism. He had encouraged numerous individuals to be true to the Sabbath. Now his own son was going to join the Air Force; would more than likely violate the Sabbath and could possibly walk away from the church and the faith of his upbringing.

Mrs. McHenry, a missionary in India at that time, heard about my plans to become a pilot. She started talking to me about going back to Spicer College to complete my studies while I waited for the results of my interviews with the Air Force. I knew the agony and the anguish my decision was causing my father and how much happier everyone would be if I went to Spicer. Yet, I felt that God had opened the door for me to become a pilot because He hadn't placed any obstacles in my way. (Oh! I had so much to learn about the way God leads and how to understand His will.) But college had already begun, and I hadn't registered. I was sure the door to college was closed.

Soon, an official-looking piece of mail arrived. My heart raced as I wondered what the news might be. The message was very plain and brief. I had been accepted into the non-commissioned officers training program and had to report to the training station in three weeks.

Though my friends were excited for me, there was anything but rejoicing at home. But the missionary lady, Mrs. McHenry, didn't give up. She offered to call the college president and ask if I could enroll that term as a late registrant.

Now I really had a decision to make. Do I go on to college and make my parents and church happy? Or do I go ahead and do what I want to do, even if it means displeasing my family and my church and, perhaps, even my God? It wasn't an easy choice. The challenge, the excitement—the temptation—of the military opportunity was practically irresistible.

After much prayer and soul searching, I went to Mrs. McHenry and said, "Would you call the college president to see if they will take me?" She did, they did, and I went.

I believe God used people around me to let me understand His will for my life. And I have not regretted my decision to this day.

I am the Lord your God, Who teaches you what is best for you, Who directs you in the way you should go. Isaiah 48:17 NIV

Thambi Thomas is principal of San Gabriel Academy in San Gabriel, California.

LESSON FROM THE PICKLE FACTORY By Sallie Alger

The summer after I graduated from Adelphian Academy, I searched and searched for a good paying job to earn enough tuition money to attend Andrews University the next fall. In the rural area where I lived, on the east side of Michigan, there were very few choices. One could detassle corn, babysit, work in the local grocery store, or do farm work. Having grown up on a farm, I'd had my fill of weeding, picking apples and, worst of all, helping to raise five acres of cucumbers for the local Vlassic Pickle Factory. Those who haven't had the privilege probably don't realize how much hot, back-breaking, prickly work is involved in raising just the "right-size" cucumbers for pickles.

Life being what it is, instead of raising pickles on a farm, I ended up getting a job at the Vlassic Pickle Factory. I worked on the assembly line—packing tiny cucumbers into jars as they passed by on conveyor belts.

I've always had a struggle with motion sickness. Watching those jars go round and round on the line and enduring the strong smell of vinegar from the canning process quickly became almost more than I could take. It wasn't difficult to lapse into thoughts about quitting. I considered it often. But soon I discovered that whenever I focused my attention on my goal and the money I was earning and told myself that I was going to stick with this job, the motion sickness lessened. What's more, I actually began to enjoy going to work each day and getting to know my fellow workers. One finds a lot of "characters" in assembly-line work. After we all shared backgrounds and experiences, we became friends. I was able to do some witnessing and I developed an appreciation for what some people go through to support their families.

As a young person, the experience taught me to focus on a goal, to develop patience, and that sometimes the opportunity to witness comes when we least expect it. My determination to stick with the job, and God's leading while I was there, ultimately enabled me to attend Andrews where I prepared myself for never *having* to work in a pickle factory ever again.

Whatsoever thy hand findeth to do, do it with thy might. Ecclesiastes 9:10

Sallie Alger is head of technical services of the James White Library at Andrews University in Berrien Springs, Michigan.

THE MONEY IN THE TOP DRESSER DRAWER *By Richard Barron*

One day, as was usual during my senior year in college, I went home after my morning classes to enjoy lunch with my wife and two children. As we ate, I asked, "What are we having for supper tonight?"

She replied, "This lunch we're eating is the last food we have in the house."

"That's no problem," I told her. "After my afternoon classes, I'll take you to market."

She paused a bit and then said, "It's not a problem of having no food, it's having no money."

"No," I assured her, "that's not a problem. We'll simply use the money in the top dresser drawer."

She looked at me as if I had lost my mind. "That's tithe. That's the Lord's money!" she exclaimed.

Well, of course I knew that. But I saw no problem using it now. My children needed to eat. I had Scripture on my side, and I quoted: "'. . . If any provide not for his own, especially for those of his own house, he hath denied the faith, and is worse than an infidel' 2 Timothy 5:8."

So, in between bites, I told my wife matter-of-factly that I was not an infidel, and that we would use the tithe money to purchase food for the family.

"Infidel or not, we will not spend the Lord's money!" she declared.

We had, as they say, a few words. I vigorously defended my position. She, with equal vigor, insisted that even though, as the mother of these children, she was more concerned about their health than anyone, she nevertheless was determined that we would be obedient to God in this matter. "God's tithe comes first, before any other considerations." she maintained.

So, seated at the table, eating my very basic lunch, I finally agreed with my wife that we would never use His tithes for our personal needs. That afternoon I decided to put my trust in Lord and to let Him care for us. Then I bowed my head and apologized to Him for having entertained the thought of using that which was holy unto Him.

As we resumed our meager meal, someone knocked on our door. I opened it to find a fellow student, a close friend of ours. "Hello," he said, "I stopped by on my way to market. I have to shop for my family. Why don't you come along?"

"Thank you very much for being so thoughtful, but much as I need to go, this is a bad time, well, uh, we're a little short on money."

I'll never forget his next words.

"That's why I've come by. I've got some extra money and you all are welcome to use what you need to buy groceries."

Praise the Lord!

Bring ye all the tithes into the storehouse, . . . and prove me now herewith, saith the Lord of hosts, if I will not open you the windows of heaven, and pour you out a blessing. Malachi 3:10

Richard Barron is associate director of the youth department at the General Conference of Seventh-day Adventists in Silver Spring, Maryland.

THE SECOND MEETING

Gordon Bietz

Elly Economou

James D. Chase

Robert Kyte

Peg Bennett

Karl Konrad

H. Roger Bothwell

Sheila E. Clark

Dave Village

Henry Zuill

Come and hear, all ye that fear God,
and I will declare what He hath done for my soul.

Psalm 66:16

CONFRONTATION WITH THE LAW *By Gordon Bietz*

It was 1967, and the Hippie movement and the war in Vietnam were in full swing. I was taking a class on the youth culture at Claremont School of Theology and writing a paper on the Hippie movement. Aside from researching magazine articles and reading books on the moral development of young people, I determined to do some primary research. I took a small tape recorder and hit the streets in Hollywood. I interviewed the publisher of a counter-culture Hippie newspaper and others who would submit to my questions.

One Sunday I heard that a "love-in" would take place at a park near my home. A "love-in" was like a "sit-in," except the objective was simply to experience the warm vibrations of happiness typically induced by some chemical substance. It was a beautiful day in southern California, and it appeared the "love-in" would be a great success. The Hells Angels were there to police the place, and undercover narcotics agents were there to police the Hells Angels and to follow the sweet, pungent smell of marijuana to some arrests. Buddhists were there meditating, musicians were seeking an audience, and, generally a rather broad selection of counter-culture Hippies were doing their own thing.

I wanted to do some interviews with my tape recorder but was too timid to accomplish much. As the time passed and the afternoon sun lowered its rays, I noted a disturbance in one area of the park. My curiosity piqued, I walked toward the disturbance and found a large gathering of police with

Hippies seated and standing in a long line across an open field. A confrontation was building. Apparently, the police had been ordered to clear the park, and the Hippies were not inclined to leave. A lot of shouting, sirens and general confusion followed.

This was a new experience to me. I was a suburban kid and my only experience with police was my parents telling me to go to the police anytime I was in trouble. They were my friends, and I was a "reporter." I walked past the line of Hippies to where the police were, turned on my tape recorder and stood by a tree waiting to watch the action. It never occurred to me that I would be seen as the enemy. I didn't have really long hair, tattoos or beads, but I was hardly dressed in a suit and, as far as the police were concerned, I was a rather arrogant, insubordinate Hippie who had no respect for the authority of the police.

The next thing I knew, a very large policeman shoved his stick into my ribs and in a very unfriendly voice he said, "Get out of here!" Before I caught on to what was happening and before I could move or tell him that I would be happy to leave, another policeman next to him cracked me on the side of the head with his billy club. It sounded like a bat hitting a pipe inside my head. I heard a girl scream and suddenly realized she was screaming for me. My knees buckled ever so slightly and I mumbled something about my car being close by, and I started a wobbly walk that direction. Apparently, the police were satisfied and they didn't pursue me. Others weren't so lucky and were incarcerated in the waiting police cars.

The moral of my story? Ignorance is not bliss and appearances are more important than you think.

A man who strays from the path of understanding comes to rest in the company of the dead. Proverbs 21:16 NIV

Gordon Bietz is president of Southern Adventist University in Collegedale, Tennessee.

JOY IN BLUE AND WHITE By Elly Economou

When I enrolled at Pacific Union College, I began to live my dream. College had started for me in my homeland of Greece, but for years, I'd been yearning to continue my education at an Adventist school. My every attempt had been blocked by my beloved but agnostic father. For years, he had exercised all his considerable influence to keep my mother and me from affiliation with any religious environment.

Father's tragic death left me deeply grieved, but free to pursue my dream. Now I could attend a Christian school in my adoptive country of America. But dreams fulfilled are often accompanied by pain. I mourned my father, and I missed my homeland, but most of all I missed my dear mother who had been a constant source of inspiration and support all along the difficult road we had walked together.

Now I had to depend on her letters, and wondrous was the strength of her cheerfulness and her power of endurance as letter followed letter, twice each week, all those long months of separation. In each letter of reply, I bubbled with exhilaration over my college life, my wonderful teachers, my classmates and my dormitory room at Andre Hall #300, the only private room on the whole campus. I needed that room, because I was studying long and hard to complete a triple major to improve my job prospects after graduation. I needed a good job so I could invite Mother to America so I could live happily reunited with her as God would guide. After turbulent years of dissent, rejection, hatred and persecution, it seemed that life was smiling on Mother and me at last.

Then my dream world collapsed. Mother's letters stopped coming. I feared the worst. She would never have left me in limbo like this even if she were seriously ill. She would've asked someone to contact me.

Day after day, I waited at my mail box while the monitor distributed the mail. I longed to see the familiar blue and white envelope. Day after day, I returned to my room with empty hands, a heavy heart and tearful eyes seeking comfort in prayer.

By the third week without a letter, I was sleeping little and eating less. My studies suffered, too, because I had lost my purpose. If Mother was gone, my whole reason for college was gone too.

Shortly before the week of finals, Elder N. R. Dower came to campus as speaker for the Week of Spiritual Emphasis. I went to see this saintly man at his study and tearfully poured out my fear that Mother was no longer alive. Because of where she was living after Father's death, I had no way to find out, not even by telephone.

Elder Dower then prayed the most simple, sincere, heart-warming prayer I'd ever heard. I returned to the dormitory and looked once again in my mailbox. Eight or nine familiar blue and white envelopes were piled there waiting for me. I clutched them to my heart as I raced up the three flights of stairs to my room where I savored every word Mother had written. Later, I learned that the postal workers in Greece had been on strike for a whole month.

My finals were successful. I graduated with honors. And a few months later Mother joined me at my new post at Andrews University.

More College Faith

He heals the brokenhearted, and binds up their wounds. Psalm 147:3 RSV

Elly Economou is professor of religion and biblical languages at Andrews University in Berrien Springs, Michigan.

DO CORVAIRS TALK? *By James D. Chase*

Absalom's donkey talked. The serpent in the Tree talked. But do Chevy Corvairs talk?

I met one that did. Or so it seemed.

During the summer of 1967, I worked as Boys' Division Leader at Pinecrest Camp to earn a college scholarship. One day I asked our Camp Director, Charles Edwards, "May I borrow your Chevy Corvair to pick up a staff member in Placerville?"

"Why certainly, Jim," he said. "But I hope you don't mind driving a car with a little spirit."

The next morning, with a prayer for protection on my lips, I pulled out onto Highway 50. All was serene as I whizzed past tall Ponderosa pines. Passing Lover's Leap, Horsetail Falls and Mount Ralston, I quietly expressed my gratitude to God for the gift of life.

Suddenly, the serene turned surreal. The car's horn started beeping—all by itself. Or had it? Had I accidentally bumped the sensitive horn area on the steering wheel?

A mile later, the horn beeped again. Could the sound actually be coming from another car? None were in sight. I decided to consciously keep my fingers away from the horn area of the steering wheel. Suddenly, the borrowed Corvair let out another strident "BEEEEEP!"

"This is strange," I thought to myself.

I whizzed by another mile of Ponderosa pines. No beeping. Then suddenly, unexpectedly, one more very loud, insistent "BEEEEEEEEEEP!" And with it came an incredulous thought: "I wonder . . . could it be . . . is it possible that an Invisible Intelligence is trying to get my attention?"

"God," I prayed, "this is too strange. Are You, indeed, trying to say something to me? If this horn beeps one more time . . . I don't know why—but I'll pull off to the side of the road."

Nothing happened. For the next three miles, all was quiet. I began wondering if all this was the product of an overactive imagination.

Then, as the narrow mountain road approached a totally blind curve, I was jolted by another very loud, intense burst of sound. "BEEEEEEEEEEEEEEP!" Immediately, I swerved off the pavement onto the gravel. At that precise instant, two cars dashed from behind the blind corner, and one of them, a sports car, sped toward me in my lane. I felt the Corvair rock to the right from the compressed wind as the sports car whizzed past—missing a head-on collision with me by a fraction of a second.

Skidding to a stop, I bowed my head and most sincerely thanked God for His incredible personal care. Humbly, I rededicated my life to His service.

The angel of the Lord encampeth round about them that fear Him, and delivereth them. Psalm 34:7

James D. Chase is professor of communication at Pacific Union College in Angwin, California.

MY BROTHER'S KEEPER *By Robert Kyte*

I graduated from a small day academy in Canada, in a class of only six students. When I arrived at Walla Walla College, I found an amazing collection of people—people with widely diverse views of life, religion and freedom.

During college, many young people engage in at least a little unhealthy experimentation. Often, they grow and mature and get their lives moving in a positive direction. And, sometimes, they don't.

Steve* lived on my floor in the dorm, where I was a resident assistant. In fact, we were both business majors and took some classes together. While we probably had other things in common, our paths didn't cross regularly. About the only times I saw him were in class or when I made the nightly room check on my floor.

Steve seemed like a fellow who was enjoying life—maybe too much. He hung around with a group that was "on the edge" of campus life. They attended classes, but on weekends they generally vanished.

I didn't think much about Steve. After all, I had work, classes and a hundred other distractions. I was too busy to be tied up in the lives of each of the fellows who lived on my floor. Beyond a groggy "Good morning" on the way to the shower, or a quick "Hello" at room check, Steve was just another college student who was doing his own thing—whatever that was.

One morning, well before six o'clock, a loud pounding on my door rudely jarred me awake. The events of the next few hours are still etched in my memory.

Steve was lying on the shower floor. There was blood.

Steve was dead.

The police arrived first, then the coroner. Answers given to their many questions left little doubt as to the cause of death. How Steve died was really of less significance than why he died at all. He was barely 20 years old. His whole life was ahead of him. But like many others, he was experimenting with his new freedoms and he paid a price that none of his friends would've foreseen in their worst nightmares.

Steve hadn't seemed that much different than me. Our paths at college had started very close together. What had led him to such a tragic end?

Could I have done anything to prevent it from happening? Should I really have been "my brother's keeper?" Can we really be expected to care for those who should know better?

In John 10:25-37, a lawyer questioned Jesus on His commandment to "Love your neighbor as yourself." No doubt the lawyer thought it clever to ask: "Who is my neighbor?"

So Jesus told the story of the good Samaritan and concluded with a question of his own. "Which . . . was a neighbor to the man who fell into the hands of robbers?"

The answer was obvious. "The one who had mercy on him," the expert in law replied.

And Jesus told him, "Go and do likewise."

*name has been changed

Let each of you look not only to his own interests, but also to the interests of others. Philippians 2:4 RSV

Robert Kyte is president of Pacific Press Publishing Association in Nampa, Idaho.

GOD'S TEST SCORE By Peg Bennett

Though not a Seventh-day Adventist, I quickly adapted to the routine and lifestyle of mid-fifties Southern Missionary College (now Southern Adventist University). And, more surprisingly still, I enjoyed it. *All* of it; not only the social activities, but vespers, chapels, and Weeks of Prayer, too. During that semester I grew to love the Lord and His message, and at the end of the semester, I was baptized as a Seventh-day Adventist.

Because I was a chemistry major, I needed to take General Physics during the summer session—*eight* semester hours of it. I registered with fear and trembling, since my experience with high-school physics assured me that this was *not* my best subject. With classes from 7 a.m. to noon, work all afternoon, and study all evening, little time was left to assimilate each day's information. We were moving fast and I was lost. The light just was not coming on. Day by day, the confusion intensified. As if I didn't know already, the quizzes left no doubt that I definitely was not getting it, and a major exam was approaching.

Money was scarce, too. I couldn't afford to take this class again. *I had to pass.* But passing this exam would take nothing less than a miracle.

My life and experience the previous year had impressed me that God could work wonders. Just my presence at Southern had evidenced that. So I studied harder. Still, I wasn't understanding the concepts. In my desperation, I recalled a text presented in one of the spiritual meetings I'd attended. My weak faith laid hold of that promise with a death-like grip.

The day of the exam, I walked into the classroom so filled with fear that I couldn't recall a single formula, much less its application. Breathing a prayer, I began to read the exam. Unexplainably, formulas began to pop into my mind. For the first time since I began the course, I could see clearly the solution to each problem and I finished the test filled with amazement.

The Lord scored a very high grade on that test, for it's certain I couldn't have done it. Perhaps God knew I needed an incontrovertible answer to that prayer to strengthen my fledgling faith; I can't be sure of His reasons. But I do know that He stayed with me the rest of the way through that course. Even today, as I reflect on that experience, I'm astonished at the way God answered a weak, new Christian's prayer. Best of all, He's *still* answering.

If any of you lack wisdom, let him ask of God, that giveth to all men liberally, and upbraideth not; and it shall be given him. James 1:5

Peg Bennett is director of libraries at Southern Adventist University in Collegedale, Tennessee.

UNDRAMATICALLY DRAMATIC *By Karl Konrad*

The Friday evening academy vesper service was inspiring. I listened carefully. One of my classmates shared his conversion story. God had certainly turned his life around, and I was glad for what he let the Holy Spirit accomplish in his life.

I left the meeting with a wistful feeling. It was the same feeling I had whenever I listened to someone speak about a dramatic religious experience. My spiritual life seemed so ordinary: no bright lights, no thunder, no trumpets, no loud voice, no hand on my shoulder to turn me around.

Why doesn't God do something exciting with me and for me? I wondered. The spiritual experiences of others were the exciting ones. Mine were most unremarkable, even boring. In a way, I felt cheated because all I ever got were quiet impressions.

I enrolled as a freshman at Emmanuel Missionary College (now Andrews University) intending to major in engineering. During the Fall Week of

Spiritual Emphasis, I received one of those quiet impressions which became more insistent as the week progressed. In analyzing my discomfort, I realized that God and I had unfinished business. I wrote some necessary letters to right some unresolved wrongs. While this exercise was helpful and cheering, it didn't remove my uneasiness.

I examined my plans for the future. I realized, reluctantly, that for me, engineering would be a selfish choice. God might have other plans, if I was willing to listen. I wrestled with the idea of becoming a minister, but that didn't bring relief either. It would be years later, in graduate school, that I'd understand how easy it is to misinterpret God's call to surrender as a call to the ministry.

I found peace of mind when I committed myself to becoming a science teacher and majoring in chemistry. Wouldn't all of this have been much simpler if only God had used a more dramatic method of communication with me? If Paul got bright lights, a voice and a miracle—why not me?

During my senior year, my major professors encouraged me to consider graduate school. I applied, was accepted and was offered a much-needed teaching assistantship. That summer, my fiancee and I were married and shortly thereafter I began my graduate program.

The assurance that God was leading in my life grew even though the communication was on the quiet side. Eventually, my thesis research was completed and I began teaching at Southwestern Adventist University. Over the years, I've come to see that while God communicated with me in ordinary ways, the results in my life have been dramatic. I married the woman of my dreams and have a wonderful family. I was enabled to achieve more in my career than I thought possible. And now He gives me the privilege of working with, and influencing, bright and earnest young people who, like I was, are listening for His voice.

And behold, the Lord passed by, and a great and strong wind rent the mountains, and broke in pieces the rocks before the Lord, but the Lord was not in the wind; and after the wind an earthquake, but the Lord was not in the earthquake; and after the earthquake a fire, but the Lord was not in the fire; and after the fire a still small voice. 1 Kings 19:11,12 RSV

Karl Konrad is professor of chemistry at Southwestern Adventist University in Keene, Texas.

JESUS AND THE STUPID QUESTION *By H. Roger Bothwell*

When we saw his hand go up, we groaned inside, wondering what inane question he would ask this time.

It was a seminary class in Christology taught by Dr. Thomas Blincoe. Several of us looked forward to Dr. Blincoe's class as the brightest spot in our education and we were covetous of each minute. On more than one occasion I left class in tears, with my heart bursting with a love for Jesus I'd never known before. Others in the class were affected deeply in the same way.

As a group, we were regularly annoyed by one student who somehow always managed to interrupt with what we thought was stupidity.

On this day his question was right on par. Even the Christlike Dr. Blincoe was disturbed by the insipid question and responded: "I'm sorry. I don't have time for that now."

Several of us nodded with approval, eager to have the lecture continue. We all thought Dr. Blincoe had done the right thing. Everyone but Dr. Blincoe.

At the start of the next class period, right after the prayer, Dr. Blincoe turned to the young man whose question he had brushed off and said, "Last class period, you asked a question that was very important to you. I was rude and didn't answer. Because I was rude in front of the entire class I now apologize to you in front of the entire class. What was your question, please?"

I was stunned. I was totally overwhelmed. No longer did I see a teacher standing in front of a class teaching us about Jesus. I saw Jesus. That one simple act of kindness and humility taught me more about Christlikeness than any other experience during my stay at the seminary.

Thank you, Dr. Blincoe.

Who is wise and understanding among you? Let him show it by his good life, by deeds done in the humility that comes from wisdom. James 3:13 NIV

H. Roger Bothwell is associate professor of education at Atlantic Union College in South Lancaster, Massachusetts.

SAYING GRACE By Sheila E. Clark

"Welcome. I'm so glad you could come. Are these your parents? How do you do Mr. Clark, Mrs. Clark. It's good to meet you. Please let me know if I can do anything for you. Your places are over here with Professor and Mrs. Brundin."

Julie, who had been my classmate for the past two years, glowed in her evening gown. "Oh, Sheila, would you mind saying grace, something inclusive, uh, something that won't offend Jews or feminists. You know me."

I thought I knew Julie. Strong feminist? Yes. The type that would ask me to say grace at our graduation dinner? No way.

"I'll think of something. I won't say Dear Jesus or Our Father," I promised.

I remembered eating lunch in the student lounge. I'd bow my head silently in the middle of the conversation. During my second year, a classmate smiled when I finished. "You say grace before every meal. My grandmother used to do that."

"I'm thankful," I remarked as I munched a sandwich, and then we discussed an upcoming assignment.

One time, a group planned to relax in the Power Plant, the graduate student hangout. "Please come with us," they invited. I hesitated. "You don't have to drink or anything. Just come and be with us." I went. Our orders were five beers and one Sprite.

Then there was my adviser who carefully helped me select courses that would help me in a small, Adventist college library or in the mission field.

"Comparative Librarianship will definitely prepare you for work overseas," she advised. And then when the total enrollment for her Academic Librarianship course was three Adventists, she re-designed the course, changing the focus from massive university libraries to the small, college libraries where we likely would be employed.

Classmates who wanted me to just be with them, professors who actively prepared me for work in my church—this was far more than simple tolerance and respect. I hadn't expected it in a large university. Had my university attendance been a time of startling, dramatic, faith-building experiences? No. How much of life is? Had it been a time of growing confidence in my own faith, of learning how faith works outside the sheltered Adventist college environment? Yes.

And now they wanted me to say grace. Julie spoke from the podium. "A buffet is served at the back of the room. Roast chicken is the main course. For those with special dietary needs, there is vegetarian lasagne. Before we begin, Sheila Clark will say grace."

So my faith journey was from the quiet prayers in the lunchroom to public acknowledgment at a graduation dinner. I was thankful again, thankful for learning to serve in the place I least expected it, thankful for my classmates and professors, thankful that God gave me a sustaining faith others could respect.

And I was with you in weakness and in much fear and trembling; and my speech and my message were not in plausible words of wisdom, but in demonstration of the Spirit and of power, that your faith might not rest in the wisdom of men but in the power of God. 1 Corinthians 2:3-5 RSV

Sheila E. Clark is assistant librarian at Walla Walla College in College Place, Washington.

A FALSE BARGAIN AND A DREAM CROSS *By Dave Village*

During my second year in community college, faith began its good work in me. Poor choices over the past several years had led me to into heavy substance abuse and lawbreaking. Though I would never have considered myself religious, a troubled conscience would not allow me any peace and I knew that if I persisted in this course of action, it would lead only to disaster and despair.

Concerned individuals and several startling experiences changed the course of my life. First, a bad drug experience nearly killed me. I pled with God for another chance at life. I also feared that an investigation could send me to jail. I bargained with God, "If you keep me from getting caught and going to jail, I'll give You my life. I'll stop doing all these bad things."

That was the best I knew and I really meant it. Determined to keep my end of the bargain, I started reading the Bible and attending church. I quit drinking, smoking pot and lawbreaking. Now God would have to keep His end of the bargain. Nobody could doubt that a major change had taken place in my life. I even thought I was converted.

Then I met Larry Isaac, a classmate, who began sharing his newfound faith in Christ with me. He invited me to church. I met Pastor Sal Larosa who gave me a copy of *Steps to Christ* by Ellen White. I began reading it immediately. Then I had a troubling dream.

Standing before me was a tall, brilliant, gentle-faced Jesus, or, at least, what I thought Jesus must look like. To my horror, I found I had a large, sharpened sword in my hand, and I was stabbing Him repeatedly. He didn't try to defend Himself. The look on His face was unforgettable. His eyes were piercing, questioning, as if He was pleading with me: "David, why are you doing this to Me?" I awoke distraught, and for days I was troubled by that horrible dream.

Two sentences from the "Repentance" chapter in *Steps to Christ* especially struck me: "Most do not understand the true meaning of repentance. They lament the suffering caused by sin and not the sin itself." My dream came back to me. I saw the bargaining I'd been doing with God. I didn't really love Him, only the blessings He brought to my life. I hadn't really been sorry for my sins; I was just afraid they would catch up with me. I felt for sure that I'd burn in hell.

But I kept reading. I began to see that Jesus loved me so much that He was willing to die on a cross for me. My sins crucified Him. With tears of repentance, I confessed, "If You loved me that much, I am Yours. I love You."

And that was the beginning of my college faith. I spent many evenings studying God's word with Pastor Larosa, and in 1976 I was baptized, giving my life fully to Christ. Now the meaning to my life is knowing Jesus Christ as my Savior and Lord.

This is how God showed His love among us: He sent His one and only Son into the world that we might live through Him. This is love: not that we loved God, but that He loved us and sent His Son as an atoning sacrifice for our sins. 1 John 4:9,10 NIV

Dave Village is associate professor of physical therapy at Andrews University in Berrien Springs, Michigan.

TWO LOST JOBS AND A LESSON IN TRUST *By Henry Zuill*

After several years of teaching high school biology, I had begun graduate studies at Loma Linda University, borrowing money to get started. With that year passing and the money running out, I didn't know how to continue. Where would money come from? My wife and I had two sons, so further indebtedness was not sensible. I began looking for a teaching job again and wondered if I'd ever get back to graduate school.

A call soon came offering an attractive teaching position in a far away place. The director of my graduate biology program cautioned: "If you leave your studies now, it will be difficult to return." I felt I had little choice, so I told that school that I would accept their position when I received their official letter of employment.

The next day, the principal of an Adventist academy came to campus looking for a science teacher. I liked him immediately, and told him that I would like to work for him. But I also explained that I was waiting for the official letter from another school confirming my employment in a position I had promised to accept. He replied that I should call him immediately if anything changed and I became available. So one way or another, it seemed, I would leave graduate school and start teaching again.

Days passed. I grew anxious. Where was the letter from the first school? What was happening? When the letter finally arrived, I saw that it had been returned once to the sender for additional postage. Why hadn't they phoned, I wondered. Opening the letter, I learned they had found someone nearer, thus costing them less moving expense, so they had hired him. I thought that at least they could have had the courtesy to call me with this information rather than wasting my time waiting for their delayed letter.

I immediately called the academy principal I had liked so much. Another disappointment. "We hadn't heard anything from you and assumed you were committed to the first institution. So we filled our position with someone else."

Now, both doors were closed. The thoughtlessness of one potential employer had ruined my opportunity with another.

To my surprise, however, I wasn't worried. Somehow, I felt our future was secure, though I certainly couldn't see the details.

This special sense of assurance was inspired by a religion course in "Righteousness by Faith" I was taking that term from Graham Maxwell. I can't think of any single course that had more impact on my life. Dr. Maxwell painted a beautiful picture of the Lord, and I felt my faith and trust in God growing every day.

So I remained calm, despite having just received news that otherwise would have been devastating. I didn't know how the Lord would lead, of course, but I was certain He would.

And He did. One door after another soon opened. I received a tuition waiver and an assistantship for my graduate work. Congress renewed the GI Bill and I was eligible. It didn't provide much, but it was what we needed to cover food expenses. Then, unexpectedly, the managers of our apartment building decided to leave and their position became ours, giving us free rent.

God evidently had wanted me to stay right where I was and continue studying. As I see it, He used the strange events of those teaching positions and an inspiring religion class to teach me an important lesson about trust. I'm still learning.

[He] is able to do immeasurably more than all we ask or imagine, according to His power that is at work within us. Ephesians 3:20 NIV

Henry Zuill is professor of biology at Union College in Lincoln, Nebraska.

THE THIRD MEETING

Robert S. Folkenberg

Gary Land

Rhondda E. Robinson

Philip G. Garver

Hamlet Canosa

Sue Mercer Curtis

Ralph Perrin

Meriam C. Fabriga

Ronald M. Barrow

John Brunt

Come and hear, all ye that fear God,
and I will declare what He hath done for my soul.

Psalm 66:16

SCHEMING, GODLY PARENTS, A FLEECE AND A BRIDE
By Robert S. Folkenberg

With sweaty palms I approached the apartment door that sultry summer evening in 1961.

The idea for me to contact this young woman began ten months before when I, a junior theology student at Andrews University, received a cryptic note from my father. Along with the note he sent a photograph of a stunning young woman in her Loma Linda University student nurse's uniform. Dad's terse note read simply: "This is a wonderful girl. You're a nut if you don't write to her."

Dad's parental counsel was always right to the point, and shared just once. The rest was up to me. During a Wednesday morning chapel I drafted a letter of introduction to the beautiful young lady at Loma Linda.

With increasing astonishment, Anita recalls, she read through the letter, wondering who would be writing her from Andrews. After considering her options momentarily, she wadded up the letter and tossed it into the nearest wastebasket. Dottie, her roommate, laughingly dared her to reply. Anita took the dare, smoothed out the crumpled letter and drafted a polite reply.

Now, many letters and several months later, I was standing at her door in Maryland, where she was home from Loma Linda for the summer. After what seemed an age, the door opened and there she was. "Yes," my heart shouted, "she's the one I've been looking for!"

We saw each other twice during the summer of 1961, yet it was enough for me to know in my heart that this was the woman with whom I wanted to spend the rest of my life. But I also needed to know if this was the Lord's will.

At the end of the summer Anita returned to Loma Linda and I returned to Andrews University. The weeks seemed to crawl. I longed to see her at least once before the next summer. Then, as Christmas vacation approached, my mother called.

"Bob," she said coyly, "student fares to California are reasonable now. We can provide you a ticket if you would like to visit the Magans and other relatives in southern California over Christmas. But," she added, "you'll have to leave before December 16. After that the student fares aren't available."

December 16 posed a big problem. Christmas vacation at Andrews didn't begin until December 21. The dean of students, W. E. McClure, had just announced in chapel that no early departures would be authorized. He even added, "Don't even bother to ask."

I knew I wanted Anita to be my wife, and I wanted to ask her at Christmas. I also had dedicated my life to the Lord and felt certain this included extended years of service outside the United Sates, a dream I knew had to be shared by both partners in life. Only the Lord knew the future. Only He knew if Anita and I should serve Him together. The question with which I struggled was simply whether I was willing to submit to His will and trust Him to lead.

After a restless, prayerful night, I made a decision. I put out "the fleece," a very brief letter addressed to Dean McClure. It simply said, "For reasons that I cannot explain, I am asking for permission to leave the campus for Christmas vacation on December 16."

After two prayerful and troubled days, I received an envelope from the dean's office. Nervously I tore it open and read the terse reply: "Departure December 16 authorized as requested." Yes! The Lord had verified what I knew was in my heart. Now the remaining question was, Did Anita feel the same way?

A few days later I landed in California and rushed into Anita's welcoming embrace. One quiet evening in the home of Dr. and Mrs. Magan, I asked Anita to be my wife. And she said, "YES!" I could hardly contain my joy.

We were married in San Francisco in July, 1962, on the first Sunday of the General Conference Session held there that year. On that happy weekend Anita and I were startled to learn the role that our parents, who had known each other as college classmates and during their service in the Inter-American Division, had played in our courtship. Her mother had given Anita's photo to my father for him to send me. And her parents and mine had shared the cost of my plane ticket for that momentous Christmas trip to California.

Godly parents are truly wonderful.

He who finds a wife finds a good thing, and obtains favor from the Lord. Proverbs 18:22 NKJV

Robert S. Folkenberg is president of the General Conference of Seventh-day Adventists in Silver Spring, Maryland.

BUS RIDE TO A BETTER PLACE *By Gary Land*

That Sabbath morning in September, 1966 dawned bright and clear. A few days before, I had arrived in Santa Barbara and moved into a small apartment in Isla Vista, the student community adjacent to the University of California campus. I was truly alone, not yet knowing anyone at the university or in the Santa Barbara area.

For the first time in my life, no one would notice whether I went to church. Sixteen years of Adventist education had provided a cultural environment that both supported and expected church-going. Not being particularly rebellious or non-conformist, I'd always attended.

But now I was on my own. I neither owned a car nor knew where the local Adventist church was. Getting there wouldn't be a simple matter. Furthermore, the Southern California coast beckoned. I considered walking to the beach that morning. But all those years of training and practice within an Adventist home and educational system won out. I decided to attend church. A public telephone book provided the address. A map gave me an approximate location. I made my way to the bus stop, map in hand.

Paying my ten cents, I boarded the bus and after a while began anxiously reading street signs and checking my map, trying to figure out the best place to get off. After leaving the bus, I wandered several streets of a sun-washed middle-class neighborhood, eventually finding the church.

The Sabbath School lesson study had already begun by the time I arrived, but I was greeted by a friendly woman who directed me to the young adult class in the balcony. With surprise, I saw an old academy friend and an acquaintance from Pacific Union College. No longer did I feel a stranger in the city where I planned to spend the next few years.

That initial church attendance proved to be significant, for that friendly congregation welcomed me with open arms. Over the next four years, church members invited me to their homes for dinner, included me in church social activities and took me on backpacking trips. Meanwhile, I became involved with the youth Sabbath School and the Missionary Volunteer Society and was ordained a church elder. In the process, I became an active member of the church community.

To be sure, the members of that congregation couldn't always help me with the intellectual and political issues that sometimes challenged my faith during my studies (this was the late 1960s). But they offered a warm environment that both supplemented and contrasted with my daily campus experience. I wanted to return each week because these people's faith in God manifested itself in an outreach to others, an outreach that included me.

If I'd gone to the beach that first Sabbath morning, it probably would've been even easier to skip church subsequent Sabbaths. That simple, yet significant decision to attend began a new stage in my life when joining the family of God was my personal decision.

Let us not give up meeting together, as some are in the habit of doing, but let us encourage one another—and all the more as you see the Day approaching. Hebrews 10:25 NIV

Gary Land is professor of history at Andrews University in Berrien Springs, Michigan.

NOTHING TO LOSE *By Rhondda E. Robinson*

I had been accepted to two of the top ten journalism graduate schools, Syracuse University and the University of Georgia. But I had no way of earning enough money during the summer between college graduation and fall registration to pay my own way. My parents already had fulfilled their promise to finance my education through undergraduate school, so now, financially, I was on my own. I didn't qualify for federal financial aid. An early offer of financial assistance from Syracuse had fallen through.

While spending the summer working for temporary agencies, I miserably anticipated taking a year off from school to work full-time. However, near the end of June, my mother encouraged me to visit the University of Georgia which was only about an hour's drive from our home in Atlanta. I called and made the appointment with the dean of university's School of Journalism.

The next day, one of my temporary agencies offered me an assignment that would require me to work on the same date as my appointment at the university. I needed the money and decided to reschedule my interview. My mother, however, urged me to keep my appointment, maintaining in her faithful way that God would provide more jobs through my temporary agencies. I reluctantly decided to follow my mother's advice.

The dean convinced me that the university had a good program, but the extensive campus overwhelmed me. The school was so large that some of the university's 25,000 students had to take buses from class to class. Housing was provided in high-rise dormitories and apartment communities.

As I was leaving, the dean informed me that because there had been a change in administration the previous spring, no decisions had been made about departmental financial assistance. He urged me to fill out several applications, assuring me that I had a good chance of receiving aid. I politely took the forms but had no intention of completing them.

My parents, however, had other ideas. Sensing my reluctance to attend such a large university and my despondency over making only pocket change from temporary jobs, they encouraged me to complete the applications. "What do you have to lose?" they asked. So I grudgingly filled out the applications.

Although God continued to provide temporary work throughout the summer, by early August I nearly had given up on my dream to attend graduate school. I had not heard anything from the university.

Then, just three weeks before school began, I received a letter from the dean informing me that I had been awarded a research assistantship. My piercing scream of joy brought tears to my mother's eyes; she thought I had horribly injured myself. About a week later, a second letter arrived with news that I would be awarded a scholarship also.

The assistantship and scholarship not only covered my tuition but provided enough money to pay for all of my living expenses.

My [daughter], keep your father's command, and do not forsake the law of your mother. Proverbs 6:20 NKJV

Rhondda E. Robinson is assistant professor of communication and English at Columbia Union College in Takoma Park, Maryland.

WHERE TO NOW? *By Philip G. Garver*

The spring of my senior year at Southern Missionary College (now Southern Adventist University) was filled with anticipation, expectations and anxiety. Where would I teach that fall? Who would want me? What if I didn't get hired by even one of the Adventist academies?

Our professors started gathering the calls from academies for physical education teachers. But a host of other tasks always seemed to be tied to a coach's job description. Teaching physical education was all I wanted to do and I was confident God had a place for me.

One academy principal from the West Coast talked to me, interviewed me and then offered me a job. It seemed perfect until one of my classmates told me that school was exactly the place he wanted to work because he had friends there. For some reason, I turned down the offer and my friend got the job.

Time went on. Another academy principal offered me a position with at least five responsibilities in addition to P.E. and intramurals. It was getting late in the spring, but for some reason, I turned down this job also.

By the end of April, I was getting quite concerned. My wife was pregnant with our son and I was about to graduate with no job. We prayed constantly. The waiting wasn't easy. Those jobs I had declined, for whatever reasons, looked pretty good now. Had I made a mistake?

One evening, the newly hired principal of Mt. Vernon Academy called. He needed a P.E. teacher and asked if I could meet him in the Atlanta airport the next day. I could and I did. He offered me the job right there in the airport. I accepted, even though I had never seen or even heard about Mt. Vernon Academy.

I learned the school had more than 375 students, and all I'd be responsible for was P.E., health and intramurals—exactly what I'd hoped for.

The blessings that followed in my life were beyond my fondest dreams. To add to the obvious blessing of finding satisfying employment, God led us to adopt a little girl while we were in Ohio. Her story and the circumstances that surrounded our adoption of her is a miracle in itself. I often remember those other jobs I might have accepted. None of them could've allowed our family to come to what it is today. To me, it is all an unbelievable miracle, a constant source of faith and inspiration in my life.

I'm convinced that God knew years in advance that a mother in crisis with a little girl would help our family fill a void. He directed me to the right place at the right time.

God does care, God has a plan. Keep close to Him.

Commit your work to the Lord, and your plans will be established. Proverbs 16:3 RSV

Philip G. Garver is professor of health, physical education and recreation at Southern Adventist University in Collegedale, Tennessee.

LATIN AND LIFE *By Hamlet Canosa*

Long before Robin Williams popularized the phrase *carpe diem* in the movie *Dead Poets Society*, I had learned the importance of "seizing the day." The lesson was provided not in one day, but every day by George Yamashiro, who taught biblical languages at Atlantic Union College. Patiently instructing a young, impetuous newcomer to the college in the fall of 1966, Dr. Yamashiro taught more than Latin. Taking me "underwing," he determined to teach me about life.

"Call me George," he would stress, recognizing my discomfort to do so. "Don't worry about your grade. Do the best you can and allow me to guide you through."

While at the time I could neither understand nor truly appreciate his thoughts and intention, in retrospect I learned, soon after graduation, that his desire was to broaden my horizons. He realized that while the Latin language was my "key" (his gift) to unlock the thoughts of scholars past and present, his greater gifts of friendship, trust and unending encouragement could better prepare and equip this young man to commence life's journey beyond those wonderful college years.

What did my good friend impart that, in time, made so great an impact?

debile fundamentum fallit opus: A weak foundation renders vain the work built upon it.

"Life," he would say, "is a work in progress; a building that grows brick by brick upon the foundation you choose to lay."

Dr. Yamashiro realized that the "bricks" that would build my life could not, and would not, be from his vast store chest of knowledge, though he would not hesitate to provide for my spiritual, academic, and even social needs at the time. In his wisdom, he knew that the greater gift he could provide was to help me discover those riches (gifts) I already possessed but of which I knew not.

finis unius diei est principium alterius: The end of one day is the beginning of another.

"Do not take your anger, frustration or concerns over which you have no control to your pillow at night. Let yesterdays be yesterdays. Deal with today's realities, harsh though they may be. Start all tomorrows anew." Our Lord gave much the same counsel, in different words, saying: "Therefore do not worry about tomorrow, for tomorrow will worry about itself. Each day has enough trouble of its own." Matthew 6:34 NIV

invite benefit etum non dater: A benefit is not conferred upon one who is unwilling to receive it.

"Keep your eyes, ears and especially your mind open," were Dr. Yamashiro's words. "Be sure of what you receive as well as what you give, including your word."

Often I've considered this advice in the context of what God gives to us: "How much more will your Father in heaven give good gifts to those who ask Him!" Matthew 7:11 NIV

Blessed is the man who finds wisdom, the man who gains understanding, for she is more profitable than silver and yields better returns than gold. Proverbs 3:13,14 NIV

Hamlet Canosa is vice president for education of the Columbia Union Conference of Seventh-day Adventists in Columbia, Maryland.

WINNING WITHOUT WAVERING By Sue Mercer Curtis

All I needed to do, so they said, was make arrangements with the chairman of the department.

That should be easy enough, I thought.

My comprehensive exams for completing my master's degree had been scheduled for Saturday, and I needed to have them rescheduled to some day other than Sabbath.

At the hour of my appointment, I was shown into the office of Dr. Smith,* the department chairman. After introductions, I began to make my request. As I talked, his expression changed. From the looks of it, it was probably not in my favor.

When I finished, he began asking me a series of stern questions. "Do you know that the testing period is long because every class offered in the department is covered? Do you realize how complicated it would be to offer the exam at a different time for just one student? Do you know that other students who worshiped on Saturday took the exams anyway? Can't you get a dispensation from your minister? Isn't this like the story in the Bible about the ox being in the ditch and it being perfectly fine to pull it out of the ditch on Sabbath?"

As our conversation progressed, I tried to address each question as best I could. My heart raced. I prayed silently—and earnestly—that I would say the right thing. I wanted to stand firm on what I believed. Yet, I felt I must do it without alienating this man. After all, he held my whole academic future in his power.

I was making little headway. There seemed to be no way to sway him. Finally, I said, "Dr. Smith, I want to finish my program here, but if it is a choice between taking the exams on the Sabbath or not getting my degree, I just won't get the degree."

A moment passed, his face relaxed and he said, "Well, I guess we can do this for you. Would taking the exams next Tuesday be okay with you?"

"Yes, yes, Dr. Smith, next Tuesday is perfect."

On Tuesday, Dr. Smith seemed to treat me with an extra measure of pleasantness. He had the exams ready, gave me a very comfortable place to take them and told me I was allowed a break when I needed one.

I can only guess that in our first encounter he had wanted to see how committed I was to the practice of my faith. Once he saw that I was resolved to stand by my beliefs, he obviously found that giving the exam on another day was really no problem.

*name has been changed

Let us hold fast the profession of our faith without wavering; (for He is faithful that promised). Hebrews 10:23

Sue Mercer Curtis is director of residential life and dean of women at La Sierra University in Riverside, California.

A BED AND A BENEFACTOR *By Ralph Perrin*

My wife and I still had unpaid undergraduate loans when we decided I should pursue a doctorate at Loma Linda University. With assurance that God was leading us, we quit our jobs in Colorado, packed up the truck and moved to California, trusting that everything would work out. For awhile, it seemed to. We found affordable housing, Patti secured employment and I was able to get two part-time jobs on campus. Finances were tight, but we were going to make it.

After two quarters we decided that with careful budgeting we could afford to purchase a much needed bed. The one we had was a family hand-me-down that was no longer adequate for comfortable sleep. We searched the newspaper and shopped the bargain stores looking for that elusive super deal. And then one day Patti came home excited. She had found the perfect bed for a very low price. In fact, the deal was so good that she was able to get a whole bedroom set for not much more than one would normally pay for a good bed.

The only drawback was that Patti had to pay for the whole set up front, on the spot. She reassured me that the store owner promised not to cash her check until we had a chance to discuss the purchase. The store was 30 miles away and the first opportunity that I had to go see it would be the next Sunday.

Unfortunately, the next day our dependable VW Dasher became undependable and was in great need of expensive engine repair. I also got a phone call *that same day* informing me that one of my part-time jobs had been given to a full-time person.

We quickly decided we didn't need the new bed after all. We called up the furniture store owner, who graciously offered to tear up our check.

Imagine our dismay when we received our bank statement at the end of the month to learn that the check had been cashed. We called the store repeatedly, but no one answered the phone. We drove to the store and found the doors chained and padlocked, with big foreclosure signs posted everywhere.

Sadly, Patti pointed out "our" bedroom set, still visible on the showroom floor. We went to the address given on the sign and filed our claim, only to be told that we would be lucky to receive back ten cents on the dollar. How were we going to pay our bills, particularly with car trouble and the loss of one of my jobs.

I'll never forget the moment I opened my school mailbox and found $100. There was no note, only cash. Who did this? Who knew? Several months later I found out surreptitiously that our benefactor was one of the administrators of the School of Health. Thank you, Elder Richard Hammond. Your timely, anonymous sacrifice made a difference and helped restore our faith.

When you help someone out, don't think about how it looks. Just do it—quietly and unobtrusively. Matthew 6:4 The Message

Ralph Perrin is dean for student affairs at Loma Linda University in Loma Linda, California.

A SILLY REQUEST *By Meriam C. Fabriga*

In March 1983, Mountain View College, an Adventist school in the Southern Philippines, offered to send me to Philippine Union College to take a Master of Science in Nursing degree. I had only worked for MVC for four years, so to be singled out for upgrading at the school's expense was an honor.

But I had other plans in mind. That same month, I was planning to take the CGFNS (Commission on Graduates of Foreign Nursing Schools) exam, a qualifying test to work in the United States. I accepted MVC's sponsorship offer on a trial basis. I told the administration that I would give it a try by enrolling in summer-school classes, but I'd make a final decision before fall. I didn't tell them I was taking the CGFNS exams and thinking seriously of going to the United States.

Six weeks of summer classes convinced me that I liked graduate school but I still wanted to go to the United States. I was in a quandary. I had only two weeks vacation before the start of the regular fall classes and the release of the results of the CGFNS exams. I had to make a decision. This time I asked God's guidance. However, I tried what Gideon did in the Bible.

I asked God for two definite signs if He really wanted me to remain in the Phillippines to attend graduate school full time.

First, I asked God to let me pass the CGFNS, if only because I'd be quite embarrassed as a clinical instructor not to be able to. Second, I asked for a "boy friend." I'd broken up with my boyfriend some time before and I thought it was time to have another.

I knew the last request was silly, considering the limited time I gave God, but I believed He'd do it if only to show me the way.

Ten days passed, but there was no sign of a boyfriend. I was beginning to believe that God wanted me to proceed with my plan to go to the United States. Then, things began to happen. Just three days before the start of my graduate classes, God answered my request for a boyfriend through an old acquaintance. Now I was sure that God wanted me to stay in graduate school, even before I received my CGFNS results, informing me that I had passed the exams. I finished my master of science in nursing degree in 1985, and served MVC for four more years.

Little did I know that God prepared everything for me so I could fulfill *all* my dreams. I was able to come to the United States in August 1989, I got married to a wonderful man in April 1992 and in November of 1992, God opened the door for me to return to the work I've always wanted to do: teaching. When you let God take control of your life, He will show the way.

The Lord delights in those who fear Him, who put their hope in His unfailing love. Psalm 147:11 NIV

Meriam C. Fabriga is assistant professor of nursing at Southwestern Adventist University in Keene, Texas.

A TAPPING ON THE WINDOW *By Ronald M. Barrow*

One January day, a couple of days before second-semester classes began at Washington Missionary College (now Columbia Union College), I nervously entered the assistant business manager's office to plead my case.

Hardly lifting his head to acknowledge my presence, he said tersely, "Your account is not current."

I explained, "I'm a brick layer and the weather was unusually bitter cold during the Christmas holidays, so I've been able to work very little. My account has always been paid by the end of each semester before. I'm sure that as soon as the weather breaks I'll be able to work again and I can pay my bill."

"Go to the local bank," he said, "take out a personal loan, pay your bill and then you can register for classes."

I knew I couldn't get a loan from a bank. I had no collateral, I owed this small bill at the college, I was hundreds of miles from home and I didn't know anyone who'd co-sign for me.

Once more I tried to explain my situation. I asked him to please check my financial records and see for himself that I was someone who could be trusted.

Instead, he said, "You can't begin classes until your account is current."

I was very dejected when I left his office and made my way out of Columbia Hall. I stood just outside the door contemplating my dilemma. Looking down the steps of that old administration building, I said to myself, "How can this be?"

Just then I heard a tapping on a window behind me. Turning, I saw the business manager, Mr. Peak, motioning for me to come back inside the building. As I entered, he was standing at his office door waiting for me. He said he had overheard my conversation with his assistant and had checked my financial records for himself.

"Be at registration. I'll take care of it," he said quietly.

The weather broke and work commenced. I kept my word and had my bill paid in full before the year was over. I've never forgotten Mr. Peak's words and the confidence he placed in me.

Today, at a sister institution, I sit on student financial review committees. On many occasions, I've heard that tapping on the window.

Do not withhold good from those who deserve it, when it is in your power to act. Proverbs 3:27 NIV

Ronald M. Barrow is vice president for admissions and university relations at Southern Adventist University in Collegedale, Tennessee.

EPISTEMOLOGY AND PEANUTS *By John Brunt*

For me, college started with a peanut. My first day as a student at La Sierra College in 1960 began with a religion class. I wasn't sure what to expect. I had heard that, unlike academy classes, college classes would be tough right from the start, including religion classes. Teachers would be deep and theoretical; and they would talk about Greek and Hebrew.

Much to my surprise, on that first day of class, Dr. Wilbur Alexander, the teacher, spent the entire period talking about peanuts. At least, we assumed we all were talking about peanuts. We couldn't really see them. He simply came to each of us with a bag and asked us to feel what was inside without looking. We all agreed that we were feeling peanuts, but our teacher wouldn't let us stop at that. He pressed us with questions: What makes you think they're peanuts? How do you know they're peanuts? Before long we were humbled into acute awareness of our naivete about matters of epistemology, though, he hadn't used the term.

After awhile, the discussion moved from philosophical questions about how we knew, to a very mundane discussion about peanuts. What did we know about peanuts? What could we say about peanuts? Before long, members of the class were contributing interesting tidbits about peanuts I'd never heard before. I started to learn more about peanuts than I ever cared to know. Nevertheless, it was interesting to find out how much I didn't know about a topic as mundane and simple as peanuts.

Before the class was over, Dr. Alexander had led us to a simple but profound point. A point that awakened both a sense of humility and a desire for discovery. There was much more to know that we didn't already know: more than we would have ever guessed even if the knowledge was just about a simple peanut.

With a few words at the end of class, Dr. Alexander led us to apply this simple lesson to the study of the Bible. Through years of Sabbath School and religion classes in elementary school, junior high, and academy, we were tempted to think we knew it all. But if there was so much we didn't know about a simple peanut, think how much there still was to learn about an infinite God.

Through other teachers and other classes during the next four years, the seed planted that day grew. The desire to discover would bring both rewarding fulfillment and yet a deeper desire to know. And along with that search for knowledge came other wonderful experiences: fellowship with friends that remain close after a third of a century, and meeting my wife in the religion office where we both graded papers for another teacher, Dr. Fritz Guy.

But it all started with a peanut.

Oh, the depth of the riches of the wisdom and knowledge of God! How unsearchable His judgments and His paths beyond tracing out! "Who has known the mind of the Lord? Or who has been His counselor? Who has ever given to God, that God should repay him?" For from Him and through Him and to Him are all things. To Him be glory forever! Amen. Romans 11:33-36 NIV

John Brunt is vice president for academic administration at Walla Walla College in College Place, Washington.

THE FOURTH MEETING

David A. Faehner

Noelene Johnsson

Lyn Bartlett

Jim Greene

April R. Summitt

Ben Clausen

Jerry Chi

Martha Mason

David S. Gerstle

Bill Knott

Come and hear, all ye that fear God,
and I will declare what He hath done for my soul.

Psalm 66:16

TWO OF A KIND *By David A. Faehner*

Six of us fellows from New York City decided, in the fall of 1960, to give Atlantic Union College a try. We loaded up my brother's 1959 Pontiac Catalina convertible, and off we drove. We weren't very serious about college, and we spent most of our freshman year in pranks and dares and having fun.

We soon learned of a Friday night tradition among more serious students at Lenheim Hall, the men's dorm. After vespers, they'd gather in the lobby and walk with the men's dean to a remote area of the campus for singing and prayer. Although our New York group had never participated, we were always restless for new challenges. My friends dared me, one cold New England evening, to join the dean's faithful group—wearing only my under-wear and my topcoat. There was some type of financial remuneration, though the exact amount I can't recall.

Of course, I couldn't resist. The dean and the faithful students gathered in the lobby and left through the back door. I tagged along near the back of the group, hoping my bare legs wouldn't be noticed. We walked across the parking lot and down the road past the gym and the athletic field toward the barn.

After I got over the initial shock of the cold, I found myself enjoying the old songs and the prayer session. What touched me most was when Dean Paul Riley requested his favorite song, "I Come to the Garden Alone." His deep love of that song and the level of the singers' commitment were a moving experience for me.

I became one of the regulars on Friday nights. I was also the only one of those six New York fellows who returned to college the second year.

In my junior year I transferred to Columbia Union College and was surprised to discover that on Friday nights the men's dorm there had a similar tradition. Dean Mike Loewen, a tall, imposing man, took the fellows out to a hilltop behind "the San." He'd raise his arms high above our heads and encourage us to sing with vigor and volume. His favorite song was "Redeemed!" As we sang and prayed, it was obvious to me that Dean Loewen loved the Lord, the song and us.

The examples of these two residence hall deans left a lasting impression on me. Since those days, I've devoted more than 35 years of my career to Adventist colleges—20 of them as a men's dean.

I will sing of the mercies of the Lord forever; with my mouth will I make known Thy faithfulness to all generations. Psalm 89:1

David Faehner is vice president for university advancement at Andrews University in Berrien Springs, Michigan.

WHAT TO DO ABOUT BILL? *By Noelene Johnsson*

As I entered my final year at Avondale College, many assumed that I would marry my college sweetheart. In fact, I'd already said "yes" unofficially. My heart was definitely engaged to be married. But my mind was another matter.

I had lived a sheltered life, having lots of decisions made for me. Those I made myself, I tended to make too quickly. When Bill popped the question, we were sitting listening to a performance of the *Messiah*. He looked and sounded so confident that I had no idea of the nervousness he felt. But wishing to sound as poised as he was, I replied, "Hmmm. I'll have to think about that."

But, in fact, I gave my heart right then and there. I wanted this, but I had unfinished business.

As a teenager, I had played false with fellows, losing my interest about as quickly as I gained theirs. I wasn't sure how I would be, staying with one man for the rest of my life. Could I do it? How could I know that this was the love that would last?

I knew that God alone could tell me, and I meant to take the time to ask Him—sometime. But I hadn't done so yet. So I let things ride, assuming that I would marry Bill, but not feeling that I had an assurance from God that he was the one. And that's where things stood at the beginning of my final year.

About a month after school started, Dr. Ivan Higgins told Bill and me that he wanted to recommend us for a teaching position at Vincent Hill School in India. This brought my procrastination to an end. I needed to discover God's will, not only in the matter of a life partner but also in being ready to go overseas.

One evening soon after our conversation with Dr. Higgins, I set aside everything else, determined to seek God's answer and to stay in my room until it came.

After much anguish and loss of sleep, I felt impressed to ask the Lord that if Bill was the wrong person for me, that I would be filled with doubt. But if he was the right person, I would have peace and certainty. God answered that prayer immediately, completely and thoroughly.

Bill and I married after graduation and went to India a couple months later. Ever since that experience in college, I have not quailed when asked to serve the Lord in some new place. I have come to recognize His will and have had no reason to regret following His leading.

Who, then, is the man that fears the Lord? He will instruct him in the way chosen for him. The Lord confides in those who fear Him. Psalm 25:12,14 NIV

Noelene Johnsson is Director of Children's Ministries at the North American Division of Seventh-day Adventists in Silver Spring, Maryland.

GETTING THE COWS By Lyn Bartlett

I've always liked early mornings. Perhaps it came with growing up on a farm. So when I went to Avondale College, it seemed appropriate that I was assigned to work on the dairy and farm.

Milking the prize dairy herd meant getting up early mornings, at least three days each week. The "dairy boys" had to rise from slumber at 4 a.m. In winter this was three hours before dawn.

I recall waking before I was ready, dressing half unaware, and trudging in heavy footwear to the dairy. I knew that somewhere between the dormitory and the dairy, I'd suddenly feel consciously awake. In winter, the morning chill penetrated all three layers of clothing; in summer, the cool breeze and shorts seemed complementary.

Once we reached the dairy, I always volunteered to go to the night paddock and bring the cows to the dairy. This was the beginning of my time alone with God and my surroundings. It was my reality check for the challenges of the day ahead. It was the forming ground of my "good attitude" toward my friends, my teachers, my study and my future. Tracing the shapes of the silhouetted trees in the approaching dawn and the outlines of the Wattagan Mountains beyond, encouraging the cows and scanning the sky for clues about the day ahead were all part of "getting the cows." These were moments when a fragile youth pondered the bigger questions of life in the company of his God. Even today, recalling those moments gives me strength and courage to embrace the vicissitudes of life as a college administrator.

As dawn approached, we fed and milked the herd of about 100 cows. We laughed, we joked, we talked about our studies, our teachers, our futures. Our discussions were honest and frank. We respected each other. This was part of the traditional camaraderie expected of the "dairy boys." All the while, we were part of the unfolding of a new day; sometimes bringing sunshine, sometimes rain. We saw clouds, birds and the colors of sunrise. We experienced cold, heat, wind in the trees and rain on our faces. We were a team and often we felt in the presence of God and always part of His creation.

By 7 a.m., the job was done. Morning had broken. The cows were back in the fields. The dairy was spotless and ready for the afternoon milking. I remember thinking, time and again, as we made our way back to campus, that all was right with the world and I could cope with my small place in it no matter what lay ahead.

What a blessed way to begin a day! What a marvelous way to gain a healthy self-concept in the presence of God!

How grateful I am for those cows, those early mornings and the "dairy boys."

I lift up my eyes to the hills—where does my help come from? My help comes from the Lord, the Maker of heaven and earth. Psalm 121:1,2 NIV

Lyn Bartlett is vice president for academic administration at Columbia Union College in Takoma Park, Maryland.

"LORD, YOU'RE NOT LISTENING!" *By Jim Greene*

While enrolled at Southern Missionary College (now Southern Adventist University), my wife Joyce and I planned our future. We agreed we wanted to work for the Lord as employees of the Adventist church. And we talked about where we would like to live and work after graduation.

We had grown up in the South, so we had no desire to live or work far from that area. In fact, we said that there were three places we *didn't* want to live: New York City, Southern California and overseas as missionaries.

During my senior year, several calls came to me to work for the church—one in Southern California, another in Boston. It was easy to turn down those offers; they didn't meet our guidelines. After graduation, we moved to Wisconsin and began our career of working for the church. At the time of the 1970 General Conference session, we were invited to go to South America as missionaries. Again, we found it easy to turn down the call.

In the spring of 1971, we were invited to move to New York and work for *Faith for Today*. Once again, we turned down the call. A few months later, *Faith for Today* contacted us again and asked if we would reconsider our decision.

Joyce and I prayed about that decision. We thought back over our career and wondered why God had been giving us so many opportunities to work where we had said we didn't want to live. Finally, we decided that maybe the Lord was trying to tell us that if we were going to work for Him, He would lead us where *He* wanted us to go. We accepted the call and moved to New York.

While living in New York, the Adventist Media Center in Southern California was formed and *Faith for Today* was relocated to Southern California. Soon we were living and working in the second place where we had said we never wanted to live or work.

In 1975, we were called again to enter mission service, this time in Indonesia. We accepted that call and six months later found ourselves living in the warm tropics.

Now when we look back over our career, we realize we've enjoyed each place God has called us to work. We've learned that sometimes the decisions made in college are not always the best. It makes little sense to say, "Lord, you're not listening, didn't I tell you I wouldn't go there." When you decide to accept God's call to service, you can't tell God what you will and will not do.

For My thoughts are not your thoughts, neither are your ways My ways, saith the Lord. Isaiah 55:8

Jim Greene is secretary-treasurer of the Rocky Mountain Conference of Seventh-day Adventists in Denver, Colorado.

THE MYSTERIOUS LOIS GREEN *By April R. Summitt*

I was in the middle of my Ph.D. program in history at Western Michigan University and was studying for my comprehensive exams. The work was intensive and required me to be extremely careful in budgeting my time and money.

I had always believed that God required good time and money management from me, and that I had been doing that well. And yet, somehow, I was running short of money and didn't have the $350 I needed for rent that month. I dropped my head to my hands and breathed a prayer. God had helped me so much until now. He had helped me pay off some debt and learn to manage money better and had helped me through some illness that threatened to end my studies. Why was He letting this problem happen now?

Four years before, I had been strongly tempted to stay in the business field. But I had become convinced that if I were to be the best steward of my talents, I should go back to teaching. Hadn't God led me this far?

What I needed was a miracle, something to give me some assurance that I was where God wanted me to be. But what reason did I have to expect a miracle?

Two hours later, the phone rang. It was my mother in Tennessee. "April?" she said. "I have found the strangest thing in my mailbox at the nursing home. Someone put an envelope there with your name on it. I opened it to see what it was, and it's a card from someone named Lois Green. Do you know a Lois Green?" she asked.

"No." I answered, puzzled. "What does the card say?"

My mother read the card to me. It said, "The Lord has impressed me that you may be having trouble making ends meet. I hope this helps, Lois Green." Enclosed was $300 in cash.

I told my mother in a rush of words about my financial trouble, that I had not told anyone else about it, and that this must be some kind of miracle.

We both spent the next couple of weeks asking around my mother's home for information about Lois Green, but we have never found her.

I thank God frequently for His help, which He continues to provide everyday. Whenever I am tempted to take an easier road or give up, I remember my miracle. All God expects of us is our best: our best use of time, money and talents. And I believe that if we are good stewards with our gifts, the Lord will provide us with all the support we need.

He certainly has for me.

Ask, and it shall be given you; seek, and ye shall find; knock, and it shall be opened unto you. For every one that asketh receiveth; and he that seeketh findeth; and to him that knocketh it shall be opened. Matthew 7:7,8

April R. Summitt is assistant professor of history at Andrews University in Berrien Springs, Michigan.

DISSERTATION WITNESS *By Ben Clausen*

Can a graduate student make a positive Christian impact at a secular university? After attending only Seventh-day Adventist schools up through college, I didn't have a clue. But advice from a college professor helped: "Just be a friend; don't avoid fellow students, and don't 'preach.'"

Research in my area was turning to large accelerators at national laboratories, providing more opportunities for interaction with scientists and for experience on several machines. The requisite travel to different sites also gave us plenty of chances to room together, eat together, hike together and work together: an accelerator runs 24 hours a day, seven days a week.

Through all this interaction with colleagues, I rarely initiated a conversation about my beliefs, but because of my lifestyle, I often was asked questions. Others knew I took Saturdays off. In fact, my professor regularly made sure I was gone by sundown Friday night and asked if I needed transportation to church the next day.

During the time I was writing my dissertation, I went hiking every Sunday. It cleared my mind; and it built friendships—with a professor who gave his free time to the Rocky Mountain Search & Rescue Team and with a fellow student I still keep in contact with.

Eventually, the time came to write the acknowledgments for my dissertation. I expressed the usual words of appreciation, including those to my wife for her patience and to a pre-school daughter for keeping me excited about learning. Then I got the idea of including a paragraph of appreciation to God. Nobody on my dissertation committee mentioned anything about the acknowledgments. I wasn't sure they were even read—until several years later.

While attending meetings at one of the national accelerators, I went to an evening banquet and sat with a post-doctoral student doing research at the university I had attended as a graduate student. His wife mentioned that my name seemed familiar. She said she occasionally visited the physics laboratory and waited for her husband in the library. Having nothing else to do, she often pulled dissertations off the shelves just to read the acknowledgments—the only non-physics reading in the library. She had noted, and now remembered, my mention of God and asked why He was so important to me. I told her.

I was inspired and affected in positive ways by my professors and fellow students in a secular university. In some small way, I believe that as a friend, I did the same for them.

In the morning sow thy seed, and in the evening withhold not thine hand: for thou knowest not whether shall prosper, either this or that, or whether they both shall be alike good. Ecclesiastes 11:6

Ben Clausen is associate research scientist at the Geoscience Research Institute in Loma Linda, California, and adjunct assistant professor of physics at La Sierra University in Riverside, California.

A THANKFUL STEWARD By *Jerry Chi*

My own learning experience as a student in higher education has been full of challenges and struggles in faith. When I decided to attend an Adventist college, my father severely punished me and terminated all financial support. So I had to work 40 hours a week on and off campus and spend every summer as a literature evangelist in order to finance my tuition.

In my first year of college, I had the opportunity to take the national university entrance exam and was blessed to pass it. I regarded this privilege to attend university as an honor and thought I could learn more in a public institution. However, after one semester, I had to quit my program because I had a chemistry lab during the entire Sabbath. The professor would not tolerate any absence. Even at the time, I felt that probably it was God's will to turn me around. So I returned to our Adventist college and devoted myself to becoming a minister.

Two years later, the government ordered me to fulfill the military-service requirement for two years. Because of my uncompromising attitude about keeping the Sabbath, I was sent to military prison in the first two months. After repeated torture and persecution, I was released and given a concession that allowed me to keep the Sabbath for the rest of my military life under probation, with limited vacation.

After that two-year nightmare, I went back to college to work on my unfinished theology degree. One day, a church leader encouraged me to take a business major in order to help improve our church administrative system. I regarded his suggestion as God's calling again. I believed that switching to business would help me to achieve my goal to make a significant contribution to our church.

After studying for five years and teaching for three years in our Adventist college in Taiwan, I went to Andrews University and completed M.B.A. and Ph.D. degrees by 1995.

As I was completing my dissertation, I prayed that God would allow me another opportunity to explore more from a state university so that I could serve our schools better. I was amazed at how quickly God answered my prayer. He provided me with several full scholarships, including free tuition, regular salary and grants that sufficiently supported the pursuit of my second Ph.D.

Away from the Adventist education environment, I found it easier to envision the needs and necessary reforms in Adventist schools. Again, I had to live out my convictions as a Sabbathkeeper when I knew my student colleagues used the day for intensive study in the library.

In the beginning of 1996, I received offers of teaching jobs from three state universities, including the one where I was finishing my second Ph.D. But I decided to dedicate myself to Adventist education. Very soon I found a position at Southwestern Adventist University.

Now, I regularly remind myself that I am just the steward of the opportunities God has given me for His service. I have nothing to be proud of about myself and every reason to be thankful for His great blessings. This is my testimony.

Not to us, O Lord, not to us but to Your name be the glory, because of Your love and faithfulness. Psalm 115:1 NIV

Jerry Chi is assistant professor of business administration at Southwestern Adventist University in Keene, Texas.

TWILIGHT ZONE *By Martha Mason*

I was mystified by the badges. FBI? "Come in," I said. Taking that enormous walk between the hallway and the kitchen table, I couldn't remember anything I had done—ah-h-h. There must be a mistake. I smiled. Should I offer them some tea?

The two agents, middle-aged Caucasian men born without smiles, were barely polite. Sober. They'd have none of my hospitality. I began to worry.

Where were you on the morning of April 19, 1970?

Twilight zone! What? Who could remember that? It was a year earlier, and my mind is not one for dates. Help me. Something about a fire. Fire? My car? Yes, my little car, that's the license number all right. Yes, now I remember. We were headed out to see New York. Yes, we passed a fire that morning and we kept on rolling.

It was an arson fire in town. Yes, at the Selective Service records office, downtown Urbana. Early in the morning.

"Burn, baby, burn!" She *had* said that. The times were crazy, and, in fact we—along with most of the students at the University of Illinois—hated the

Vietnam War, and the draft. "Burn, baby, burn!" She shouted it out the back wind-wing of my VW bug. A thoughtless comment—made in the excitement and unconnected to the world of real danger. But someone had been listening.

Me? They couldn't get anything on me, the innocent driver. Would they care that once I had carried a hand-made placard saying IMPEACH NIXON. It was just after the massacre of students at Kent State.

But I had laid the placard down. I laid it down when I saw the riot gear of the National Guard. I was scared out of my wits when I saw the gas masks. It gave me a sickening feeling—a feeling more like a smell. It was the smell of war and death. That smell memory was around during my childhood, at the end of World War II. Now it seemed that I could die. In sheer terror, I fled instinctively. I laid that placard in the bushes and got out of there.

Our class had missed our graduation: there was the demonstration and we went on strike. Out of our class, we four women simply got together and decided to at least go to New York to see the art there. We were headed there that morning.

As we sped out of town, we heard the radio news: arsonists had targeted the draft records. We paid little attention to the story then. Later we were very concerned, and had to defend our innocence at considerable emotional expense. Once exonerated we still had to deal with an issue: we had indulged in a lot of tough-sounding talk. Now, painfully, we were forced to recall the difficult line between truth and hyperbole, between posturing dangerously for dramatic effect and careful sifting of facts.

For whatever is hidden is meant to be disclosed, and whatever is concealed is meant to be brought out into the open. Mark 4:22 NIV

Martha Mason is assistant professor of art at Walla Walla College in College Place, Washington.

GOD'S CHRISTMAS GIFT By David S. Gerstle

"One hundred and ten dollars," replied the campus bookstore clerk. That's how much our next semester's textbooks were going to cost. In 1975, at Southwestern Adventist College (now Southwestern Adventist University), $110 for my wife Nettie and I might as well have been $1,010.

Christmas break began in two days and our campus jobs that year didn't offer any hours the first week of break. After making financial arrangements for tuition, we didn't have enough cash left over for books. In fact, we didn't have enough for living expenses for the next week, since payday didn't come until after the first of the year. With no work for a week and little cash, we simply didn't know what to do about the present or the bills coming due in January.

With great relief, we accepted my parents' offer to pay for gas if we drove home for Christmas. Since we couldn't work, at least we could get some home-cooked meals.

With just enough cash to buy gas for the 250-mile trip we gladly packed my yellow 1966 Chevy Caprice after our last final exam. Driving down Interstate 35 to Houston, we looked forward to Christmas decorations, holiday goodies and visiting family. We made our finances a matter of prayer and tried not to worry. During our visit we didn't mention our needs at school. We didn't want my parents to worry, as parents often do.

As we gathered around the Christmas tree with my parents and two brothers and their families, my father began handing out envelopes to each of us brothers. He'd never done this in the past, but this year, he had decided to give each of us a $100 bill for Christmas. Nettie and I were quite taken aback. Dad had always been generous, but not that generous. We thought to ourselves that the Lord was certainly taking care of those books we needed.

After a wonderful visit, we returned home. Just after arriving, we checked our mail. Among the bills, advertisements and Christmas cards was one card from some friends we hadn't heard from since their move to California the year before. Inside the card was a check for $10 and a note that said, "We were thinking of you and were impressed to send you the $10. Have a Merry Christmas."

We were awed by how God took care of our needs. Those were the most appreciated textbooks we ever had, knowing how the Lord "purchased" them.

When the righteous cry for help, the Lord hears, and delivers them out of all their troubles. Psalm 34:17 RSV

David S. Gerstle is associate professor of nursing at Southern Adventist University in Collegedale, Tennessee.

ROMAN HOLIDAY *By Bill Knott*

O*h, there's no place like ROME for the holidays,*
No matter how far away you . . . roam.

My friends and I sat on the edge of the famed Trevi Fountain in Rome on Christmas Eve, belting out the carols and ditties that you're never sure you know until you sing them. Passersby strolling near the fountain that warm Roman evening looked puzzled or amused. Here were three crazy American college kids in a public place doing something no sane European would have dared.

Dashing through the snow in a one-horse open sleigh,
O'er the fields we go, laughing all the way.

It took a powerful imagination to transport me from the warm, flickering light and the sound of gently lapping water at the Trevi Fountain to the nose-biting cold and snow of my New England-childhood Christmases. Though I had dutifully thrown my three (American) coins in the fountain, at that moment I would have given a thousand times that amount to have been home just then.

I looked across at Connie singing with a far-away look in her eyes. Where would home have been for her? A daughter of missionaries, she had grown up in Asia, attended school in the United States and was now enrolled at Newbold. There was certainly a mixed set of Christmas memories for her.

Robin was staring into the water of the pool, a gentle smile on her face, quite obviously seeing some other place than Rome as she sang. I reviewed what I knew of her background: suburban home in Virginia or Maryland, traditional family. Christmas for her usually would mean an all-day, whole family gathering in some cozy Takoma Park neighborhood where nieces and nephews played among mounds of wrapping paper.

Silent night, holy night; .
All is calm, all is bright.

We three (hardly kings) sang that night with a devotion and a harmony I've never been able to forget. Perhaps it was the great acoustical setting— lots of stone buildings clustered around—that made us sound terrific. Or perhaps, on the night when the world celebrates His birth, there was a choir somewhere, joining us. Thousands of miles from home, in a land where none of us spoke the language, we learned that night what the Incarnation truly means:

My dwelling place shall be with them; and I will be their God, and they shall be My people. Ezekiel 37:27 For where two or three are gathered in My name, I am there among them. Matthew 18:20

And He was with us that night, in a wordless but Word-filled way, wrapping our unusual celebration of His birth with a peace and a joy we saw reflected in each other's faces. Far from home, far from family, far from all things familiar, we found the Christ-child in a city where we didn't expect Him.

O come to us, abide with us, our Lord Immanuel.

Bill Knott is associate editor of the Adventist Review *in Silver Spring, Maryland.*

THE FIFTH MEETING

Garland Dulan

Robert E. Kingman

Zerita J. Hagerman

Ben Maxson

Bryce Cole

Philip Follett

Terrie Dopp Aamodt

Michael F. Cauley

Randy Roberts

Peter D. H. Bath

Come and hear, all ye that fear God,
and I will declare what He hath done for my soul.

Psalm 66:16

SOMETHING BIGGER THAN BIG RED *By Garland Dulan*

Big Red was playing today. As an avid Big Red fan and athlete, I found it difficult to keep my mind fixed on Sabbath School and the church service. Big Red was the University of Nebraska Cornhuskers football team. They always played on Saturday, and all Union College students knew it.

The stadium wasn't far from Allon Chapel where I often attended church services. As I rode in the direction of the chapel on Sabbath morning, it seemed the whole world was dressed in red and white, the team colors. In a place as American as Lincoln, Nebraska, what could be more exhilarating on a bright fall Saturday than thousands of committed fans cheering and chanting at the top of their voices: "Go Big Red, Go Big Red."

I was well acquainted with the feel of that chant and the infectious excitement it generated. I had attended several Monday-night basketball games at the university, including one in which Nebraska beat the number-one-ranked Michigan State in the last two seconds of the game. Now, that's *excitement*.

So here I sat in a pew at Allon Chapel. Would anyone ever know if I slipped out to the game? Football was important to me. All *good* Adventists would be attending church and couldn't possibly assume that if I was missing, I was at a football game. If I ran into any not-so-good Adventists like myself at the game, they wouldn't tell on me because they'd incriminate themselves. What a temptation!

Years later, my wife and I were comparing notes. She mentioned that one of the things that persuaded her to consider me as her life partner was my value system that was so obvious to her during our college days.

"What are you talking about?" I asked.

"Well," she replied, "Sabbath after Sabbath, while other Adventists I knew slipped out to see Big Red at the stadium, you were always present in Sabbath School and church. That convinced me that your commitment to God's values would serve well in a lifelong match with my commitment to God's values."

What a life of joy with a loving wife I might have traded for a few momentary excitements provided by Big Red.

Our God has a way of rewarding us both in the here-and-now as well as in His kingdom to come. Many things deemed vital now will pale in significance to the much greater joy He has for us as we commit to Him.

But seek ye first the kingdom of God, and His righteousness; and all these things shall be added unto you. Matthew 6:33

Garland Dulan is professor of sociology at La Sierra University in Riverside, California.

YOU ARE CALLED *By Robert E. Kingman*

M y mood didn't match the brightness of the beautiful day in Tucson in 1971. I'd just completed my doctorate in physics at the University of Arizona and I wanted to return to Walla Walla College where I'd taught from 1963 to 1967. Being the independent sort, I'd gone to Tucson without accepting support from my employer. I preferred having no financial obligation that would require me to return.

Now I was ready to return, but there was no job offer. Every other job prospect that failed to materialize added to my growing flood of discouragement and frustration. I had to find a job to support my wife and four children. Since our home was in the Pacific Northwest and most of our relatives lived there, that was where I wanted to teach. Also, I wanted to teach for the church, but not at an overseas church institution. I wanted to spend as much time as possible with four aging grandparents.

In my frustration on that beautiful, sunny day, I reflected on how God had provided for us over the past four years. Soon after starting my course work, I had been awarded an unexpected fellowship under the National Defense Education Act. The pay I received was more than I had received the year before for teaching full time at Walla Walla.

I had been allowed to write (and had passed) two language exams privately in the graduate dean's office to avoid Sabbath conflicts. I was awarded the third year of a fellowship vacated by another student. In all, I had completed four years of additional graduate work and my wife Lillis had completed a master's degree in music education. We certainly had been blessed.

But now, on this beautiful day in Tucson, I struggled. What were we supposed to do? I reviewed my wants, my plans. I thought they were very reasonable. But why weren't they happening?

Like a bombshell exploding in my head, the thought flashed through my mind: *Bob, the problem is that you've decided what you want to do. What does God want you to do?*

In a flood of emotion, I sat down and wrote a letter to the education secretary of the General Conference. In it I noted God's leading in my life and my willingness to serve the church *anywhere* I was needed.

With a great sense of relief, I gave the letter to Lillis to type. While she typed, the telephone rang. The caller was Richard Hammill, president of Andrews University, inviting me to visit Berrien Springs to explore the possibility of teaching there. I told him I would consider his invitation, but my first choice was to return to Walla Walla.

Immediately I contacted Walla Walla College and soon received an offer. After my visit to Andrews, I considered both situations and thought of God's perfect timing. I accepted the teaching position at Andrews University and, despite occasional struggles, I continue to celebrate God's call. A quarter century later I'm even more confident of His leading.

Through Him and for His name's sake, we received grace and apostleship to call people from among all the Gentiles to the obedience that comes from faith. And you also are among those who are called to belong to Jesus Christ. Romans 1:5,6 NIV

Robert E. Kingman is professor of physics at Andrews University in Berrien Springs, Michigan.

ENOUGH FOR THE MOMENT *By Zerita J. Hagerman*

The phone rang early on my 21st birthday but the message was not one of greeting. My oldest brother—the father of three children, with a wife six months pregnant—had been killed by a drunken driver.

When the funeral was over, I returned to Union College where I was a nursing student. I had an overwhelming sense of loss and questions based on feelings, not faith, about why God had allowed such a thing to happen. After all, as a single college student, I'd hardly started my preparation for life and didn't have a young family counting on me. I had little to offer. But my brother had so much depending on him. If someone had to die in my family, couldn't God have gotten along easier without me than without my brother? *What could God use me for, that I should remain and my brother be gone?* My need was to accept, but my questions were about the mercy and justice of God.

A friend in California sent me a bus ticket and I went to visit her family during my short, four-week summer break. I needed that rest, to get away for a time and put the funeral and the sorrow of my family out of mind for awhile.

Three days before I was scheduled to return home, I suddenly felt impressed in the night that I had to take the next bus home. When I told my friends in the morning, they were perplexed but helped me pack to catch a late morning bus.

As I rode along, I wondered about my actions. I could've been water skiing instead of sitting on this crowded bus. Was this something silly and impulsive, or was I following some prompting from the Lord?

As the miles rolled by, I took out my copy of Ellen White's *Education*. At least I'd finish my goal of reading this book on vacation.

At Prescott, Arizona, a woman got on the bus and took the empty seat next to me. She asked about my reading. I told her that the book was about the principles of Christian education. She said that she had attended all the churches in the area but hadn't found one that really followed the Bible. When I asked what she meant, she said that as she read the Bible, she found that Saturday was the Sabbath, and none of the churches were keeping the day God had set aside for His Holy day. I told her about the Seventh-day Adventist Church. We found we shared a mutual understanding of the Bible.

Then the woman told me how she had prayed that God would send someone to help her find others with whom to share her understanding of what she was reading in the Bible. She had started out from Flagstaff the day before, but her car broke down. She had an important meeting in Prescott so she borrowed a car to make the trip. But on this morning, in Prescott, the borrowed car wouldn't run either. She left it in a garage and took the bus in order to get back to her work in Flagstaff. She told me she was sure that God had answered her prayer for help by sending me.

God had answered her prayer. What about *my* questions, the ones that had been troubling me? God hadn't answered all the big ones, to be sure. But at least He had made it plain that *He could use me to accomplish His purposes,* even if it was just to be on a bus in Prescott, Arizona.

And that was enough for the moment.

I waited patiently for the Lord; and He inclined unto me, and heard my cry. He brought me up also out of an horrible pit, out of the miry clay

and set my feet upon a rock and established my goings. And He hath put a new song in my mouth, even praise unto our God. Psalm 40:1-3

Zerita J. Hagerman is professor of nursing at Andrews University in Berrien Springs, Michigan.

ONE FRIDAY NIGHT By Ben Maxson

Friday night in a college dorm was not where I wanted to be. I was taking 18 semester hours of class work, working more than 50 hours a week, and courting the woman who would become my wife. It had been a bad week. Things were not going well on any of those fronts, and that Friday night I needed to find something beyond myself. The stress of the unrealistic schedule had mounted to the point of desperation. The activities of the men's dorm on Friday night didn't provide the answer to the heart's cry for God. I asked the dean for a late leave to go out driving alone. Somehow he understood my need and signed the late leave form, with no definite return time.

In desperation, I reached out to God and even opened the passenger door of my car as I invited Him to ride with me. The drive through the countryside was spectacular. The night was lit by the moonlight glinting on the snow which had fallen that day. The combination of distance from the hectic pace, the peace of the night and a growing sensitivity to God's presence began to penetrate my confusion and stress.

I talked with God as I never had before. I shared my burdens, my frustrations, my trials and my loneliness. I imagined God sitting beside me. I paused to listen and reflect on ways in which He had touched my life and ways in which my busy schedule had isolated me from Him.

As I opened my thoughts to Him, Bible verses came to mind. I remembered different choruses and sang them as prayers. I paused from time to time and, in silence, sought to hear God through the convicting of His Spirit. Slowly, He did His wondrous work of grace. The stress and pressures began to slip away. I gained a growing sense of God's ability to make a difference in my life. I began to realize how much I had been trying to do on my own, without Him. Opening my heart more fully to Him, I surrendered my classes, my work and my courtship to His control.

Hours later, I became aware of the time and of how far I had driven. I headed back to the dorm. The weight was lifted. I still would have to struggle with the pressures of my intense schedule. The load was not lightened by walking away from anything. Instead, as I opened these areas of my life to God,

He was picking up my load and carrying my burden. The load was lightened, not by the removal of any part of it, but by His added strength and presence.

As I parked my car, I thanked God for the wonder of His presence. I invited Him to continue to walk beside me in each area of my life. I walked into the dorm awake to the reality that God was real and was making a difference in my daily life because I now was giving Him room to do so.

Be still, and know that I am God. Psalm 46:10 NIV

Ben Maxson is director of stewardship at the General Conference of Seventh-day Adventists in Silver Spring, Maryland.

SABBATH SCHOOL DISASTER *By Bryce Cole*

I studied German in my freshman year and spent my sophomore year at Seminar Schloss Bogenhofen in Austria. Upon returning to Walla Walla College, I found few opportunities to use my German. The major forum for applying my skills was in a Sabbath School class that was taught by two or three German-speaking faculty at the college. This was a most enjoyable experience. We sang German hymns and discussed the week's lesson. I looked forward to this Sabbath School class as the high point of my week.

One Sabbath, one of the teachers asked whether I would teach the lesson the following week. Since I had led out in Sabbath School discussions previously in English, I accepted. However, I had spoken in front of a crowd in German only once previously, and on that occasion I had made a grammatical mistake that left everyone laughing.

Needless to say, I didn't look forward to the following Sabbath with as much relish as I had in previous weeks. I put off preparation. Friday night came rolling around and I still hadn't thought of anything to talk about in Sabbath School the next day. Finally, by 4 a.m. Sabbath morning, I gave up and went to bed with only the smallest idea of what I would do.

Sabbath School was rough from the beginning. The songs were new and my short presentation didn't seem to catch on for the discussion. I panicked. I looked at my watch every 30 seconds, excused myself to get a drink of water, and finally, convinced myself that I was sick enough so I couldn't continue and headed back to my dorm room, less than 15 minutes after the start of the lesson study.

What a miserable failure I was! Further, what was previously my favorite event of the week now had became the most dreaded, simply because it reminded me of how I had made a fool of myself.

Fortunately, through patience and the grace of God, I gradually felt more comfortable discussing philosophical topics in German, particularly after another stay in Munich working at a testing laboratory.

One weekend, Reinhard Czeratzki, the German teacher at Walla Walla College, had to be out of town on a Sabbath he was slated to teach the Sabbath School. I offered to teach in his place. I remember his hesitation in allowing me to do it. But this time, I started preparing that evening with prayer. On Sabbath morning, I still glanced at my watch every 10 minutes, but, the first three chapters of Matthew have never seemed as beautiful to me as they did that day.

Many years later I have known few more personally painful experiences than that first Sabbath School disaster. Yet, through the grace of God, I've learned to focus on God's Word instead of my failures. I've even preached once in German at a small church in central Germany when a friend needed some help. I spoke from God's Word that day and never once did I have to glance at my watch.

My grace is sufficient for you, for My power is made perfect in weakness. 2 Corinthians 12:9 NIV

Bryce Cole is assistant professor of engineering at Walla Walla College in College Place, Washington.

AN IMPERFECT SERMON AND A PERFECT CRITIQUE By *Philip Follett*

At last, I had reached the top. I had passed the last hurdles of Greek language study, late nights working on the student newspaper and cleaning chicken coops to pay tuition. I had achieved that exalted status of college senior.

Four of us, all senior theology majors, decided to conduct evangelistic meetings in a nearby village. Often we had walked door-to-door in that town to distribute tracts, but this time we determined to conduct a full-fledged evangelistic series.

Kenneth Richards, the son of H. M. S. Richards, Sr., and I had given Bible studies to a family in the town. We wanted that family to be the first-fruits of our evangelistic work.

We rented a hall, distributed advertising and took turns preaching. The opening night, I was surprised and honored to see Kenneth's mother, Mabel Richards, walk into the hall. It was a two-hour drive from her home to the meetings. I doubted that she would come often.

But she did come often. Every night, in fact. I expected her to come when her son spoke. But every night, when we other student preachers stumbled through our sermons, Mrs. Richards was there.

One night I preached on one of the prophecies. I had wanted the message to be perfect. It wasn't. I got through the sermon, but I knew that some points weren't clear. After the audience left, our team, along with the sponsoring pastor, met for the critique of the night's presentation. That night, everybody "helped" me by pointing out my mistakes. I felt miserable.

When we left the back room to walk out the door, I saw Mrs. Richards. She had waited after the meeting especially to see me. I really didn't want to see her right then but she wouldn't let me get past her. She stepped up and said, "Brother Follett, I want to thank you for that message. I learned some things I hadn't thought of before. It was a blessing to me."

I was surprised, stunned, and visibly revived. I mumbled a "Thanks" and left the auditorium. I left with a gift of hope from Mabel Richards, who chose to arrive at her home late that night in order to speak a word of encouragement to an embarrassed student preacher. She helped me to learn from my mistakes rather than to let them destroy me. And I'm sure the Lord forgave her for exaggerating the blessing she received from my fumbling efforts.

Years later, I had many opportunities to spend time with Mother Richards. One of her spiritual gifts was the gift of encouragement. She never used it more effectively than that night when a mighty senior was humbled by his own mistakes and restored by a few words of gracious encouragement.

Among those baptized was the lady from the family where Ken and I gave Bible studies. Soon, a small group of believers was organized. Now a thriving church stands in that community.

Pleasant words are like a honeycomb, sweetness to the soul and health to the body. Proverbs 16:24 RSV

Philip Follett is general vice president of the General Conference of Seventh-day Adventists in Silver Spring, Maryland.

PART OF A BLANKET OF LOVE By *Terrie Dopp Aamodt*

I came home disappointed from a year of student mission service teaching at an Adventist college in Korea. I wasn't sure that I was a better person or that I had left Korea a better place. Had I done something wrong? Had it been a mistake to go?

I wondered what would happen to my former students, especially the top student, Susan. The first day of class, she had written about why she came to an Adventist college. "It wasn't my will. It was my lot."

Although she had attended a mission school for several years, she did not attend church or believe in God. But college had begun to change her. She later wrote: "Now, I think I know why I came here. Perhaps God called me directly."

After I came home from Korea, I learned that shy, silent Susan was becoming a confident leader. She had a major role in the school play during her junior year.

Then I learned of the tragedy. The warm, heated floor of Susan's bedroom had leaked charcoal fumes from the flue underneath, asphyxiating her. Susan's father ran with his precious grown-up daughter in his arms, limp as a rag doll, to the nearby Adventist hospital. It was too late. Susan was dead.

Memory took me back to the classroom where Susan had sat every day in the same short-sleeved, crisply ironed, light blue cotton dress. Like all my women students, she never spoke up in class, but mischief darted from her eyes, and sometimes she giggled behind her hand to her friend, Gloria. What I remembered most was her consistently first-rate work, penned in neat, careful handwriting.

I wished I could see Susan again. For the first time in my life, heaven became a real place. My grief made me want to touch people who knew Susan, so I got the address of her non-Christian parents. I wrote to tell them about what an outstanding student their daughter had been, about how I looked forward to seeing her again in a better place.

Months went by, and I went to work at a summer camp where a twice-forwarded letter caught up with me. It was from Susan's father. "It's been a long time since I intended to write you," he wrote. "To obtain your address took quite some time. Then I wanted to write you my first letter after I am baptized. On the Sabbath day, June 4th, I and my wife were baptized at Yongdungpo Church, the south Seoul."

The letter made me cry. I cried for Susan, but I also cried for the sense of joy and hope I found in her father's letter. I cried for the sense of warmth and connection I finally felt about my year in Korea. I had been a tiny part of the blanket of love and support that Susan's teachers and college classmates had wrapped around her family. I look forward to seeing all of them in heaven.

Even so, come, Lord Jesus. Revelation 22:20

Terrie Dopp Aamodt is professor of English and history at Walla Walla College in College Place, Washington.

More College Faith

AN ELEVENTH-HOUR ANSWER   By Michael F. Cauley

In June 1974, my fiancee Dottie and I worked at summer jobs to pay our fall tuition at Southern Missionary College (now Southern Adventist University). Dottie worked in her hometown of Orlando, Florida. I was a task-force worker in Soddy-Daisy, 40 miles north of Chattanooga, Tennessee, cutting my pastoral teeth as I helped with the small church there. I gave Bible studies and assisted with plans for an evangelistic meeting to be held later in the summer.

One weekend, Dottie and I arranged to meet back at the college in Collegedale. Dottie had found a ride on Friday from Orlando to Collegedale. The next morning, Sabbath, I drove south out of Soddy-Daisy to pick her up before Sabbath School and church. Just as my 1968 Ford Fairlane gathered speed along the country road to Collegedale, its hood sprang open, blocking the windshield. Quickly I edged to a stop. Grabbing some stereo-speaker wire a friend had left in my car weeks before, I wired shut the now-corrugated hood. This wasn't the best way to keep the hood closed, but it worked, at least for the weekend.

When I called my father a day or two later, I found to my surprise that I was not covered by his insurance. I inquired of the conference and found that I was not covered by their insurance either. The husband of one of the Soddy-Daisy church members agreed to fix the car for me, but it would cost $78—a relatively small sum today, but not then when I had no money at all. Except for the scholarship that I would receive at the end of the summer, I was living on faith.

At the beginning of the summer, I had made a covenant with the Lord. Following His counsel to prove His promises, I had promised that I would give Him 25 percent of all the money I received that summer.

In a car with a hood that flopped as I drove down the road, I was able to maintain my schedule of giving Bible studies and attending church functions. But I was planning to drive to Orlando in a few weeks, and I didn't think it wise to travel several hundred miles with a car in that shape. I was desperate. I needed help and had exhausted my resources.

For weeks, no money came. I continued to plead with the Lord, who owned everything, to help me with my problem. By the last Sabbath before my scheduled Wednesday departure for Orlando, I still had no money.

Arriving home from church, I checked the mail—since nearly every day brought a letter from Dottie. I found three letters: one from the treasurer of the conference with a check enclosed for $75; the second from my mother with a $20 bill; the third from my grandmother with a $10 bill—a total of

$105. Quickly calculating the 25 percent I had promised the Lord, I realized I'd have $78.75 left. On Monday, I had the Ford's hood replaced by one from a junkyard; on Tuesday, it was repainted; and on Wednesday, as scheduled, I was on my way to Orlando.

When the righteous cry for help, the Lord hears, and delivers them out of all their troubles. Psalm 34:17 RSV

Michael F. Cauley is president of the Pennsylvania Conference of Seventh-day Adventists in Reading, Pennsylvania.

THE TOWER CLIMBER *By Randy Roberts*

I was climbing a 180-foot tower that was fairly old and not very straight. Its supporting guy wires needed replacing. My college buddy Bill and I were to help do it. The further I climbed up the tower, the more I questioned by sanity.

We were college students, studying for the ministry and spending one summer as student missionaries in Guatemala. Our job was to help build a new Adventist World Radio station by building several antenna towers and strengthening an existing one. The first day on the job the engineer threw a couple of tower climbing belts at our feet and gruffly said, "Climb that tower. You'll have to learn to trust this belt, or you'll be of no use to me."

I don't have a selfish bone in my body, so I said to Bill, "You go first!" He looked at me and said, "My feet aren't leaving the ground."

I finally caved in, looped the belt around the tower, and started to climb. Every twenty feet I had to unfasten the belt and climb over the guy wires. The higher I climbed, the more scared I got. Forget the belt! I'd rather trust my own hands! I clung tenaciously to the tower.

I didn't want to look down, that was too frightening. I quickly discovered that when I looked up, the scurrying clouds gave me the sensation that the tower was falling. So I couldn't look up! I finally just looked out at the horizon. I arrived at 160 feet, and quit climbing, refusing to go any higher. The engineer left me there for a few minutes, and then yelled, "Lean back!"

I considered that a couple of seconds, and then screamed back, "No!" But he was persistent. As the minutes ticked past, he continued to press me to do more. First it was to lean back. Once I could do that, it was to look up. Then it was to look down. And then came to the worst of all.

"Let go!" he shouted.

I almost passed out! Let go?! What if the belt broke? I remembered what he'd said, "You'll have to learn to trust this belt, or you'll be of no use to me."

Once again, he left me there to think about it for a while. Finally, one finger at a time, by sheer force of will, I pried my clutching fingers from the tower.

Incredibly, by day's end, he had me leaning back, looking up, and placing my hands behind my head! He had me trusting that the belt would hold me.

I have often reflected on what I learned as a college student missionary perched atop a tower in Guatemala. The belt will hold you. You just have to let go.

Sometimes our greatest lessons come in the classroom called life.

Now faith is being sure of what we hope for and certain of what we do not see. . . . And without faith it is impossible to please God. Hebrews 11:1,6 NIV

Randy Roberts is assistant professor of relational studies at Loma Linda University in Loma Linda, California.

TO BE OR TO DO *By Peter D. H. Bath*

I'm a "do-er" struggling to be a "be-er." This characterized much of my life as I approached my studies in the seminary at Andrews University. My view of life was that I'd do well if I worked hard, did my best and gave people little to quibble about.

As such, I was very happy, doing my best, working hard on my courses and at the two jobs I held. All this work was done, I think, not so much to glorify God as to find strength for self-esteem and acceptance in the presence of others.

I had experienced unconditional love, but conditional man that I am, I struggled to let it really take hold of my life and my marriage. My focus on "doing" even expanded into a habit of reminding my wife of the things that needed to be done.

I well remember a class that I took with Dr. Ivan Blazen entitled "Love, Marriage, and Divorce: A New Testament Perspective." Dr. Blazen spent most of the time in the course focusing upon what love really is—from Christ's point of view and as demonstrated in His ministry. He beautifully illustrated Christ's compassion and caring, showing how grace was meted out in the presence of wrong, and how the transforming power of unconditional love, given to us so freely, should be extended to others.

About halfway though the quarter, the lights started to go on in my head. I recognized that my "doing" nature needed to be much less conditional and much more unconditional in its expression of love. Right after class one day, I ran from the seminary building all the way back to Garland A-14 where we lived. I dashed into the apartment and found Cathy sitting in a chair. Breathlessly, I asked her to put her book down because I had something important to tell her. I looked into her eyes and said, "Dear, I'm not the easiest person in the world to live with, but I've just learned what unconditional love really means in my life. And I've seen you give that to me. I see the Lord giving that to me and it's something I want to give to you. I won't be cajoling you or telling you what needs doing. I'll just let you be—and love you."

I well remember the look I got from her when she said, "Well, isn't that nice?" Apparently, she didn't believe me. But, thank the Lord and a New Testament professor, she does today.

To be confronted with ourselves in the context of a Christian education is a wonderfully transforming experience, even though it's painful to come face to face with our own shortcomings. To do so in the context of the Gospel, of Christ's love, is to experience redemption. I'll always be grateful for Ivan Blazen's eloquent emphasis on God's unconditional love.

But I am like an olive tree flourishing in the house of God; I trust in God's unfailing love for ever and ever. Psalm 52:8 NIV

Peter D. H. Bath is president of Kettering College of Medical Arts in Kettering, Ohio.

More College Faith

THE SIXTH MEETING

Lourdes Morales Gudmundsson

William G. Johnsson

Wayne Wentland

Robert K. Lehmann

Ruth F. Davis

Gregory A. Gerard

David G. Rand

Joseph G. Galusha, Jr.

Chris Blake

Sharon Weaver Pittman

Come and hear, all ye that fear God,
and I will declare what He hath done for my soul.

Psalm 66:16

THE TRUNK *By Lourdes Morales Gudmundsson*

"You mean it's okay for me to go?" I asked incredulously of my mother.

She couldn't help chuckling at my delight. "Yes, you must go." Her voice trailed off absentmindedly, but I was too young and too restless to grasp the enormous pain that choked off my mother's words.

Mom understood well why I HAD to go. We were a poor family, recently moved from the inner city into a comfortably upper-middle-class Adventist neighborhood in Southern California where both our ethnicity and our economic status made us stick out like sore thumbs. I often looked at the girls who attended my school and wished that I could have the clothes they wore. I knew I couldn't ask Mom for more clothes because she was already doing heroic deeds to see us through Christian schools. But none of that kept me from eyeing greedily the possessions of my classmates.

To make matters worse for my already seriously compromised self-esteem, my brothers, Ralph and Raul, and I were grappling with the tentacled implications of our older brother Tito's recent diagnosis of schizo-phrenia. Our life had suddenly taken on a surreal quality with regular visits to the mental hospital carrying large jars of carrot and celery juice and other imaginative provisions for miraculous healing. Now, in my irrational and self-preserving adolescent form of thinking, going away to college seemed wrenchingly necessary—going far away from my house.

The speaker for the Spanish version of *The Voice of Prophecy* had just returned to our community from studying in Argentina. Now there was a solution, I thought. I'll go to college in Argentina.

Ever the thorough and sacrificial provider, Mom packed my trunk to the brim with endless quantities of clothes and shoes. After all, I'd be gone a whole year, she reasoned. I was ecstatic about having so many new things to wear. I wasn't as thrilled about my grandmother's old fur coat and the ubiquitous vegetable juicer.

Providence would have it that I got to the school in Argentina before my trunk arrived. I looked around and noticed the spare wardrobes of my Argentine counterparts: two skirts, three blouses, two pairs of shoes, one or two Sabbath outfits, and that was it. For the *whole* school year. Then I remembered that overgrown footlocker floating inexorably south and began praying with all my heart for it to sink into the ocean somewhere, anywhere between California and Argentina.

But the embarrassing evidence of my comparative wealth inevitably arrived. And what a ruckus it produced. All the girls in the dormitory (or so it seemed) came down to inspect the contents of the "americana's" trunk. They gawked and oohed and aahed at everything they saw—all of this interspersed with questions asking my assurance that all of that stuff REALLY was all mine. I had never imagined I would ever in my life be wishing to have less rather than more than I actually had.

Necessity eventually relieved my discomfort. My parents didn't have enough money to pay my way back to the United States, so I sold that old trunk and all its contents to buy my ticket home.

Therefore do not worry, saying, "What shall we eat?" or "What shall we drink?" or "What shall we wear?" But seek first the kingdom of God and His righteousness, and all these things shall be added to you. Matthew 6:31,33 NKJV

Lourdes Morales Gudmundsson is professor of Spanish at La Sierra University in Riverside, California.

LETTER OF CREDIT   *By William G. Johnsson*

"These papers are all very well, but we want cash! I'll give you a week or ten days to come up with cash, or you'll have to withdraw from the university."

A few months before, our first term of mission service in India drew to a close. Leaders of the Southern Asia Division voted that, in addition to a short visit to relatives in Australia, Noelene and I should proceed to Andrews University for me to earn a master's degree in religion.

During our mission service, we had built up savings, but all in rupees. The Government of India had strict regulations concerning hard currency—you couldn't simply go to a bank and convert rupees into dollars. To get us on our way, the division treasury gave us a letter of credit drawn on the Southern Asia Division. We were told we could present this at any church office in the world and draw out what we needed.

About a month later, we arrived at Andrews University. We were about broke—our first paycheck hadn't yet arrived from the General Conference. But we had the letter of credit. It had worked for us in Australia, it was our security now.

The last step in registering for the summer session required that I see Mr. Smith* for financial clearance.

I went into his office. I gave him an introductory letter from the Southern Asia Division, stating I was at Andrews under the division's sponsorship. And then I showed him the letter of credit.

He looked askance at it, then handed it back.

"We want cash!" he said.

He wasn't a bad man; he was simply following procedures. We hadn't understood those procedures. Andrews University was only just beginning to see itself as an institution for the world church.

If I have ever felt a heel, it was when I stumbled out of that office. A stranger to the United States, a stranger to the campus, I suddenly felt very much alone.

But God sent us an advocate. Dr. and Mrs. Dick Banks, who knew us from their own service in India, heard of our plight. Incensed, Dick contacted a senior financial officer of the university, who in turn called the General Conference and told them to get a check to us *pronto*.

Our troubles were over—almost. The check didn't arrive: either the United States mail was unusually slow, or someone in the General Conference was. After waiting several days, we figured the check must have gone astray. I walked out to the Berrien Springs post office, about a mile each way, and inquired if they were holding a letter for us. I walked back empty-handed.

I walked out and back again the next day. And the next. And the next. And the next. Those were very long walks. Walks of frustration, walks of pleading, walks of faith.

At last the check came.

Exactly ten years later we arrived back on campus. No longer were we strangers—I was joining the faculty of the seminary. But I hoped to do more than teach classes in the New Testament. I wanted to help Andrews University become more sensitive to the needs of students from abroad. And I hoped to become someone like Dick Banks.

name has been changed

The Lord is my rock, my fortress and my deliverer; my God is my rock, in whom I take refuge, my shield and the horn of my salvation. He is my stronghold, my refuge and my savior. Psalm 22:2,3 NIV

William G. Johnsson is editor of the Adventist Review *at the General Conference of Seventh-day Adventists in Silver Spring, Maryland.*

THE FORMULA By Wayne Wentland

Go to school without your book, pen or paper, and you'll have a difficult time. If you fail to read or listen in the classroom, you'll have a bad time. If you don't finish your school work or if you forget your assignment and skip class, you'll have an impossible time. I learned each of these truths in college by personal experience. Most of all, however, I learned that if I didn't pray, I'd experience *all of the above*.

I had a very difficult first quarter at college. I enjoyed all the excitement my new environment offered: new friends, new freedoms and sports. I didn't, however, enjoy my 1.63 GPA. I received the standard letter from the academic dean, "Study or prepare to find another school." With all of my bad study habits firmly in place, I was prepared to accept my fate.

My mother reached me by phone to provide a wake-up call. She told me that I was capable, needed to try harder and should find an easy class or two to increase my GPA. Before she ended the conversation, she challenged me, "Son, you need to study more and pray."

I smiled inside and told her I would. But I didn't believe any such formula would provide a miracle, and that's what I needed, a miracle. I decided to prove her wrong by doing exactly as she had asked.

For the next quarter, I used every available moment to study. Time that had previously been filled with all of the other excitements of college was now devoted to the application of this new formula. Before I studied any subject, I'd pray, read a chapter of the Bible, and then give my best effort to accomplish the task. I did this faithfully for one quarter, and even before the final examinations, I knew the result would be vastly different. My second quarter GPA was 2.93.

This formula has never failed me. In graduate school, I've used the Bible, the writings of Ellen White and prayer before studying my subjects, with even greater success. I recommend this formula for all the challenges we face in education and life.

Study to shew thyself approved unto God, a workman that needeth not to be ashamed, rightly dividing the word of truth. 2 Timothy 2:15

Wayne Wentland is principal of Rio Lindo Academy in Healdsburg, California.

MIXED MOTIVES AND CHANCE ACQUAINTANCES *By Robert K. Lehmann*

It had been a good ball game. My curve had been breaking sharply and my buddy, Rod, had caught well for me. With cleats crunching under foot, we walked back up the hill toward the campus of Canadian Union College (now Canadian University College) and the custodial jobs awaiting us there.

I had plenty to think about. I was finishing my studies in preparation for a teaching job. To date, however, no prospects for employment had turned up. As we walked up the hill, I fell silent as the future zeroed in on my mind. Rod's words brought me sharply back to the present.

"You and I are going Ingathering on Monday," he proclaimed. Apparently, he was trying to spoil a beautiful Alberta spring day.

"Not on your life, buddy!" I replied. I'd grown up in the shadow of the little prairie church ministered to by my grandfather. I had come to know about this business of Ingathering funds for the support of the church. I wanted nothing to do with it. I wasn't going.

"Well, *we are*. I already signed us up, three of us. What's more, the girls are going as a team. It's kind of a competition."

Monday morning I was out Ingathering with two other buddies and our driver, Elder Mel Erickson, a man from the Alberta Conference office whom I didn't know. We set out for the nearby countryside, along with 50 other carloads that spread out through central Alberta. During a brief lunch break, Elder Erickson, a congenial man, quickly became acquainted with this unlikely trio of Ingatherers—out only because the girls were going.

The results of the day were discouraging. Early 1950s farmers, so recently out of the depression era and not yet ten years out of the Second World War, had not yet developed any great humanitarian ethic. Yet, gracious to the end, Elder Erickson uttered no word of complaint as my two buddies and I ended the day with less than five dollars for the cause of the Lord.

The school year wound down. I looked forward to graduation and worried about a job. The future seemed uncertain at best.

Just before graduation, "mail call" brought a letter from Elder Erickson, the conference director of education.

"I enjoyed my day Ingathering with you young men; and Bob, I have taken note of your hopes for the future. I have an opening for a teacher in Northern Alberta and I would like for you to consider the position."

So began my 40 years of service to the church in education, pastoral ministry, and administration. I've found that the Lord often works this way. He gives us direction in many ways. Of course, He speaks through His Word. But He also works through the lives of sincere Christians and the mundane, off-hand events, mixed motives and chance acquaintances of our every-day lives.

And we know that all things work together for good to them that love God, to them who are the called according to His purpose. Romans 8:28

Robert K. Lehmann is president of the Maritime Conference of Seventh-day Adventists in Moncton, New Brunswick.

THE LORD WILL PROVIDE By Ruth F. Davis

As I approached the end of my senior year in college, I wondered what I would do after graduation.

My adviser told me she had received a letter from the General Conference requesting a home economics teacher for a mission appointment. So she had sent pictures of me presenting a nutrition seminar in the community. Immediately, the call came requesting that I teach at the Bekwai Training College in West Africa.

I told my mother and the young man who was my special friend about the call. My mother told me to forget about Africa. She didn't want me to go. My special friend said he wouldn't wait for me the two and a half years I'd be away because he wanted to get married.

After graduation, I went home to Greensboro, North Carolina, and prayed earnestly that God would guide me in my decision to work in His vineyard. Like Gideon, I wanted a sign. I asked God to change my mother's heart if it was His will that I go to Africa. Almost overnight, it seemed, she said, "You know, Ruth, I think it's a good idea for you to go to Africa."

On hearing my decision, my special friend was very upset. He again said, "If you go to Africa, I won't wait for you." I told him God would provide someone better for me.

God gave me the strength I needed to go to West Africa where I spent two years and nine months teaching courses at the Bekwai Training College in Ghana and six more months at the Konola Secondary School in Liberia. My special friend married someone else while I was still in Africa.

When I returned to the United States, I enrolled at Michigan State University for my master's degree. During the summer, I was invited to speak at Elder Joseph Hinson's tent meetings about my African work. There I met a young man, and the beautiful relationship that began there has blossomed into 34 years of married bliss with my husband Oliver James Davis.

I've told my story many times at women's retreats and to my students who are discouraged and think that God has forgotten them. I'm a living witness that God's promises are true. I waited patiently on the Lord and He provided for all my needs according to His riches in glory. He'll do the same for others.

Those who seek the Lord lack no good thing. Psalm 34:10 NIV

Ruth F. Davis is professor of family and consumer sciences at Oakwood College in Huntsville, Alabama.

MY PLANS, GOD'S PLANS *By Gregory A. Gerard*

By the end of the fall quarter of my freshman year at Andrews University, I had made a major decision concerning my studies and future. I sensed a strong desire, perhaps a "call," to become a teacher. My first step was to change my major and minor and it felt right.

After changing my academic program, I became infatuated with the idea of changing schools. I tried out that concept on a few of my friends. Since I was the product of 12 years of public schools, I felt I was best qualified to become a public-school teacher. And to my way of thinking, my desire to be a witness to Christianity by ministering in public schools could best be accomplished by graduating from the state university near my home. The combination of the strong statement of desire to witness, with the logic of my situation convinced several of my friends, and even one professor with whom I talked.

With my decision reaching the point of finalization, I ran into two people I greatly respected. The first was Ken Blanton, who was assistant dean of men. I shared my idea and waited for him to agree. Rather than agree, he cut through the witness and logic arguments and put his finger on the real issue—homesickness. He agreed that my "call" to teach came from God, but thought my methods to answer that call were my own confused way of escape.

I left his office and ran right into Nancy Mauro, a fellow freshman I respected as a friend and sincere Christian. With no reference by me to what Dean Blanton had just told me, she quickly came to the same conclusions.

A few days later, I went home for the weekend and found support for my ideas from several friends, even a couple of fellow Adventist family members. Then, at the end of the weekend, I tried out my idea on my very secular, non-Adventist father. Surely, he would agree with me. He did agree with my desire to be a teacher, but he told me I hadn't given Andrews enough time and that I should stay.

My heavenly father had spoken to me through my earthly father; through the one faculty member, Dean Blanton, who knew me best; and through the one person who would know me best for the rest of my life. For Nancy Mauro and I were married the same day we graduated together, from Andrews, four years later.

Many are the plans in a man's heart, but it is the Lord's purpose that prevails. Proverbs 19:21 NIV

Gregory A. Gerard is vice president for advancement at La Sierra University in Riverside, California.

FRIENDS AND NEIGHBORS AND CHARIOTS OF FIRE *By David G. Rand*

I came home from work, went to my room, and there it was: a large, brown, very official-looking envelope. The letter inside began with the ominous greeting: "From Your Friends and Neighbors."

In the fall of 1949, I had enrolled as a religion major at Emmanuel Missionary College (now Andrews University). When my money ran out, I dropped out of school and went to Detroit to get a job. That's where my "friends and neighbors" caught up with me.

So, on November 30, 1951, at the request of those "friends and neighbors," I reported for duty in the United States Army at Fort Custer, Michigan. Not having the prophetic gift, I was unable to see the future and properly judge the value of what had happened to me. It was not the happiest day of my life.

Soon, however, a miracle began to take place. Not the instantaneous kind, but the kind that occurs slowly, over an extended period of time. My unhappy attitude began to change, without my awareness. I began to like military life. The Lord reminded me of two things: one, make the best of a situation not to your liking; and two, military service is only for two years.

Time flew by much faster than I anticipated, and with a lot less stress. I was discharged from active duty on November 6, 1953.

Immediately, I began my second year at EMC in January 1954. That's when I truly began to appreciate my "friends and neighbors." My two years of military service entitled me to the benefits of the GI Bill—benefits that continued all the way through my graduation from the Seventh-day Adventist Theological Seminary on June 4, 1959. Years later, I also learned that those two years of military service also counted toward my retirement benefits.

When I graduated from EMC and the seminary, I was given the real thing—a diploma, not a blank piece of paper meaning I had unpaid bills. I owed no debt to the schools and had no bank loans to worry about, thanks to the GI Bill and the jobs I held. I was poorer than Job's proverbial turkey, but richer than I had ever been. God had given me an undergraduate and a graduate degree. Praise God from Whom all blessings flow. To my friends and neighbors, whoever you are, and wherever you are, I thank you from the bottom of my heart.

How often do we not appreciate our many blessings just because we can't see what God is doing for us. How His heart must ache as He sees us blindly missing blessings that, if seen, would result in more praise to His Name and a lot less complaining.

And Elisha prayed, and said, "Lord, I pray, open his eyes that he may see." Then the Lord opened the eyes of the young man, and he saw. And behold, the mountain was full of horses and chariots of fire. 2 Kings 6:17 NKJV

David G. Rand retired in 1997 as chaplain at Andrews University in Berrien Springs, Michigan.

WAITING TO SHARE *By Joseph G. Galusha, Jr.*

It was exhilarating to be walking the halls of a major research university. It was even more exciting to belong in an office there with other graduate students.

Only a few months before, I had come to Oxford University to study animal behavior. I had been invited to bring my passion for, and my master's thesis on, the social behavior of Glaucous-winged gulls and have them tested by some of the best minds in the English-speaking world. Professor Niko Tinbergen was about to win a Nobel Prize for his fascinating research on why animals act the way they do. And though I didn't know it, he had decided that I would be the last of his graduate students. Life felt just too good to be true.

So good, in fact, that I began to worry about my spiritual witness. I knew friends who left church tracts with every new friend and acquaintance. I'd heard of salesmen who left small books with the boys who filled their gas tanks. I felt obliged to do something—but none of these ways seemed appropriate.

In an attempt to resolve this persistent conviction, I began to walk alone very early in the morning in University Parks. Often I'd stop and sit quietly with a tattered Bible in my lap. Watching. Listening. Wondering what to do.

One foggy morning, I selected a favorite spot on the end of a well-worn wooden park bench. What should I do? What could I do? My thoughts were in a gentle whirl—like a foggy vortex.

Sluush, sluush, sluush came the approaching sound of someone moving, but invisible in the fog. And then, there he was with wellys, raincoat and the neck of a thick wool sweater. My eyes dropped back to the dew-drop splotch on Acts, chapter one. I expected him to pass; but he stopped.

"Would you like to study the Bible with a group of new friends? Try Oxford 33265. We meet on Thursday nights."

Barely had I looked up, and there were no earthly signs that he had stopped. Sluush, sluush, sluush, and more tiny, foggy vortices.

My phone call to that number began many months of Thursday nights when I heard the voice of God from the mouths of fellow graduate students. They spoke openly of Jesus. They spoke of life. Of mind. Of reason. And hope. There were questions about my faith, which I answered candidly. There were questions about my diet, which I described enthusiastically. There were questions about my Sabbath, which I answered humbly. There were even more questions about the future, which allowed me to talk of prophecy and hope.

And all that didn't seem so hard. Meeting God's appointment to fellowship with others and to talk together of Him was worth waiting to share.

But you will receive power when the Holy Spirit comes on you; and you will be My witnesses in Jerusalem, and in all Judea and Samaria, and to the ends of the earth. Acts 1:8 NIV

Joseph G. Galusha, Jr., is dean of graduate studies at Walla Walla College in College Place, Washington.

I DIDN'T KNOW By Chris Blake

Even before I began college, I knew quite a lot. For example, I knew college would be different from high school, and it was. I intuitively knew Mark Twain's counsel, "Never let schooling get in the way of an education." I didn't. I also knew my roommate Billy and I would become friends.

We were the only freshmen on our floor. The peeling, two-story athletic dormitory was officially Chase Hall, but students tagged it The Zoo, for reasons we knew too well.

Acid rock and marijuana assaulted our senses day and night. We encountered rooms set on fire, gunshots fired though closed doors, roommates beaten unconscious. We muttered when the water fountain was again torn from the wall.

We spent our first year eating, playing and laughing. We wrestled, talked and traveled home together. Together, we endured the indignities of Zoo life.

Billy was a 6'5" forward who could jump and run. I was a 6'2" guard who could pass and play defense. We knew that both of us would be stars at Cal Poly San Luis Obispo, and we were half right. Billy became the university all-time scoring leader. Quick and powerful, he would streak for a lay-up, score on a fadeaway jumper, and tip in a shot. More than once, however, he also dealt elbows, delivered curses and drew technicals.

Billy held one tangible dream—to play in the NBA—and he had an excellent chance. Apparently, our coach branded Billy "uncoachable." He never received a tryout.

After our senior basketball season, we went our own ways. Billy played pro ball in Mexico, winning league-most-valuable honors (I knew he would). I started attending classes and began student teaching.

Then a curious thing happened. I was converted. After becoming a Christian, I prayed every night for family, for friends, for Billy. I invited him to my wedding, but he didn't come.

Three years passed before I talked with Billy again. One night he called me. His speech was slurred, and he said he might come by sometime. He wasn't working much, he was playing ball and he had seven girlfriends. Eventually, I told him I was a Christian.

He seemed surprised. "You?" he said. "I never knew that. What religion are you?"

"Seventh-day Adventist."

"Hey, that means I can't bring in my brew when I come over. I can't go anywhere without my brew."

I told him he would be welcome with or without his brew. He laughed. He said he'd come by to see me. He didn't. I kept praying for him, knowing he was in trouble and hoping he would just stay alive.

Two more years passed. From out of nowhere Billy called.

"I'm a Christian," he said.

"What?" I said.

"Yeah, I go to church four times a week now. Sing in a men's quartet. It's true." (It's still true today).

I remember thinking with wonder, God can save ANYONE.

I should have known that.

But God, who is rich in mercy, out of the great love with which He loved us, even when we were dead through our trespasses, made us alive together with Christ (by grace you have been saved). Ephesians 2:4,5 RSV

Chris Blake is associate professor of English at Union College in Lincoln, Nebraska.

FAMILY TRAP By Sharon Weaver Pittman

"It always seems to work out this way," I fumed. "Why do my parents always think they know me better than I do?"

I had just finished one of those parents-always-know-best sessions that as a college student I would have avoided at all costs. I had three hours to mull this over as I drove back to Andrews University in my rust-bucket Chevy Vega.

As I traveled the littered maze of Interstate 94, I felt unlucky to have parents who not only valued higher education, but always expected that we, all six of their children, would not only go to college, but would be on the Dean's List and in the honors program.

"I just wish I wasn't a Weaver," I thought, albeit half-heartedly. Being a Weaver meant that medical school was my only academic option. I felt trapped—suffocated—a victim of genetic predestination.

By the time I reached the dorm, depression had engulfed my being. The ghost of melancholy followed me everywhere for the next week. I couldn't seem to shake it off. I met it during Anatomy I, Introduction to Chemistry, English Comp, Life of Christ, and P.E. The dark cloud hung over me at the cafeteria and while I was working. Night times were especially difficult. It seemed to me that my life was in a lose-lose downhill spiral.

One night the pressure intensified. I left the dorm, walking aimlessly, ambling among the campus shadows. "How am I to escape this trap?" I cried, as the pent up tears flowed freely. "Lord, where are You?" I challenged. "You know that I need to escape this bondage."

I spent the night in a personal "Jacob's wrestle." What did *I* really feel called to do? How could I still belong in my over-achieving family if I settled for doing other than what was expected? Would I still be loved?

Then through the darkness cracked a ray of light. It dawned on me that this bondage had been self-induced. The Lord and I could shake it off. I could create my personal identity and become the "black sheep" in a medical family. I loved working with people. I realized I wanted to be a social worker.

Morning was here. I triumphantly arranged my drop-adds and signed up to take Introduction to Psychology and Sociology. With relish, I sold back the "hard science" books that symbolized my bondage and purchased the texts of my new personal identity. What freedom! I could now be what I was, a professional helper committed to making the world a better place. I could follow the calling of Isaiah 58 and Matthew 25 with the peace and assurance that I could be a Weaver *and* a Christian social worker.

Let me tell you the kind of fast that is acceptable to Me. It's to remove the chains of injustice, to untie the heavy burdens, to let the oppressed go free and to lift the spirits of those who are brokenhearted. Isaiah 58:6 Clear Word

Sharon Weaver Pittman is associate professor of social work at Andrews University in Berrien Springs, Michigan.

THE SEVENTH MEETING

W. Richard Lesher

Janet S. Borisevich

Greg A. King

Anees A. Haddad

Mario Veloso

Wilma McClarty

Jack McClarty

Jacqueline L. Kinsman

Keith J. Leavitt

George H. Crumley

Come and hear, all ye that fear God,
and I will declare what He hath done for my soul.

Psalm 66:16

A DREAM AND THREE PROVIDENCES   *By W. Richard Lesher*

From the first dawning of consciousness about what I wanted to do in life, my choice was the ministry. My college years raised three big roadblocks to the fulfillment of my dream and each road block was removed, but not by me. The first problem began during my last year in high school.

In the fall of 1942, I was a senior at Shenandoah Valley Academy. I would turn 18 years old in November. America had been at war for nearly a year and the Selective Service (military draft) was in high gear. It didn't take a genius to figure out that I'd be in the army right after academy graduation in May of 1943. So I reconciled myself to the inevitable draft and joined the Medical Cadet Corps in preparation for it.

When I registered for the draft that fall, I went through the motions of requesting a ministerial deferment. I had no real reason to hope it would be granted. No matter how earnest, fellows still in high school aren't viewed as ministers or even ministerial students.

One day, the Bible teacher told me there was a man he wanted me to meet. I went with "Prof" that afternoon and was introduced to the chairman of the local Selective Service Board. "Prof" explained the purpose of our visit. He obviously had been there before and knew how things were done. The chairman told us that the board would consider my request to be allowed a deferment to study for the ministry. They did, and, incredibly, sent me a deferment for that purpose. I could hardly believe my good fortune.

Ministerial students already in college were being denied deferment, and yet I, still in academy, was recognized as a ministerial student.

With my entrance to Atlantic Union College came another typical problem: money. My father was ill and had no savings or income. After several semesters, my meager resources were exhausted and I began to owe money to the college. Because I was taking classes year-round to comply with the Selective Service requirements, I had no opportunity to recoup my finances with serious summer work. If I had to quit school for lack of money, I'd certainly lose my deferment and would be drafted. My dream seemed to be slipping away again.

One day, after hitch-hiking home for a visit, two men from my home church came to see me. To my complete surprise, they offered me a loan to help with my college expense. How grateful I was. That unsolicited loan saw me through college.

But why college if no job? In 1945/46, not many openings were available for ministerial interns, especially in the part of the country where I was studying. In fact, I hadn't even been interviewed as ministerial students usually were. Where would I find a "call?" Just before Christmas of 1945, I received, out of the blue, a letter with an invitation to serve as a ministerial intern. After the holidays, the offer was canceled for budgetary reasons. A few weeks later, it was reinstated.

Thus began 48 years of work that I had dreamed of since some of my first remembered thoughts.

Before they call I will answer, while they are yet speaking I will hear. Isaiah 65:24 RSV

W. Richard Lesher retired in 1994 as president of Andrews University in Berrien Spring, Michigan.

ARABIC, ALLAH, AND A CAN OF BEER By *Janet S. Borisevich*

As I walked into the vast cafeteria for the first time, I suddenly realized more than ever that I was a stranger in a strange territory. This was my first day at the University of Washington as a linguistics graduate student. It was also the first time in my life to be a student on a non-Adventist campus.

After choosing some items from the meal line, I looked for a seat. My heart thumping, I spotted an empty chair at a table with five others who graciously allowed me to sit with them. I heard them speaking Arabic as I approached, but they stopped as I sat down.

"Please continue your conversation," I said. "I enjoy listening to other languages."

They smiled, thanking me, "You are very kind. Would you like a beer?" One can remained of their six-pack.

"No, but thank you very much," I replied.

"Please, take the last one," they encouraged me.

"Thank you very much for your generosity. I don't drink," I responded.

"You don't drink? Really?" They were very surprised.

"Yes, really," I smiled. "I honestly do not drink."

"But we thought that all Americans drink." They were still amazed. "Are you a Muslim?"

"No, I'm not. I'm a Christian."

"Then why don't you drink? Other Christians we have met drink alcohol. It's okay for them. What kind of Christian are you?" They seemed determined.

"Well," I started, "I'm a Seventh-day Adventist Christian. Drinking alcohol is discouraged by my religion because we believe that our bodies are the temples of God and that we should take the best care of them that we can. Drinking destroys brain cells and makes it difficult to make wise decisions."

"Actually, we are ashamed," one of them confessed. "We are not supposed to be drinking either. We are Muslims."

"Yes, I know," I said. "Don't you think that Allah has eyes outside of the Middle East?"

"How did you know that we were Muslims?" they asked in surprise.

"You were speaking the same Nadji dialect of Arabic that my other Arab friends speak," I continued. "I figured that you were probably followers of Islam."

One of them got up from the table and gathered all the half-filled cans of beer and placed them in the garbage can. He then sat down again. "From our hearts, we thank you for sitting with us. We know that Allah has sent you, a Christian, to our table to guide us back to the straight path. What did you say the name of your religion was? Seven days . . .?"

"Seventh-day Adventist."

"What does this name mean?" they asked. "Tell us more about your religion. We want to know more about it."

Several hours later, my new friends and I had discussed the beauty of the Sabbath invented by our Creator, why most Christians worship on Sunday, the difference between the Old and New Testaments, health issues, the earth's last days and Jesus' Second Coming.

From that day on, I realized the magnitude of every word that we say. I could have simply declined their offer of the beer. But I had also said,

"I don't drink." That simple statement gave my Muslim friends an opportunity to hear aspects of the gospel they had never heard before.

Be wise in the way you act toward outsiders; make the most of every opportunity. Let your conversation be always full of grace, seasoned with salt, so that you may know how to answer everyone. Colossians 4:5,6 NIV

Janet S. Borisevich is assistant professor of English at Pacific Union College in Angwin, California.

WHO I KNOW *By Greg A. King*

I can remember very little about the class, just a few peripheral details: the building it met in, where I usually sat in the classroom, that the class was in Adventist history and the name of the teacher.

Try as I might, I can remember virtually nothing else, except for the events of one day.

As the professor lectured on some aspect of Adventist history, he somehow got sidetracked. Or perhaps I should say he got "main tracked." As the name of Jesus was mentioned in the class discussion, the instructor began sharing a moving testimony of how much Jesus meant to him personally.

He didn't quote what renowned theologians and scholars had said about Jesus Christ. He simply shared what Jesus meant to him.

He spoke of the Lord's unfathomable love and His wonderful gift of salvation for undeserving sinners. He included himself as a sinner in need of God's grace. He declared his own love for a Lord Who had loved him first, Who had died for him, forgiven him, and promised to return so that they could share eternity together.

As my professor testified of his love for Jesus, his eyes clouded with tears. I realized something I hadn't known about this teacher. From the information he shared in class day by day, it was already clear what he knew: a wealth of information about Adventist history—dates, events and numerous details. Now it was clear *Who* he knew.

The fact that my learned professor with an advanced education was so deeply committed to Jesus that he was not too proud to be moved to tears as he spoke of his love for Him, touched me deeply. That testimony etched an unforgettable example in my mind, an example I strive to honor as I stand in front of my students at Pacific Union College. The facts and details that I relate in class will soon be forgotten. But if I, like my professor of two decades ago, can speak movingly of my personal relationship with Jesus, if I am not ashamed to declare my love for the One who suffered and died for me, perhaps it will leave a lasting impression with my students as my teacher's testimony did with me.

My students will soon forget what I know. But maybe, just maybe, they will remember Who I know.

For I am not ashamed of the gospel; it is the power of God for salvation to everyone who has faith, to the Jew first and also to the Greek. Romans 1:16 NRSV

Greg A. King is associate professor of biblical studies at Pacific Union College in Angwin, California.

FROM LONDON TO JERUSALEM *By Anees A. Haddad*

" Now get out of my office, think seriously of my London offer, and don't fail again to come to school on Saturday. You understand?"

That was the curt directive on a Monday morning of Dr. Clay, principal of Quaker High School, which I had attended for the past three years. He had become agitated that my sister, my brother and I had accepted the Gospel truth according to the Adventist Church and had stopped attending school on Saturdays.

On another Monday, it was more of the same: "I told you last Monday to come to school on Saturday, but you didn't," he thundered. "Don't let me have to call you again. This is more serious than you think."

Before these unpleasant encounters, Dr. Clay had known about and been touched by my deep love for music, especially my dream of becoming a cello player. He brought our case before the school board and their headquarters in London. He arranged a scholarship for me to study cello in London, with all expenses paid.

He dangled this carrot before me several times before he became more belligerent and informed me that all I had to do was "renounce the foolishness of being a Sabbatarian" and I would realize my dream and have the scholarship.

Since my father had died when we were babies, an anonymous benefactor had been paying our tuition at this high school all along. I weighed the situation with great concern and serious misgivings. The London scholarship was the biggest temptation of all. Persisting in my new faith could cost me both the free tuition at the high school and the London scholarship.

By the grace of God, the fire and faith of my first love prevailed. The only school I went to on Sabbath from then on was Sabbath School.

Unknown to me, the Lord already was setting in motion a plan to compensate for my coming loss. Two professors at Middle East College in Lebanon pledged to support me the first year at college if I had to leave my high school. Though my grades were very good, missing many tests during the last term of that year and especially missing the finals gave the principal the ammunition he needed. At the end of the school year, he wrote a letter to my mother "regretting the fact" that all three of her children would not be permitted to return to school the following year because we had "failed" our classes.

With a sad heart, I left my friends and my high school. Attending Middle East College demanded quite an adjustment. The first three months were a trial, especially as I reflected on what I was "giving up" for my faith. I was hurt deeply to lose the prized London scholarship—one of my most cherished dreams.

Soon, however, I found the new school atmosphere much more to my new liking. There I trained for my lifework and eventually found my life companion. The journey of life has been exciting and fulfilling. Those first three months of spiritual battles in the Middle East were a great turning point in my life. Often I wonder how different my life would've been had I gone to London. But the Lord took London away from me and instead gave me a New Jerusalem.

May the God of hope fill you with all joy and peace as you trust in Him, so that you may overflow with hope by the power of the Holy Spirit. Romans 15:13 NIV

Anees A. Haddad is professor of sociology and family studies at La Sierra University in Riverside, California.

I WILL HELP YOU *By Mario Veloso*

At the end of my freshman year at Chile College, I sailed to the far south of Chile to Puerto Aysén, where I intended to sell books in the Aysén province.

On the ship, I met Philip de Commines, who was returning to his home in Chile Chico, a small lake-side town in the middle of the Andes Mountains on the border with Argentina. We became fast friends during those few days. When we arrived in Puerto Aysén, Philip made me promise to visit him later that summer.

My work went well and toward the end of the summer, after a long trip, I began to canvas in Chile Chico where Philip lived. One Sunday, I had dinner with his whole family and enjoyed being able to tell them about the teachings of my church.

I soon learned about the town of Puerto Cristal, a five-hour boat trip to the west. A lead mine there employed about 4,000 workers. I thought those people also should benefit from the gospel and the books I was selling. So I set sail on the *Don Edmundo,* a ship owned by the mining company, and the only way to get in or out of Puerto Cristal.

My canvassing work went very well until the mine workers decided to go on strike. Everything in the small town stopped. The administrator of the mine suspended the sailing schedule of the *Don Edmundo* because he didn't want the workers to have contact with the outside world or to receive supplies. The strike continued day after day. Soon it was time for me to go back to college for my sophomore year, but it was not possible for me to leave. The *Don Edmundo* was being held back in the Chile Chico bay by the mine administration. I reluctantly began making alternate plans for the coming semester since it was obvious I would not be able to get back to college in time for the beginning of the school year.

One day, as the strike dragged on, I was greatly surprised when Philip's eldest brother showed up at my room in Puerto Cristal. "Hurry up! Pack your stuff, and let's go back to Chile Chico," he said.

Quickly I packed and boarded the de Commines' family boat and set sail for Chile Chico.

I soon learned that a day or so before, the de Commines family were at the dinner table. They were discussing a telegram they had just received from Philip which said he had returned safely to his college in the north of Chile.

Then Philip's father asked, "And what about Philip's friend, Mario?"

Someone replied, "He went to Puerto Cristal and hasn't come back due to the strike." The family all agreed they should do something to help Philip's friend. So Philip's brother took a boat and sailed five hours to come and rescue me.

The Lord had provided a means of escape for me through the family of someone I'd met by chance a few weeks before. I was so happy and grateful. And, even more, I was confident that God was watching over me.

You whom I have taken from the ends of the earth, and called from its farthest regions, and said to you, "You are My servant, I have chosen you and have not cast you away: Fear not, for I am with you; be not dismayed, for I am your God. I will strengthen you, yes, I will help you, I will uphold you with My righteous right hand." Isaiah 41:9,10 NKJV

Mario Veloso is associate secretary of the General Conference of Seventh-day Adventists in Silver Spring, Maryland.

DEFINITIONS AND A DEFINING MOMENT   By Wilma McClarty

When I attended Andrews University, I lived in the village. One rainy day I was walking home when a car stopped beside me and the driver offered me a ride. Pleasantly surprised to see the driver was the senior pastor of Pioneer Memorial Church, Elder James Rhoads, I gratefully accepted the chance to get out of the storm.

As we drove to my house, we exchanged social chatter until I thought of something. Here was my chance to question my pastor about a characteristic of his preaching. As I had listened to Elder Rhoads speak Sabbath to Sabbath, I repeatedly was impressed with his unusually large vocabulary. The spiritual messages poured from his soul in compositions of flawless rhetoric and precise diction. Every topic was couched with exactness and style. Actually, I had never heard anything quite like his word crafting. As an English major, I was most impressed.

"Pastor Rhoads," I said, "I have noticed your extensive vocabulary as I listen to your sermons every week. How do you know so many meanings?"

Never have I forgotten his explanation. "Wilma," he explained, "during World War II, I was imprisoned. I was permitted to have a dictionary. So you know what I did? I studied the words in that book until . . . well, until I knew the basic meanings of all the words in the whole dictionary."

I will always remember that rainy day ride with my kind, brilliant pastor. I think of Elder Rhoads when I teach my own writing composition students the value of word study. I think of Elder Rhoads when I need an example of a person who took a stifling prison experience and turned it into an enriching professional exercise. I think of Elder Rhoads when I need to illustrate how the people we often envy because they have "such natural talent" have attained success or fame because they took that native ability and honed it with practice. And I think of Elder Rhoads when I meditate on how God ultimately can use the darkest days of one of His children to enlighten the lives of many of His sons and daughters.

Thank you, Pastor Rhoads for picking up a rain-drenched parishioner that damp autumn afternoon; the experience has soaked into my soul these many years.

And we know that God causes all things to work together for good to those who love God. Romans 8:28 NASB

Wilma McClarty is professor of English at Southern Adventist University in Collegedale, Tennessee.

SO FAR SO FAST *By Jack McClarty*

The crossroads of my life can be traced back to my graduating in music from the University of Montana. I was excited to be hired as the director of a high school band. Then, in the middle of the year, I received my draft notice. In order to finish the year at my job, I joined the National Guard, which allowed me to continue working if I attended monthly meetings and promised to take my six months of active training in June.

During my active training, my buddies back home who were in the National Guard were having farewell parties. Our Howitzer battalion was shipping out for Laos. Laos? I braced for the inevitable. Then, suddenly, political and military events changed and we didn't have to go after all.

My six months of training was over by Christmas. By law, my former teaching job was still mine. But it had its limitations. Perhaps I should consider graduate school? Should I head back East, or go back to the University of Montana, which I knew so well?

I had a friend at Andrews University who suggested I come there. Why should I go to an Adventist school? I had no official profession of faith even though my father and brother were Catholic and my mother and sister were Adventist.

I arrived in Berrien Springs in January. There were no extra rooms for single graduate students to live in so I had to search for a place in the community. Another graduate student, in the same predicament, teamed with me to search for a room.

We checked out the bulletin boards where we found an advertisement of a new home with a room and bath for rent near the campus. We took a look, met the homeowners and another woman at the house who had a little girl sitting on her lap. The room was what we needed and we rented it.

Little did I know how God was leading. In the days that followed I learned more about that other woman we had met. She, too, was attending Andrews as a graduate student. She was the sister of the homeowner. She was single. The little girl who had been sitting on her lap was her niece.

I began seeing that woman quite often. It seemed miraculous that in just one semester I had ventured so far. I was not in the trenches of Laos. I was in Michigan. Graduate school was going fine, I had met the woman of my dreams and I had given my life to God.

I ended the semester well into my master's program, a baptized member of the Seventh-day Adventist church, and married to my beautiful bride Wilma.

I will instruct you and teach you in the way you should go; I will counsel you and watch over you. Psalm 32:8 NIV

The late Jack McClarty was vice-president for development at Southern Adventist University in Collegedale, Tennessee when he wrote this story. He died on September 8, 1997.

TWO SPARROWS AND A LOST CONTACT By *Jacqueline L. Kinsman*

I rushed into the locker room, undressing as I ran. I hated the hassle of having swimming class immediately following a class on the other side of campus. I threw on my suit and trailed the last classmate into the pool just as the instructor began class. A few minutes later I was doing laps, practicing a new stroke and wondering how I could get to this class sooner without all the hectic rush.

Suddenly I realized my eyes were not seeing right. I wondered if the pool was high on chlorine. I rubbed my eyes and held a hand over one eye. Then I realized that in my rush to the pool, I'd forgotten to take my contacts out. Now one was missing. (Nobody wore goggles in those days, as it is now customary to do). At that time, the loss of that contact would cost me $150.

"Dear Lord, please help me find that contact."

I called to my classmates and teacher. They immediately began searching for the tiny gray contact in this Olympic size pool.

"Dear Lord, it was pretty stupid of me to forget to take out my contacts. But even though I'm forgetful, You're still God and You know where the contact lens is. This pool is nothing compared to You. Please help us find this lens. I know You walk with me and I'm always in Your presence. Please help us find this."

Just then a classmate yelled, "I've got it!"

"Thank you, Lord!"

Since that day in my freshman year, I've known for sure that God is always with me. His eye is on the sparrow, and I know He watches me.

Are not two sparrows sold for a penny? Yet not one of them will fall to the ground apart from your Father. And even the hairs of your head are all counted. So do not be afraid; you are of more value than many sparrows. Matthew 10:29-31 NRSV

Jacqueline L. Kinsman is assistant professor of nursing at Andrews University.

A FELLOW NAMED NORM   *By Keith J. Leavitt*

At the moment, I thought the knock on the door of our apartment was just a brief interruption to my solution of a difficult differential equation. In the end, however, that knock interrupted and changed my entire life.

I opened the door and found a short, young man wearing a smile as broad as his face and holding a booklet in his hands. I recognized the booklet.

Weeks earlier, while visiting in my parents home, I had read the latest issue of the *Signs of the Times.* An Adventist neighbor faithfully had been sending the magazine to my parents for years. Even though I claimed no strong religious convictions at the time, I liked the *Signs.* In that issue, I saw an invitation to send away for a free copy of George Vandeman's booklet, *A Day to Remember.* It sounded interesting and, best of all, it was free. For a poor university student, anything free sounded good. I had sent for it.

"Hi," said young man at the door, shaking my hand. "My name is Norm. I'm from the local Adventist church and I understand that you're interested in receiving this book."

Puzzled, I replied, "Actually, I sent away for it by mail and have already received it and read it."

"Really!" he said, expressing his surprise. "Then there sure seems to have been a mix-up in communication someplace. Do you mind if I step in for a few minutes? I'd like to hear what you thought of the book."

Actually, I did mind, but I heard myself saying, "No, come on in." Before his short visit was over, Norm had invited himself back later in the week to study the Bible with me. I knew very little about Adventists and was wary. They might be a cult.

Norm showed up at the appointed time a few days later and we studied the Bible. I actually enjoyed it. After a couple more visits, Norm had convinced my brother Brian to study with us. Soon he was urging us to attend the opening night of an evangelistic crusade that was coming to the city.

Still wary of what we might be getting into, Brian and I told Norm we were too busy with our studies to go. We used this line again when Norm phoned to invite us to the second and third nights' meetings.

On the fourth day, Norm didn't call. He showed up at the door and caught us watching TV. "Well," he chided teasingly, "I can see you guys aren't too busy tonight so come on, get in the car, and let's go to the meeting!"

Norm had won. No, God had won. Brian and I experienced the drawing power of His Holy Spirit and were baptized at the end of those evangelistic meetings.

Behold, I stand at the door, and knock: if any man hear My voice, and open the door, I will come in to him, and will sup with him, and he with Me. Revelation 3:20

Keith J. Leavitt is associate professor of education at Canadian University College in College Heights, Alberta.

A BUSINESS MAN'S CHOICE *By George H. Crumley*

During my first year at Pacific Union College, I was drafted into the United States Army. After basic training, I was sent to Europe. My young bride, Ruth, joined me a short time later.

While stationed in Heidelberg, Germany, we began discussing what we should do when I was discharged. We both agreed that I should finish college. Through a series of providential events, the Lord led us to Walla Walla College where I enrolled as a business major. I chose two minors— secondary education and religion, the latter because I wanted to become not only a good business man but a good Christian business man.

Hardly had I arrived on campus when I discovered that something interesting was happening to me. I was receiving an excellent professional education but, in addition, through both my business and religion professors, God was planting in my heart a desire for a life of direct service for Him in His work.

One gray day, late in the winter of my senior year, the head of the business department arranged for us to visit the nearby Upper Columbia Conference office. He wanted us to observe first hand how the church conducts its business. I was impressed with what I saw. Here was an office employing multi-talented people who had committed their gifts in service to their God and His church. For them, this was not "just a job"; it was a life's ministry. They were professional. They were well educated. They were committed. They worked together as a team.

On the ride home that evening, I struggled with the idea that God wanted me to enlarge my dream of going into business. Perhaps I should consider serving my church as a Christian business leader in God's special work, rather than working for myself. Ruth and I talked about it long and often.

A few weeks before all the excitement of graduation, Ruth and I realized that it was time to make a decision. Should we send out resumes in order to determine if God had a place for us in His work? Or should we continue with our original plan that I go into business for myself?

Strangely, the final decision wasn't difficult. Both Ruth and I sensed that God's plan for us involved serving among the ranks of Seventh-day Adventist workers. We sent out a dozen or so resumes. A short time later, we received a call to join the staff of Upper Columbia Academy where I became the accountant and a teacher.

Some years later, I had the privilege of working with the Upper Columbia Conference treasury staff, some of the very people who had so strongly influenced our decision to serve God's church. That was nearly 40 years ago, and we still rejoice to recall how the Lord changed and directed our lifetime plans.

Commit thy way unto the Lord; trust also in Him; and He shall bring it to pass. Psalm 37:5

George H. Crumley is treasurer of the North American Division of Seventh-day Adventists in Silver Spring, Maryland.

THE EIGHTH MEETING

Kenneth H. Wood

Bertram Melbourne

Shirani de Alwis-Chand

James McGee

Dwight Hilderbrandt

Mitch Menzmer

Kathleen M. Demsky

Won K. Yoon

Jim Jeffery

James Londis

Come and hear, all ye that fear God,
and I will declare what He hath done for my soul.

Psalm 66:16

THE STRAIGHT LINE OF TRUTH By Kenneth H. Wood

In 1935 I was a sophomore at Pacific Union College. As was usual in those days, early in the school year a visiting minister held a Week of Prayer for the student body. After 61 years I have forgotten most of what was said that week, but recently something happened that brought back vividly one result of the week.

My freshman composition teacher during the 1934-35 school year was Miss Lois Christian, a daughter of the well-known Adventist leader, L. H. Christian. Though she has been married and twice widowed in the years that have passed since that time, we have kept in touch, principally through greeting cards at the year-end holiday season. As with many Christian teachers, when I became editor of the *Adventist Review,* she was gratified to note that one of her pupils was making a contribution to the church in her field of interest.

Now in her mid-nineties, she recently was reviewing her keepsakes. When she found among them a letter I had written to her on October 18, 1935, she sent it, thinking I might like to include it among my own keepsakes. Here it is:

"Dear Miss Christian:

"The past Week of Prayer has marked a new period of progress in my Christian life, and has been of very great help to me in many ways. Of course, just as any good Week of Prayer would do, it brought out sins in my life, and pointed to weaknesses in my character.

"Last year when I took freshman rhetoric, in one of my daily quizzes, or perhaps it was a period test, I unintentionally glanced at a paper containing some information that I needed. The question asked was for the different call numbers on different library classifications. And I glanced at a paper giving me one or two of them. I thought little of it at the time, but since·then I have had little peace because of it. I confess it to you, and am willing to do anything about it that you deem fit. I suppose nothing can be done now, but I feel a great deal better for having gotten it 'off my chest.'"

Miss Christian was understanding but devised a suitable way to impress me with the importance of absolute honesty. Ever since, I've had a special appreciation for these two inspired statements: 1) "Lying lips are abomination to the Lord: but they that deal truly are His delight" (Proverbs 12:22); and 2) Everything that Christians do should be as transparent as the sunlight. Truth is of God; deception, in every one of its myriad forms, is of Satan; and whoever in any way departs from the straight line of truth is betraying himself into the power of the wicked one. *Thoughts From the Mount of Blessing,* p. 68

Kenneth H. Wood, retired editor of the Adventist Review, *is chairman of the Ellen G. White Estate Board of Trustees at the General Conference of Seventh-day Adventists in Silver Spring, Maryland.*

THE LORD'S A *By Bertram Melbourne*

On this last day of the course, I felt I had thoroughly enjoyed it and had learned much. Or so I had thought until this moment. Everyone else in the room was busy writing. My paper was blank. Half an hour of the final examination had elapsed and I had written nothing. I gazed at my paper in wonderment. For the first time, I stared failure in the face.

My thoughts began racing over the events of the semester. I had turned in my assignments on time. I had done well on quizzes and tests. I had made an A on the nine weeks examination. I had studied for this examination and had expected a good grade. However, as I read all the questions, I was stunned to realize that I couldn't answer *any*.

I thought of my mother and her sacrifices for me to get a Christian education. The morning I left home for elementary school, she left home, too. I went to school with a bag of books; she went to work with a bag of books. I went to get an education; she dedicated her life to the literature ministry to ensure I would receive a good one. Together, we had made it from elementary school to this my junior year at West Indies College in Mandeville,

Jamaica. It seemed to me in that desperate moment that if I didn't pass this class, I would fail her and show lack of appreciation for her sacrificial work.

I read through the test questions one more time. Again, I found *not one* I could answer. I decided to waste no more time. I'd just turn in my blank exam paper and go to the dormitory to study for the next test. But, at that critical moment, it occurred to me to pray.

Of course, the teacher had prayed at the beginning of the exam, but that was for everyone. This was for *me*. I closed my eyes, bowed my head and prayed: "Dear God, thank You for Your blessings. You know I've studied, yet I can't answer any of these questions. I've done my part; I now claim Your promise. Please bring back to my mind what I have studied. Help me to do my best on this test. Thank You. Amen."

I picked up my pen and began writing as fast as I could. I answered the first question and continued answering questions until the time expired. Imagine my surprise when the papers were returned to learn I had gotten an A. God had helped me to recall what I had studied, and He rewarded my efforts. That was the Lord's A. I thanked Him for it.

I've found that if I perform faithfully and sincerely—whether in studying, or anything else—God rewards my efforts.

The steadfast love of the Lord never ceases, His mercies never come to an end; they are new every morning; great is Thy faithfulness. Lamentations 3:22,23 NRSV

Bertram L. Melbourne is professor of religion at Columbia Union College in Takoma Park, Maryland.

GUIDED BY GOD'S OWN EYE *By Shirani de Alwis-Chand*

Three weeks left until D-Day—my doctoral defense. My entire psyche was constricted into knots and made me absolutely non-functional. Sleep eluded me, my fat cells craved excess food, my brain cells seemed to be nonexistent, and I was engaging in the art of procrastination in its purest form.

Why were these thoughts and emotions racing through every fiber and sinew of my being? Had I forgotten that I received very high grades through all my doctoral study, or that my research papers had been highly commended? Fear, that dreadful emotion, crippled me; fear of being unable to explain regression analysis, the statistical tool I had used in my research; fear of facing a committee of all males, except for my chairperson; and fear of being unable to think on my feet.

Tossing and turning in bed one night unable to sleep, I suddenly heard a text recited aloud: "I will guide you with Mine eye." I sat up in bed with a start as I heard the text repeated again: "I will guide you with Mine eye." I got out of bed with the strong conviction that succeeding at my doctoral defense was indeed feasible. I worked into the wee hours of the morning preparing.

The days and weeks that followed were enjoyable ones for me. Ideas for presenting my research in a lucid manner were popping out at me. My creativity levels for making materials and graphs were high, and I had an "I can do it" attitude. I was rearing to go! I could hardly wait for the big day.

When that day came, my nerves were calm. God's Spirit provided me with confidence and courage. As the questions were fired at me, answers came smoothly, with no element of fear. After successfully defending my dissertation, I was even told that some people felt my defense was one of the most outstanding they had ever seen.

Today, seventeen years later, whenever I face challenges, I know that the Lord and I are meeting eye to eye. I never fear.

I will instruct you and teach you in the way you should go; I will guide you with My eye. Psalm 32:8 NKJV

Shirani de Alwis-Chand is director of the Teaching Learning Center at Loma Linda University in Loma Linda, California.

BLEST BE THE TIE THAT BINDS *By James McGee*

When I arrived as a freshman at Emmanuel Missionary College (now Andrews University), I was excited and grateful for the opportunity to learn. At the same time, I felt a keen sense of loneliness as I realized how far away I was from my home in British Columbia.

Soon caught up in the activities of school, I hardly noticed the rapid passing of time. Suddenly, it was December, and everyone was making holiday plans—everyone, that is, except me. Unable to pay for transportation to my far-away family, I resigned myself to remaining on campus. I felt sad and dejected.

Learning of my plight, one of my music teachers invited me to share Christmas dinner with him and his wife. When I arrived, I noticed in their living room a small Christmas tree with several packages scattered under its branches. I immediately wondered if I should have brought a gift for my hosts; but then, perhaps there was nothing for me under the tree either—why would there be?

After the meal, we sat in the living room while my teacher distributed the presents. To my astonishment, two of them were for me. Looking closely I discovered that the original name on the tag had been scratched out and my name written over it.

I don't remember the contents of the first present I opened, but I certainly do remember the second. It was a tie. Not just any tie, but the quintessential "Christmas Tie," one that the recipient dislikes hugely, but accepts graciously to please a dear benefactor who gave it along with their love. Truthfully, I had never seen a more bizarre tie. Its pattern was a jumble of shapes colored in shades of red, orange and yellow, interspersed with random splotches of green.

I kept that tie for decades—even wore it a few times. As visually unattractive as it was to me, it was for many years one of my most treasured possessions. It was a tangible representation of the Christian caring of a teacher whom I greatly admired and respected. It was a gift from his loving heart. Besides, nearly overcome with gratitude, I now felt as never before that I belonged to a larger family, the family of God. Christmas that year turned out to be merry and joyful after all.

By this all men will know that you are My disciples, if you have love for one another. John 13:35 RSV

James McGee is professor of music at Pacific Union College in Angwin, California.

FAITH AND A FIVE-DOLLAR BILL   *By Dwight Hilderbrandt*

Five days before my 16th birthday, I arrived on the campus of Southern Missionary College (now Southern Adventist University) to attend Collegedale Academy for my junior and senior years of secondary school as well as four years of college. That beautiful June day was special because I hoped to be the first person in my immediate family to graduate from college.

I had been told that if I was willing to work, I could earn my way through academy *and* also college. That day as I stepped off the bus in front of the college store, I was almost overwhelmed with the beauty of the valley where the school is located. The driver opened the baggage compartment and removed all my earthly belongings in a single, shiny, new footlocker that my mother had bought for me to take to school.

As the bus drove away down the narrow main street of Collegedale, I looked up the hill to the lovely old buildings of the college and began to wonder what I was doing there. Having paid for my bus trip to Chattanooga and then the bus ticket on to Collegedale (which I had not planned for) I had one single $5 bill to my name. I pulled it out of my pocket and thought, "How will I ever get through school with this?"

The next day, when I went to the business office to find work, my courage was tested even more. I was told that because I was not yet 16 years of age I wouldn't be able to work in any of the industries. I would have to do custodial or some other service-type work. Alas, my job assignment was to work on the farm at the tremendous rate of 35 cents an hour.

My next stop was the accounting office where I had to provide my social security number and all the usual payroll details. One of the questions asked of each student was, "Do you want your tithe and church expense offering withheld from your pay?"

"I've come to school to train to be a worker for the Lord," I thought to myself. "It will take all I make to put me through school. Can I afford the tithe and offering out of my 35 cents per hour?" At that moment the Bible spoke to me. I remembered that the Lord had promised His blessing if I was faithful to bring the tithe to Him.

"Yes, please withhold the tithe and two percent for church expense," I told the person in the accounting office.

I know that God keeps His promise. Seven years later, I graduated from college with my degree and all my bills paid. I didn't owe one penny for my education to complete academy and college. For the entire seven years, the tithe and church expense was always cared for first.

Bring the full tithes into the storehouse, that there may be food in My house; and thereby put Me to the test, says the Lord of hosts, if I will not open the windows of heaven for you and pour down for you an overflowing blessing. Malachi 3:10 RSV

Dwight Hilderbrandt is Secretary-Treasurer of Adventist-Laymen's Services and Industries at the North American Division of Seventh-day Adventists in Silver Spring, Maryland.

SERMON FROM A SWALLOW By Mitch Menzmer

I t could have been uncertainty in a relationship, a disappointing exam score or a tuition-related problem that left me feeling discouraged that afternoon. I don't remember what it was. But I was discouraged.

On the upside, it was a beautiful spring day in Angwin, so I took my Bible and headed out of the dorm. As I made my way across campus, I prayed, "Lord, SHOW me something!" I found the Irwin Hall Chapel empty and decided to make that my place to read and think. As I opened my Bible, I was distracted by something up above. A swallow had somehow managed to get inside the chapel and was darting around the light fixtures near the ceiling. I noticed an open window above the balcony seats and assumed that the swallow had come in that way. I further assumed he eventually would depart by the same opening. I continued to read.

A moment later, I was distracted again, this time by the sound of the swallow banging against glass, attempting to escape through a closed window.

After about 10 minutes of his distracting banging I felt impressed to help. I went upstairs to the balcony window and found my friend clinging to the lattice, exhausted.

The bird made no attempt to escape my presence as I drew nearer. Slowly, I extended my hand and grasped the tiny body. I was startled by the fragileness of his structure, and pleasantly surprised when, after a few frantic wing-flaps, he became completely calm in my hand. His heart was racing. His tiny feet gripped my finger. I walked down the balcony aisle to the open window to set him free.

I held him there for a moment and then slowly opened my hand. He made no attempt to leave until my hand was completely open, at which point he flew away. I watched him as he darted among the campus trees.

God had shown me something.

If I rise on the wings of the dawn, if I settle on the far side of the sea, even there Your hand will guide me, Your right hand will hold me fast. Psalm 139:9,10 NIV

Mitch Menzmer is associate professor of chemistry at Pacific Union College in Angwin, California.

LEAPING WALLS *By Kathleen M. Demsky*

E very now and then in life, the only thing one seems able to do is sit and stare out a window.

The window was framed with a cloud of yellow forsythia; the day was a perfect picture of spring. On the table in front of me were piles of books and papers in total disarray. My thesis project, looming like a forbidding wall before me, was due in two weeks for the completion of my degree. To add to my stress, my boss had just given me the opportunity (another wall) of chairing a committee to organize an all-day event and a luncheon to be held for a prestigious group of visitors. My position at the university, plus my heavy class load, required more then I felt I could give.

As I stared out the window, I reflected on the sense I had of God's working in my life day by day. I recognized the support and courage He gave me through the people I worked with and my family. Sometimes I'd call my children for advice on how they met their hectic college schedules, or just to ask how I should begin this paper or that project. My husband most of all was a constant encouragement. He drove me an hour each way for my nightly classes. I slept most of the way each time, yet he never complained.

As I sat contemplating, I noticed my Bible on the table in the midst of the mess. I picked it up and began reading some of my favorite passages. The Psalms are among my favorites. David seemed to be a person of passion who wasn't afraid to express his deepest needs and thoughts to God. Suddenly, I spotted a text which became the motto I lived by throughout the rest of my collegiate experience. In fact, this verse is mounted on the wall of my office as a constant reminder to me of God's great power and love.

For You will light my lamp; the Lord my God will enlighten my darkness. For by You I can run against a troop, by my God I can leap over a wall. Psalm 18:28,29 NKJV

Kathleen M. Demsky is director of the architecture resource center Andrews University in Berrien Springs, Michigan.

TOUGHING IT OUT By Won K. Yoon

Literature evangelism was one of the requirements the theology majors at Korean Union College kept putting off. We recognized the value of the colporteur experience, but none of us was enthusiastic about doing it ourselves.

I decided to fulfill the requirement during the winter vacation of my senior year. To maximize my earnings and the matching scholarship, I opted to canvass alone. After a brief orientation, the colporteur field director assigned me to a small coastal town, surrounded by a dozen fishing and farming villages scattered within a seven-mile radius.

I took a room at the cheapest inn in town. In the first few days, the sense of loneliness was overwhelming. I regretted that I had chosen to canvass alone. Even Jesus had sent the disciples out two by two. However, my loneliness inspired a new companionship with the Lord in prayer and self-talk out on the road and in the quiet hours at the inn.

In the cold winter time, the villagers had plenty of idle time, but they had neither the money to buy the books nor the interest to read them. A few of them shut the gate in my face as soon as they learned I was selling Christian books. Some days I returned to the inn with an empty wallet. Nonetheless, I kept visiting homes with a sense of mission. I was determined not to skip a day despite discouragement or cold weather.

At the end of that month-long effort, the students got together to compare sales records. I was surprised to learn that despite all my difficulties, I had brought in the most sales. I learned that my classmates had skipped a few days here and there, and some even had quit canvassing altogether.

That month of canvassing was the toughest requirement of my college education. Yet I learned a valuable lesson: perseverance is the key to success in life.

By your endurance you will gain your lives. Luke 21:19 RSV

Won K. Yoon is assistant vice president for graduate studies and research and professor of sociology at La Sierra University in Riverside, California.

UNCLE ARTHUR, ARCHIMEDES, GOD AND ME *By Jim Jeffery*

I couldn't believe what I had just done. With a sickening, wrenching thunk, I had just driven my VW Bug up onto a huge round boulder in the middle of a farm field. The car had come to rest up there, finely balanced, high and dry and unable to get traction to go anywhere.

It was summer and I'd listened once again to God's clear call to be a literature evangelist. I was selling "Uncle" Arthur Maxwell's *The Bible Story* on Cape Breton Island in Nova Scotia, Canada. Each evening I'd find some out-of-the-way place to pitch my tiny tent.

A few moments earlier I'd been driving around this farm field, trying to find just the right spot. Hidden by the tall grass, the large boulder found my VW an easy prey.

I sat in the car, thinking about my long day, the many visits and my simple desire to just set up my tent and relax. I thought wistfully about the comfortable job that I'd left in Washington, D.C., working as a night switchboard operator in a posh downtown apartment building.

"Lord," I prayed, "I've worked really hard for You today, and look at the mess I'm in. What am I going to do? There are no people around here for miles. I'm up here in the middle of nowhere and I need to rest for the night. Please show me what to do."

God knew that I needed an answer to prayer that night, and He knew that I needed to be reminded once again of His special care. His answer didn't come right away, nor without my participation.

Perspiring profusely and fighting the mosquitos, I struggled to push my car off the rock. It wouldn't budge. The back wheels spun hopelessly. I tried to jack the car up, but the jack was too short. I tried putting pieces of wood under the wheels, but they wouldn't hold. Finally, in desperation I called on the Lord again to help me out of this mess.

Just then I was strongly impressed to look around the field. Soon, I found a 25-foot wooden pole. Using a huge stump which I rolled from another side of the field, I constructed a giant lever. Then I literally pried my Bug off the rock so that its back wheels touched enough ground to allow me to roll it free.

Exhausted, I settled into my tent for that short night. The last thing I remember doing before I fell into a deep, deep sleep was to thank God for His answer to my desperate prayer.

You discern my going out and my lying down; You are familiar with all my ways. Before a word is on my tongue, You know it completely, O Lord. Psalm 139:3,4 NIV

Jim Jeffery is dean of the Division of Professional Studies at Canadian University College in College Heights, Alberta.

LIBERAL IN THE VERY BEST WAY *By James Londis*

My life in the dormitory under Paul Riley was deeply spiritual. Between Dean Riley's daily devotionals and our weekly Friday night men's prayer bands up on Kilbourn Hill, I always felt I was centered on the love of God revealed in Jesus Christ.

From the dorm to the classroom, that "center" was reinforced in the most rigorous and demanding classes I took and confirmed my call to ministry.

In my second year at Atlantic Union College, I was persuaded to take a course in Advanced Composition from Ottilie Stafford. On the basis of that course, I decided to double major in English and religion. That was also the year I was introduced to theology professor Gerald H. Minchin, just returned from finishing his Bachelor of Divinity degree at Andrews University.

In Dr. Stafford's class, I was constantly admonished not to "preach" so much in my writing, to think carefully about what I really wanted to say. In Elder Minchin's class, great poetry was always being quoted to clarify theological ideas. Dr. Stafford taught a class in biblical literature while Elder

Minchin read Shakespeare, Wordsworth and T. S. Eliot. Both professors—while scholars in different disciplines—were deeply appreciative of the range of learning included in what we traditionally have called the "liberal arts." It was they who taught me the importance of language for the preacher, that the gospel must be "housed" in language worthy of its splendor.

To this day, my primary interests are in spirituality, English, theology, and philosophy. That cannot be an "accident." It goes back to the people who most influenced me as a college student. I didn't understand then what was happening to me. Now I can see what they gave to me and I am grateful.

My heart is stirred by a noble theme as I recite my verses for the king; my tongue is the pen of a skillful writer. Psalm 45:1 NIV

James Londis is director of ethics at Kettering Medical Center in Kettering, Ohio.

THE NINTH MEETING

Rich Carlson

Denise Dick Herr

Brian E. Strayer

Jeanette Rogers Dulan

Willie J. Lewis

Y. J. Moses

Steve Pawluk

Katherine Koudele-Joslin

C. Lee Huff

Gregory P. Nelson

Come and hear, all ye that fear God,
and I will declare what He hath done for my soul.

Psalm 66:16

SUPPORT FROM THE HOME FRONT   *By Rich Carlson*

When college began to loom large in my future, my parents and my home church rallied to provide the support and encouragement I needed for such a venture.

My blue-collar, hard-working father and mother made many financial sacrifices so their children could attend an Adventist college. The local church pastor played baseball with me when Sabbath conflicts prevented me from playing on my public high school sports teams. The pastor's wife took time to drive me and my best friend to Union College to see the school I planned to attend after high school graduation. That commitment of my parents and my pastor kept me focused on Seventh-day Adventist higher education.

The greatest miracle of affirmation, however, came after my sophomore year in college. I decided I wanted to be a student missionary, but the college provided no funding for expenses and my family could not afford to pay the $535 for airfare to Peru. This was in the days before fund raising through letter writing, so I was perplexed to know what to do. I had no rich relatives and no assets I could turn into cash. The picture for fulfilling my dream of being a student missionary looked bleak indeed.

But somehow, the elder of my home church found out about my need. To this day, I still don't know how he knew. This elder was one who invested countless hours helping us in Pathfinders, chauffeuring us around town for Ingathering, driving us to summer camp and finding a myriad other little ways to help us know that we were a valuable part of that church. And, somehow, he found out that I had the opportunity to go to Peru—if I could raise $535.

One Sabbath, while I was on home leave, I listened as he stood at the pulpit and told my church family that one of "our students" could be a student missionary if we all would help. He asked for offering plates to be passed specifically for the purpose of sending me to the mission field. When the deacons counted the money, there was $535.

They called me to the front of the church and had prayer for me. I knew then how special I was to them—and to God. There was no question about my calling to serve God for the rest of my life. The combination of dedicated parents, a committed church family and the direct leading of God in that offering plate left me not the slightest doubt that I was valued.

Today, as a college chaplain, I continue to commit my life to assisting God's young people find a closer relationship with Him. I remember my home and my home church, and I offer myself as a tool for God to be that "home church" for someone else.

Have I not commanded you? Be strong and of good courage; do not be afraid, nor be dismayed, for the Lord your God is with you wherever you go. Joshua 1:9 NKJV

Rich Carlson is chaplain at Union College in Lincoln, Nebraska.

REJOICING IN THE SABBATH *By Denise Dick Herr*

Most of my life, I've lived in Adventist communities where Sabbath-keeping was a given. When I went to college at Andrews University, my friends and I attended church, took naps and then went for a walk. I kept Sabbaths, but didn't truly enjoy them.

Several years later, I joined an archaeological excavation in Israel as the pottery manager—the person who organized the washing, analyzing, marking and storing of the millions of shards that are all-important on a dig. When one of the directors, an American Jewish rabbi, asked me to be the pottery manager, I said to him, "You know I don't work on Sabbath."

"That's okay," was his reply. "Many of the students are Jewish. We finish work on Friday morning and don't return to the site until Sunday noon. Of course," he hesitated, "there is the last weekend, when we write reports . . . but," he quickly added when he saw the look of determination in my eyes, "you won't have to work then."

The long, hectic weekdays of the dig rolled by. I got up early and went to bed late. I worked hard. Sabbaths, on the other hand, were bliss: I had time to sit and talk to friends, time to walk without boxes of pottery in my arms, time to read and think. But I didn't realize how wonderful Sabbaths were until the final weekend of the excavation.

The last Friday of the dig was the day we began the serious business of writing reports and closing down camp. My Jewish and Christian friends tried to synthesize their summer findings. Coffee mugs in hand, they labored over stacks of notes and drawings.

I worked hard all day too, but when the sun went down, I breathed a sigh of relief: it was Sabbath. I was free from work for 24 hours. Sabbath wasn't a chore—something I had to do. It was a gift of time.

That evening a special meal was served in the dining room at our tables rather than through a cafeteria line. The report writers, Christian and Jewish alike, ate quickly and rushed to return to their work.

Free, because I observed the Sabbath, I chatted with the other Adventist archaeologist as we ate cookies and watermelon and watched Israeli folk dances.

Sabbath morning, I awoke later than usual and observed the bloodshot eyes and haggard faces of the writers. They had been up late and early. Several were dependant on the summer's work to get into graduate school. Others needed the data for dissertations. The pressure was evident.

I felt like an island of peace in the midst of frantic activity.

I ate breakfast with one of the dig directors, an Israeli woman—Jewish but not religious.

"You're not working today, are you, Denise?" she asked.

"No, I keep Sabbath—Shabbat."

"You know," she said, looking exhausted before the day had even begun, "I think keeping Shabbat is a wonderful idea. I'll have to try it someday."

The Sabbath was made for humankind. Mark 2:27 NRSV

Denise Dick Herr is professor of English at Canadian University College in College Heights, Alberta.

A FLOATING AX HEAD AND A TAX REFUND *By Brian E. Strayer*

As a third-generation Seventh-day Adventist who had grown up in the church, I went to college with a "borrowed" faith. It had never been tested, so it wasn't really mine experientially. But at Southern Missionary

College (now Southern Adventist University), I found Jesus personally during Elder Morris Venden's 1971 Week of Prayer.

In the spring of 1972, I received an IRS refund check for $75 in my Talge Hall mailbox. That was big money to a poor college student. Phoning my girlfriend in Thatcher Hall, I shared the great news with her and invited her for a walk on Biology Trail to plan how we would use the money. After showing her the check, I slipped it inside the envelope and jammed it into my back pocket.

It was one of those incomparable April afternoons when the Tennessee hillsides are ablaze with multi-colored crocus, golden forsythia and brilliant redbud. We must have hiked for two hours, crossing the creek several times, following the intersecting trails through the hills.

Late in the afternoon, on our way to the cafeteria, I reached for the envelope. It wasn't there! With twilight coming on, we couldn't retrace our steps to find it. With heavy hearts, we ate our supper, agreeing to pray about the matter.

That night I pleaded with God. "Father in heaven, You know exactly where my check is. Please send an angel to guard it tonight and help me find it tomorrow, if it is Your will. Amen."

Early the next morning, after another prayer for guidance, I left the dorm before breakfast to cover acres of rough, hilly ground searching for that tan envelope. At a bend in Biology Trail, I felt impressed to walk along the banks of the swollen creek. Then, just ahead in the swift current, I noticed something really peculiar—a piece of paper bobbing up and down midstream balanced only by a single blade of grass. Kneeling down, I pulled it from the water. Stunned, I recognized my very water-soaked (but still legible) IRS refund check. Somehow it had slipped from my pocket, separated itself from the envelope and floated in the creek the entire night. Still on my knees, I thanked the God, Who once floated an ax head for Elisha, for caring enough to answer my prayer in such a miraculous way.

Casting the whole of your care—all your anxieties, all your worries, all your concerns, once and for all—on Him, for He cares for you affectionately, and cares about your watchfully. 1 Peter 5:7 Amplified Bible

Brian E. Strayer is professor of history at Andrews University in Berrien Springs, Michigan.

OUTCOMES *By Jeannette Rogers Dulan*

M any times I had heard the wonderful stories of personal faith and miraculous outcomes told by my professors and classmates at

Oakwood College. I'd heard how stepping forward in faith had resulted in unexpected money to pay college bills just in time to take exams, or just in time to return to college. I heard, and saw, too, the stories when the money did not come, and I witnessed my classmates' firm assurance that God would provide other opportunities.

At Union College, I heard many stories of the Golden Cords and the lives touched in distant lands where people endured hatred and ridicule and trusted God for their needs and their lives.

All these stories were vicarious faith experiences for me. I was thankful for daily sustenance, but I had never faced academic or financial crisis, serious loss, or heartache. However, these stories had a deep influence on my thinking.

I remembered the point of those stories of faith when, years later, I faced an academic crisis of my own. Near the end of my graduate program, an individual, for reasons unknown to me, decided to withhold vital data I needed to complete my research project. Not having access to this data literally would cost me thousands of dollars and several years of additional work.

Those old stories of college faith became real to me as I put this seemingly impossible situation in God's hands. I remembered our math professor at Oakwood College telling of her graduate-school experience and how, in a dream, the Lord had provided the solution to a very difficult problem. What impressed me most was her seeming calm when confronted with difficulty. With these stories in mind, I looked at all possible approaches to completing the project without that data and came to the realization that it wasn't possible. The situation seemed hopeless.

I sat quietly and waited on the Lord. Suddenly, I was impressed to call the individual again about the missing data. Though I wasn't sure what to believe, she had told me several times that the data had been destroyed. So I felt that the impression to call was unreasonable. In astonishment, I responded in a loud voice, "NO, I can't call again. There must be another way." But the impression to call came again, even stronger.

I dialed the number, not knowing what I would say. The woman who said the data had been destroyed answered, and before I could state my request, she said, "I have the information you need. I've been impressed to help you."

Is there anything God can't do? Experiences shared by my teachers and classmates contributed to my being open to a personal relationship with Christ. Now my own experience taught me to be faithful in what I'm called to do and to trust God to handle the outcomes.

When the ways of people please the Lord, He causes even their enemies to be at peace with them. Proverbs 16:7 NRSV

Jeannette Rogers Dulan is associate professor of curriculum and instruction at La Sierra University in Riverside, California.

A MOTHER WHO NEVER CALLED RETREAT   *By Willie J. Lewis*

After two weeks of canvassing as a student literature evangelist in Atlanta, Georgia, I was a discouraged young man. I had made only enough money to pay for my housing and food. The stress, strain and struggle of trying to sell enough books to attend the seminary at Andrews University in September had gotten the best of me. Disappointed and discouraged by my failure, I went to the recruiting center in Atlanta and enlisted in the United States Army.

I had seven dollars in my pocket. A church member offered to take me to the South Atlantic Conference campmeeting in Hawthorne, Florida, for five dollars. With nothing better to do, I gladly accepted. I'd be able to see my mother, who attended campmeeting each year. The last time I'd seen her was the previous Christmas.

One day during the meetings, she and I were sitting on the bed in the family tent. She asked, "How are things going in your work?"

"Mom, I've joined the army," I blurted out. My heart was touched by the look of sadness and disappointment on her face. I told her what a difficult time I'd been having in the literature work and that I had spent four years working my way through Oakwood College. I had graduated and didn't have a call to the pastoral ministry. Now my plan to attend seminary at Andrews University on my own was ending in failure. I'd given up.

After I finished speaking, my mother said, "Let's pray about it." We knelt down in the tent and my mother prayed and cried unto the Lord. When she finished praying, she said, "Son, I want you to go to that army office and withdraw your enlistment. The Lord has not brought you this far to leave you."

After campmeeting, I went to the army office and asked to withdraw from the army because I wanted to attend graduate school. The officer on duty explained that he didn't know whether I could withdraw, but he gave me some forms to fill out.

I went back to work as a student literature evangelist and was successful. In fact, I sold enough literature to earn a scholarship to Andrews University. Approximately eight weeks after enrolling at Andrews, I received a letter stating that the army had granted my request to withdraw and return to school. Upon completion of studies and graduating from Andrews, I was hired as a pastor by the South Atlantic Conference.

Listen, my son, to your father's instruction and do not forsake your mother's teaching. They will be a garland to grace your head and a chain to adorn your neck. Proverbs 1:8 NIV

Willie J. Lewis is president of the Allegheny West Conference of Seventh-day Adventists in Columbus, Ohio.

THE BROKEN PROMISE *By Y. J. Moses*

A new president of the Malaya Mission had been elected at the mission's year-end meeting on the campus of Southeast Asia Union College (SAUC) in Singapore. I immediately made an appointment to see him.

I told him of my agreement with his predecessor—a promise that the Malayan Mission would sponsor me to Spicer College to complete my degree when I returned from teaching school for two years in Sarawak. I had taken the teaching job to pay off my debt to the SDA secondary school. Now my school bill was paid and I was ready to make final arrangements to go to Spicer.

The new president said: "Yes, Brother Moses, I heard about that commitment, but you know we have our own two-year college here in Singapore. Why don't you attend SAUC? Then we'll consider sending you to Spicer to complete the undergraduate program in religion. But Brother Moses, our budget is tight. You'll have to finance your own education here at SAUC."

The president's response shattered all my dreams of getting a college education. The mission leadership had backed out of their promise. I had no money to go to Spicer on my own, and having finished teaching in Sarawak, I now had no job. I hadn't worked to arrange one because I was sure I was going to Spicer. That teaching job had paid me enough to cover my living expenses, pay that school bill, and even help support my aging parents in Malaysia. Now I had no job, no money, nowhere to go and no way to help my parents.

I went to the dormitory guest room where I was staying temporarily and prayed earnestly, seeking God's guidance. The next morning after breakfast, I knelt by my bed and prayed earnestly, "Lord, tomorrow is the last day of the meetings. I have to vacate this room and I don't know where to go. Please show me Your will."

Ten minutes later, I heard a knock on the door. Pastor Chu was there. He had been my high school Bible and English teacher and now was the assistant principal of the local SDA secondary school. He asked if I could go immediately to the school room downstairs as a substitute teacher for three days to cover the classes of a teacher who was ill. I dressed, went downstairs and took over the class.

I didn't know what awaited me, but I was glad I would have something to keep me busy working for the Lord and doing a favor for Pastor Chu for the next three days while I waited for God's answer to my prayers.

Two weeks later I was still teaching in that classroom when Pastor Chu told me it was mine for the rest of the school year and that I could take one college class free.

The three days turned into teaching full time for four and a half years and attending college part-time with all expenses paid. In December 1967 I graduated from Southeast Asia Union College with an associate degree in education. In June 1968 I received a full sponsorship from the SDA Secondary School to attend Spicer Memorial College to complete the under-graduate degree with a major in English, and a sizeable monthly allowance for my aged parents who by then had moved to Singapore to live with me.

"For I know the plans I have for you," declares the Lord, "plans to prosper you and not to harm you, plans to give you a hope and future." Jeremiah 29:11 NIV

Y. J. Moses is professor of education at Union College in Lincoln, Nebraska.

BLAB LAB AND A STUBBORN TEACHER *By Steve Pawluk*

He refused to sign my drop slip, and I was angry, significantly more angry than a theology major probably ought to be. My grade in Greek had slipped down to dangerous levels and it was important to me and my GPA that I drop the class. I could try that required class again during my sophomore year. But there stood the teacher, telling me that I should spend more time on vocab and in "blab lab." Kindly but firmly, he told me that he wouldn't allow me to drop the class. He didn't take the drop slip that I held in my extended hand.

I was tied for last place during that winter quarter of Greek I, and I even took a certain unscholarly pride in that. Greek was hard. It seemed unnecessary. Lists of vocab words and verb endings seemed to be endless. Lots of good translations of the Bible and many scholarly Bible commentaries were available. Did I imagine that I could improve on them? Who cares, anyway, if I master the details of the ancient Greek language?

Evidently Niels-Erik Andreasen cared. He refused to let me take the easy way out. He insisted that important things were often difficult and that difficult things were often important. If my call to minister for the Lord was as genuine as I claimed it to be, he pointed out, then I could not prepare in a half-hearted way. I had to begin to care too.

And so, finding that there was no way out but up and through the course, I memorized vocab words, parsed verbs, memorized vocab words, and prayed; and memorized vocab words, and desperately claimed James 1:5, and memorized vocab words; and went to blab lab, memorized more vocab words, and prayed again. And I finished Greek I with a respectable grade. The next year, I completed Greek II.

While those classes, in fact, have enriched my ability to understand God and to minister for Him in a variety of arenas, they and Dr. Andreasen also taught me that the battleground of faith and faithfulness is easily disguised as merely a difficult course or other trying experience in college.

Oliver Wendell Holmes once wrote: "Man's mind stretched to a new idea never goes back to its original dimension." Similarly, I say that faith and faithfulness, once stretched by a growth experience, never return to their original limits.

As iron sharpens iron, so one man sharpens another. Proverbs 27:17 NIV

Steve Pawluk is associate professor of education at Walla Walla College in College Place, Washington.

THE WITNESS AND
THE WANDERING SHEEP *By Katherine Koudele-Joslin*

At the beginning of the fall quarter of my senior year, I arrived on the beautiful but huge campus of Michigan State University (MSU). It's the largest contiguous university campus in the United States, with 2,000 acres of developed campus and 3,000 acres of farms. I was there to take a class I needed to complete my pre-professional program at Andrews University, where I'd done all my previous undergraduate work.

Besides being big, MSU was full of students—more than 40,000 were enrolled. I was the product of 15 years of Adventist education, eight of which were in a two-room country school. I'd never been in a class of more than 50 students. Now I was in classes four times that size. The secular "anything goes," post-Vietnam mentality swirled around me.

I lived off-campus with another girl (and her practically live-in boyfriend) and I was free to come and go and do as I pleased. No one was checking me in at night or seeing that I had attended my quota of dorm worships. I felt the undertow of the whole experience begin to pull me into its humanistic way of thinking. My desire for things spiritual began to wane.

When the weather was pleasant, the street-corner-preachers appeared—from saffron-robed Buddhists to undisguised Marxists. They espoused almost every belief system known. The group that drew the biggest crowds, however, were the black-suited Bible thumpers. These young men seemed determined to bring down judgment on the entire student body for its sinful ways. They delighted in engaging passersby in heated debates about who would be saved or lost. Their brand of Christianity left a bad taste in my mouth.

One day, late in the fall when the preachers were in full cry, an argument broke out that almost turned into a shoving match between a Bible-thumper and an avowed atheist. This kind of confrontation made me feel quite uncomfortable, so I shrank back into the crowd.

Just as the tension peaked, a slim, dark-haired student stepped up and placed herself between the combatants. In a calm, quiet voice she began to explain the Gospel truth clearly and simply and with a depth of understanding that spoke of her personal relationship with Jesus.

The scoffing crowd settled down and listened intently as she spoke. The arguing atheist was engrossed and asked her question after question which she answered in a loving, Christ-like manner. The preacher soon realized he had lost the crowd, so he stepped over to another bench and again took up his harangue. Not a soul moved to follow him; they clustered around the girl.

Her act of bravery in speaking out for truth reached out like a shepherd's staff and hooked my heart. God used her that day not only to reach the atheist but to bring back one of His wandering lambs.

I myself will search for My sheep, and will seek them out. As a shepherd seeks out his flock when some of his sheep have been scattered abroad, so will I seek out My sheep. Ezekiel 34:11,12 RSV

Katherine Koudele-Joslin is associate professor of animal science at Andrews University in Berrien Springs, Michigan.

A LESSON IN WHITE BOOTS AND AN APRON By *C. Lee Huff*

During my junior year in college, I faced a sobering decision. I was married, had two small children and the money just didn't seem to stretch to cover all our expenses. I worked evenings at a small dairy where I was in charge of cleaning and setting up all the equipment. The most coveted and best paying job in the dairy was running the pasteurizing machine. The man who had been doing that job had quit very suddenly. Now there was considerable speculation among the dairy workers about who would replace him.

On Friday, before a final decision would be made on Monday, the assistant plant manager called me and said, "Lee, you know how to run that machine. Why don't you apply for the job? You can drop out of school for a year or two until your finances are caught up. Then you can go back to school and finish your ministerial course."

This was a new thought to me. Even though we were struggling financially, I'd never doubted that God wanted me to be a minister and that He would somehow provide the means. However, in those few minutes, when I understood that my wages would increase about four times, I was tempted. I agreed to let him submit my name for consideration.

That was a difficult weekend. I didn't tell my wife what had transpired. I wondered what I would decide on Monday, if I were offered the job.

As I walked into the dairy Monday afternoon, the plant manager saw me and said, "As soon as you punch in, come to my office." Immediately my hands started to sweat and my throat went dry. As I closed the office door he said, "Lee, this morning we agreed to offer you the job. We would be delighted to have you in that position. However, before you decide, I must tell you a little about myself. Twenty-three years ago, I started college to become a doctor. After two and a half years of school, I found myself in a similar position to what you are in today, so I dropped out of school for a year or two. That was 20 years ago last month. Lee, before you make your decision, I want you to look at me. Notice my white boots and apron and then see yourself 20 years from now."

My decision was easy to make. As I left the office, I thanked God for using my boss to cause me to look at the bigger picture and not get hung-up on challenges of the moment.

All that was 36 years ago. I've spent 34 of those years in the ministry and I've often had to remind myself to look beyond the present challenges to the bigger picture. We must not lose sight of our goals.

I press on toward the goal to win the prize for which God has called me heavenward in Christ Jesus. Philippians 3:14 NIV

C. Lee Huff is president of the Euro-Asia Division of Seventh-day Adventists in Moscow, Russia.

IMAGE VERSUS IDENTITY *By Gregory P. Nelson*

Village Hall, the old church building on the campus of Walla Walla College, ranked high on my list of favorite romantic places, especially at night. And it was located right by the two women's dorms.

One night, my girlfriend Cindy and I were returning to her dorm just before her 10 p.m. curfew. With a few minutes to spare, we were pleased to find an open door at Village Hall, and no one around in the darkened building. Our purpose in lingering there, of course, was merely to exchange some profound philosophical insights about the meaning of life and love. Our philosophical exchange was brilliant and passionate, until we heard the old, wooden swinging doors right behind us creak open. The menacing beam of a bright flashlight cut through the darkness looking for its victims. And then it found us.

The night watchman's voice shattered the romantic stillness: "You two, come here!" Timidly, with hearts pounding, mortified that we had been caught kissing, we followed his flashlight beam.

As we stood in front of him, he looked us over carefully trying to recognize us. With judgment ringing in his voice, he said, "You shouldn't be in here! Especially kissing! I may have to report this to the authorities. Let me see your ID cards!"

My pounding heart almost stopped. I thought my life as I then knew it was over. Cindy was on the Student Affairs Council and I was Religious Vice-President for the Associated Student Body. What would people think? What would happen to our "lily white" reputations? The end had come.

The night watchman studied our ID cards carefully. After what seemed like the 2300 prophetic days, he gave the cards back to us, looked at us gravely and said, "I'll let you go this time. Just don't let me catch you in here like this again!"

I could've hugged him at that moment, I was so relieved. As I walked Cindy back to the dorm and reality began to sink in, I felt like a kid who'd gotten his hand slapped because it had been caught in the cookie jar. Embarrassed. But more than that, afraid —afraid primarily of what that man, and others who would find out, might think of me. I was more concerned about my image than anything else.

Through the years I see the matter differently. I've realized how easy it is to subscribe to a "cosmetic Christianity," where we put more emphasis on how we look than on who we are, image instead of character. Contrary to Andre Aggassiz's old commercial, could it be that to God, identity, and not image, is everything?

For the Lord does not see as mortals see; they look on the outward appearance, but the Lord looks on the heart. 1 Samuel 16:7 NRSV

Gregory P. Nelson is senior pastor of the College View Seventh-day Adventist Church in Lincoln, Nebraska.

THE TENTH MEETING

Patricia B. Mutch

Warren Ashworth

Philip Nixon

Thomas J. Dunion, Jr.

Robert L. Sweezey

Laurel Dovich

Cecily Daly

Keith Mattingly

Benjamin McArthur

Marvin K. Mitchell

Come and hear, all ye that fear God,
and I will declare what He hath done for my soul.

Psalm 66:16

GOD AND THE RIGHT MAN *By Patricia B. Mutch*

The arguments were getting worse—more frequent, more hostile. I loved this man, I told myself. Why couldn't I get along with him? My mother and some of my closest friends disapproved of our friendship, which made the situation worse. I didn't want to admit, even to myself, that they could be right.

He wanted me to quit college so we could be married and I could accompany him overseas to the army base. But I was resisting; college was important to me. I loved my studies and I wanted to be able to support myself if ever I had to. So our engagement was secret—and increasingly troubled.

Though I was a junior in college, I struggled with deep self-doubts, especially about romantic relationships. My parents recently had been divorced and my father had quickly remarried his girlfriend. During a recent argument, my fiancé had flung at me: "You'll never make anyone a good wife coming from a broken home, you know." Was he right? Was I being selfish to want to finish college? If I broke off with him, would I wind up alone?

What did the commandment to honor your parents mean? Were my mother's objections valid? Where was God in all this? I went to talk things over with a religion professor whose class in Philosophy of Religion was stimulating my thinking in new ways. Wil Alexander was wise enough to listen and ask me questions instead of prescribing the "right" course of action. He encouraged me to talk about my doubts with God, just like I would to a good friend. That insight was particularly helpful to my confusion about God after my father's remarriage. After all, I had wondered, if my biological father couldn't be trusted, how could I trust an unseen, heavenly Father?

To complicate things further, about this time a good-looking chemistry major with whom I worked on a research project began lingering more often for conversation after we finished work. I admired his brains, his keen wit, his thoughtfulness. Maybe—was there another possibility? My conflict grew worse—I had a commitment to my fiancé, but—should I reconsider? Would that be fair to him?

One night, unable to study for the clamor of opposing ideas in my mind, I consciously told God that I wanted Him to take charge. It was my first real leap of faith, going beyond the rather vague acceptance of God with which I'd grown up. "God, I don't know what to do—but I believe you know what's best for me. Please show me what is right. I trust you to lead me to the right man for me, if that's your plan. If I'm not suited to marriage, that's okay, too."

My face was wet with tears, but I was at peace. It was a prayer of desperation, of mustard-seed faith. But God honored my trust. Within two weeks, my fiancé had broken off with me. To my surprise, I felt only relief, not misery. God even spared me being broken-hearted. And without any effort on my part, my new friend and fellow worker had asked me for a first date. Today, after 30 years of marriage to him, I'm still thankful for the blessing God provided—a man suited to my needs and personality.

Listen to advice and accept instruction, and in the end you will be wise. Proverbs 19:20 NIV

Patricia B. Mutch is dean of the College of Arts and Sciences at Andrews University in Berrien Springs, Michigan.

THEY CHANGED MY LIFE *By Warren Ashworth*

Near the end of my sophomore year at La Sierra College, where I was preparing for dental school, I was deeply touched by the dedication of two of my religion professors, Royal Sage and J. C. Haussler. I sensed the Holy Spirit impressing me to become a minister.

Two of my friends were going to Newbold College in England, so I decided to spend my junior year there, too. Through the influence of the dedicated students at that school, that one year changed my life.

Only 120 students attended Newbold that year, and we came from 23 countries. I'd been there only a short time when I noticed that my classmates always seemed to have their Bibles with them. If they had to wait for the dining room to open, or the teacher to arrive, or a meeting to start, they'd get out their Bibles and read. I had never developed that habit but decided to try. To my delight, I was able to read the Bible through (for the first time in my life) in about eight months just by reading it in my "spare" time.

Some of my classmates already had suffered for their faith but were joyful, committed Christians. One had been imprisoned in a cell so small he could neither stretch out nor stand up. Another had come to Newbold to improve his English in order to help his father, a minister in a Communist country, translate the writings of Ellen White. This, in spite of the fact that his father had been imprisoned on several occasions for his illegal translation work, and the son would run the same risk.

From those Newbold students I also discovered the joy of literature evangelism. Some of the students had colporteured for *two* or *three* years just to pay the expenses of traveling to and attending Newbold for just *one* year. Nearly all of my classmates had spent at least one summer selling Adventist literature.

At the end of the year, I supposed I would just return to California because I had no money to travel around Europe. My student friends, however, convinced me to be a literature evangelist in Norway. Selling one book alone, *Slektenes Hop (Desire of Ages),* God helped me earn enough to travel around Europe, to live in Spain for four months, and to catch a much bigger picture of the world Christ came to die for.

My experience with those dear students at Newbold proved true what Ellen White wrote in *Testimonies* 1:388: "The young have a powerful influence over one another." The influence and concern of those students enriched my life and immeasurably enhanced my walk with the Lord. For this I'll always be grateful.

Let each of you look not only to his own interests, but also to the interests of others. Philippians 2:4 RSV

Warren Ashworth is professor of religion at Pacific Union College in Angwin, California.

"WHY DON'T YOU PRAY?" *By Philip Nixon*

During my sophomore year at Oakwood College, my wife and I accepted a call to go to Japan as student missionaries. We taught English and Bible classes at the SDA English Language schools.

We had high hopes of witnessing to people who have no knowledge of the God we serve. We were warned that the methods used in the United States, a "Christian" country, to bring people to accept Christ would have little success in Japan, a "pagan" country. Only one percent of the total population of Japan professed to be Christian. Of that one percent, approximately 10,000 were Seventh-day Adventists. To call the Japanese skeptics on the subject of the existence of God, as we understand Him, would be an understatement.

During the summer, the student missionaries and their Japanese students traveled together by ferry to the school's summer camp. The students went for the fun. We teachers viewed the occasion as a major evangelistic effort. Through interaction together at the camp (playing volleyball, swimming, hiking, etc.), the student missionaries and Japanese students bond as friends, causing the students to become interested in Christianity. From these friendships, many a precious soul has been won to Christ.

Our camp that summer began as a flop. Clouds and rain moved in on the first day. When the heavy rain continued through the second day, it seemed all our plans for a week of "fun in the sun" would be washed away.

During group worships that second night, everyone was discussing how the weather was spoiling the camp. Then one of the Japanese students innocently asked: "Why don't you pray?"

For a moment, everyone was silent, focusing on the implications of the question. We teachers could almost hear the thoughts of the students: "Hey, that's right. Haven't you Christians been telling us that God answers prayers? Well, now is your chance to prove it." We were well aware of what was at stake, and the potential of the moment.

We bowed our heads and offered a simple prayer. Before bedtime, all the student missionaries got together, talked about the event and prayed again, earnestly, for God's intervention.

We awoke the next morning to bright sunshine. The beautiful weather continued for the rest of the camp. On the morning of the last day, we accompanied our students to the ferry as they made the return trip home. As we stood on the dock and waved good-bye, a light drizzle started, signaling the return of the weather our Heavenly Father had graciously postponed to prove His love for believer and non-believer alike.

And this is the confidence that we have in Him, that, if we ask any thing according to His will, He heareth us. 1 John 5:14

Philip Nixon is assistant dean of men at Oakwood College in Huntsville, Alabama.

IT SHALL BE SEEN *By Thomas J. Dunion, Jr.*

M y heart seemed to drop right through the floor of the small plane circling the airport a few miles out of Pocatello. The desolate, drought-stricken landscape visible out the window only heightened my sense of foreboding.

I didn't know a single soul in Idaho. I faced an 80 percent drop in income. And all in all, this didn't seem to be an auspicious start toward a doctoral degree in mathematics. True, the Lord had indicated through pastors, prayer partners and others that going back to graduate school was the right thing to do. Only weeks before I had confided to my prayer partner, "Tony, I'd have to find some way to double the meager assistantship salary the university is offering, then find a virtually free place to live. Even then, I don't see how I'll handle student-loan repayments from previous graduate studies."

My prayer partner said, "Tell the Lord what you just told me. Don't settle for anything less. After all, if God is really in this, He'll provide."

When I walked into the math department office at Idaho State University, my heart sank again: a new department chairman. Would he be as supportive as the friendly fellow I'd talked with on the phone?

At that moment, God began to show His marvelous provision. The new chairman had attended church years before with the man who was now president of the college where I had been teaching. He quickly found another class for me to teach, doubling my salary. Soon after, another professor told me about an apartment. I tried hard to suppress my feelings of amazement and joy when he told me the price. Compared to rents in the East, this rent was practically nothing. Then, my parents decided they could see their way clear to help me with those student-loan payments for the first year.

All this was just the beginning of three years of remarkable provision. A part-time summer job ended just in time for me to study for an important comprehensive exam. Someone had left-over conference funds. Would I be interested in the extra money? (Not all questions are difficult.) Then there was the "penny stock" I'd bought a couple of years earlier in response to a prayer partner's challenge to do something to expand my horizons. Suddenly, it now was peaking at a 5-for-1 payoff. Just as suddenly, after I sold it, it dropped through the floor faster than I had wanted to drop through that airplane only a few months before.

Things went very well those three years at Idaho State, and I finished my advanced degree right on schedule and even got back my old job in New England. As I drove east into Wyoming with the mountains of Idaho receding in my rear-view mirror, I thought of another mountain, another time and another place where the God of Abraham had made His provision known.

And Abraham called the name of that place Jehovah-jireh: as it is said to this day, In the mount of the Lord it shall be seen. Genesis 22:14

Thomas J. Dunion, Jr., is associate professor of mathematics at Atlantic Union College in South Lancaster, Massachusetts.

SERVICE ON ANOTHER PATH _Robert L. Sweezey_

M y earliest ambition as a child growing up on a farm was to be a preacher. Never a policeman, or fireman or chief. Only a preacher. I well remember preaching in the farmyard with a stump for my pulpit and chickens for my congregation.

While many of my friends changed their majors during our college years, I held to my goal of becoming a preacher all the way through graduation. I spent many long hours struggling with Greek. Some measure of my difficulty can best be illustrated by noting that I found calculus a far easier subject to understand. Yet I persevered.

Twenty-five theology majors were in my 1980 graduating class. These students heard Desmond Ford and Walter Rea speak of their "new" theology, and views about Adventist history. Our graduation year saw the unfolding of the Davenport financial fiasco in our church in North America. Those were confusing times for budding pastors and seasoned churchmen alike, but my dream of becoming a preacher persisted.

Graduation came and went. For me and more than half my theology classmates, no "call" came. I understood there were far more graduates than employment opportunities. Yet I was very disappointed not to have an immediate opportunity to exercise my response to the personal call to pastoral ministry I had felt at such a tender age.

After graduation, I remained in the Walla Walla College area doing what I could to make some money to pay my many bills. In the fall, I enrolled again to convert my minor in business into a major. During this term the General Conference Risk Management Service came to our campus looking for potential business interns. I knew nothing about them or about insurance. I went for an interview because they represented the church. I knew that God was using them and sensed that He might want to use me through them.

As I consider how God has led me to become the president of Adventist Risk Management (the Adventist Church's world-wide insurance service), I now believe that nothing could have prepared me better for my later graduate studies in business and law, or for God's service, than His leading through the most disappointing times. For where God leads, He provides.

More College Faith   143

I will instruct you and teach you in the way you should go; I will counsel you and watch over you. Psalm 32:8 NIV

Robert L. Sweezey is president of Adventist Risk Management, Inc., at the General Conference of Seventh-day Adventists in Silver Spring, Maryland.

GIVING AND GETTING ON THE SABBATH *By Laurel Dovich*

The phone rang. In a sleepy grog, I tried turning off the alarm clock. I had a right to be tired and groggy. It was 6 a.m. on a Sabbath morning, and it had been a long, intense week, as it always is for engineering students. I pulled on a pair of sweats and found my way down to the dorm lobby where the phone call had originated.

Orville, a fellow student, and I set out for the apartment of a classmate who graciously got up and fed us breakfast. That was his weekly contribution to our ministry, since the cafeteria schedule didn't support the hours we required.

Every Sabbath, no matter how tired we were after a week of homework, labs, lab reports, project deadlines and work, we pulled ourselves together to head out to a small church about 70 country-road miles away. Orville had bumped into this church by accident one Sabbath when he found himself driving by it about the time Sabbath School should start.

The church consisted of seven adults and eight children. It readily became apparent that we had a lot to offer this little congregation. A core student group of three went there every week and we looked for volunteers to come and help us. Fellow students came along to present special music, play the piano and organ or just fill the pews. Two carloads of college students nearly doubled the attendance of the church.

Our core group soon found permanent responsibilities in the children's Sabbath School. We also entertained the small children during the worship service so their parents could listen to the sermon. Afternoons gave us a chance to help with Ingathering and witnessing programs in the community. We became fully involved in the church.

It was a sacrifice for us to attend church so far away from school. We had no chance to catch up on any sleep on Sabbaths. And, we had to find extra time to prepare for our responsibilities at the church each week. At times, we scrounged to come up with gas money to get us there and back. We missed the campus fellowship, socializing and special programming that happens on the only leisure day of the week.

And yet, our lives were richly blessed. The hours spent together every Sabbath helped form deep friendships within our core group, and gained for us an extended family at the church who fed us, cared for us and took us into their homes and families.

We learned that there are many rewards in giving.

Each one should use whatever gift he has received to serve others, faithfully administering God's grace in its various forms. 1 Peter 4:10 NIV

Laurel Dovich is associate professor of engineering at Walla Walla College in College Place, Washington.

KNOCKING ON HEAVEN'S DOOR By Cecily Daly

"Tomorrow's the day! I'm really excited," a youthful voice declared. "Make sure to take your washed clothes off the line," said another. "Elder Nation's going to pray for rain tomorrow during church and we'll have rain."

"How can you be so sure?" I asked.

"Oh, you've never heard of Elder Nation? Whenever there is a drought such as this, the college asks him to pray for rain, and rain falls."

"Well, I'll have to see that to believe," I said.

The corridor buzzed with excitement as students brought their arm loads of fresh, sun-dried clothes inside. Although I saw no possibility of a deluge on this parched day, I collected my clothes too. The pale, sickly flowers struggling from the dry earth eloquently explained why most of the crops had failed. College administrators were at their wit's end, for there was little or no water to avert an impending disaster. The only option open was to pray for rain. Elder Nation, known among us as a giant of faith and prayer, was the selected intercessor.

Sabbath morning dawned clear. The sun shone starkly from a cloudless sky. But expectancy filled the air, for veteran college students knew the efficacy of intercessory prayer and waited for the miracle of water on parched ground. As a curious freshman, I eagerly watched the sky.

At the appointed time in the church service, Elder Nation stood at the desk and quietly but firmly declared, "If there is anyone here who does not believe that God can perform a miracle of sending the needed rain, you may go home, now." The silence was absolute.

The prayer and sermon centered on "mustard-seed" faith and the power of God. The theme was that God still hears and answers prayers. Church was dismissed and everyone left with an extra measure of faith in the Master of winds and waves, who still works miracles.

At lunch, the cafeteria buzzed with stories of past campus miracles. Soon it was rest period. My roommate slept, but I was determined to watch a miracle take place.

About 3 p.m., I noticed one small cloud in the sky. A few minutes later a few large, dark clouds drifted across the face of the sun. Almost immediately the bright, hot sun and the blue sky disappeared and angry-looking black rain clouds crashed against each other. I watched this phenomenon and soon witnessed a "cloud burst." Water poured down from the sky in torrents for about 30 minutes. Suddenly, the rain stopped and the sky cleared.

This dumbfounded college freshman stood transfixed at the window, gazing at the freshly washed earth and sky and listening to the steady, musical drip of the water from the eaves. I savored the earthy smell of rain on parched ground. It was a moment I would never forget.

If you have faith as a grain of mustard seed, you will say to this mountain, "Move from here to there," and it will move; and nothing will be impossible for you. Matthew 17:20 NKJV

Cecily Daly is assistant professor of English and communication at Oakwood College in Huntsville, Alabama.

HE WALKS WITH ME *By Keith Mattingly*

I grew up in a religious home and was spiritually directed from the very beginning. Not surprisingly, I had a hard time understanding the full, life-changing impact others experienced when they accepted Christ later in life. I never had felt the euphoria that often accompanies a dramatic conversion. So when I'd consider those who had experienced dramatic change, I tended to wonder, even worry, about myself. Am I really walking with the Lord? I knew that a walk with God must be personal and real. I craved knowing that God was really with me and I with Him.

My first understanding of a personal walk with God occurred when I nearly got caught breaking some rules at Helderberg College. Two couples had decided to take an unsupervised walk one evening. Our venture nearly turned into disaster when we almost bumped into a couple of faculty members in an unexpected place. We could hear them talking as they discussed missing us and wondered where we were.

Quickly, I invented a story and coordinated the details with the others so that our stories would match when we arrived back at the dorms. We all took off on our separate ways. Our stories matched. Our trouble was minimal.

God is the master of bringing good out of bad. He started working on me in a big way. My lie really began to bother me and I decided I had to confess. But I realized that if I confessed, I essentially would be confessing for the other three as well, and they definitely weren't ready to confess. Finally I went to the principal, a man I trusted, and told him I needed to confess something. I also explained that my confession would implicate others, who had no similar desire to make things right. I asked the good man that he pretend that I only was confessing and ignore the involvement of others. If there was to be any punishment, I would gladly take it all. He agreed and, gratefully, I was able to unload.

What a sense of relief rolled over me. I realized as never before the great discomfort of hidden guilt, and the joy that comes with forgiveness. Of course, in the big picture of life, this was a relatively small matter. But it was a very important one for me, because it reassured me that I didn't have to have a major "big conversion" crisis in order to experience my own walk with God, and to know that He was walking with me.

He who conceals his sins does not prosper, but whoever confesses and renounces them finds mercy. Proverbs 28:13 NIV

Keith Mattingly is assistant professor of biblical studies at Andrews University in Berrien Springs, Michigan.

AN OUTPOURING OF THE SPIRIT *By Benjamin McArthur*

When I entered Andrews University in the fall of 1969, I had no idea the following year would prove so fateful for American society, in general, and for higher education in particular. Protests against the Vietnam War, which had been endemic on college campuses for several years, exploded in the spring of 1970 with the announcement of America's invasion of Cambodia. In May, the Kent State shooting shocked the country. When two students at Jackson State College in Mississippi were killed by state troopers ten days later, I recall wondering whether our nation's social fabric might unravel completely.

Although the Andrews campus never approached the level of student protest seen elsewhere, the 1960s spirit of activism was felt even there. Trivial issues, such as hair length for men, provoked mild demonstrations. The more serious matter of the Vietnam War drew some Andrews students to a Washington protest march. And Kent State prompted a campus "teach-in" devoted to the war.

Tumultuous times they were—and exciting. As an impressionable freshman, I discovered the intellectual rewards of scholarship and social observation, which led to my future career in education. Yet my reflections on that year must also acknowledge that the campus lacked a pervasive atmosphere of spirituality.

A radical change occurred the next fall. At the beginning of fall term, a number of students attended a retreat where God's spirit became manifest. Their testimonies and changed lives quickly brought revival to the full campus. There was no obvious external cause to the awakening, no tragedy or supernatural manifestation to inspire piety. It appeared as mysteriously as the tongues of fire must have at Pentecost.

The revival wasn't limited to Andrews. Student groups traveled to other Adventist campuses carrying the good news. A general renewal was effected in much of Adventist higher education, touching hundreds of lives across North America. The intensity and scope of the revival even captured the attention of *Christianity Today,* which detailed the phenomenon for its readers.

The campus tone changed markedly after my freshman year. Animosities between administration and students attenuated. If fewer students seemed caught up in the great national political debates than the year before, regard for spiritual values and of witness had trebled. My first substantial involvement in outreach came that year in one of the many groups that traveled regularly to outlying churches.

I've often pondered the campus transformation of that year and its impact on American Adventism. It showed me how rapid and unexpected change can be. It demonstrated the power of youthful energy and idealism. And it prompts the question: When—and where—will God's spirit again move that way in North American Adventism?

And in the last days it shall be, God declares, that I will pour out My Spirit upon all flesh. Acts 2:17 RSV

Benjamin McArthur is professor of history at Southern Adventist University in Collegedale, Tennessee.

THE PRANK AND THE PRESIDENT *By Marvin K. Mitchell*

S tudent Week of Prayer was upon us at La Sierra College. We had been accustomed to open seating at these meetings held in Hole Memorial Auditorium (HMA). But this year, a new rule from the administration required that we use our regular assigned chapel seats. At supper before the first evening meeting, a table full of concerned young men decided that the college had gone too far.

As we saw it, sitting in our assigned chapel seats would likely put a serious crimp in our social development. The plan we devised was simple. We'd go early and sit in a seat other than our own, thus forcing another person to do the same. Soon chaos would reign and we all could sit wherever we pleased.

We hurried through supper and arrived early at HMA to put our plan into effect. It didn't take the rest of the students long to realize what was happening and to gleefully join in. When Lou Ann Wallace, along with the other student speakers, came on stage, her eyes widened with anxiety as she sensed that something was amiss. The record takers had no idea how to proceed and made a hasty call to the deans. Upon arrival, the deans quickly decided who the likely instigators were and made valiant, though unsuccessful, attempts to sort things out and restore order.

The deans, possibly feeling the frustration of their inability to communicate effectively, wheeled out the heavy artillery. As we sat there chortling about how truly clever we were, Lou Ann and the other student speakers suddenly left the platform and were replaced by the dean of students and Dr. William Landeen, the college president.

Suddenly a deep hush fell over the audience as we waited for events to unfold. First to speak was the dean of students who began talking very earnestly about student rebellion. This had a sobering and bewildering effect on the majority of students, but still nobody moved. Student rebellion? Wasn't that a bit of an overreaction to a silly prank? Or were we in a lot deeper trouble than we had planned?

Next it was the president's turn. The silence was now palpable. Dr. Landeen moved stiffly to the podium in his usual deliberate way, and paused before speaking.

Then, something wonderful happened. Without saying a word, he smiled, and then he laughed. An eruption of applause broke out that was as genuine and heartfelt as had ever been heard in that venerable old chapel. Without a word being said, we all got up and returned to our assigned seats.

It was wonderful. It was amazing. It was almost a miracle how that wise, old scholar recognized the difference between a student uprising and a sophomorish prank, and without a word, defused the little crisis. Lou Ann returned to the platform and preached her heart out. The Week of Prayer proceeded that evening and the rest of the week with great positive impact upon the students.

Somehow the Lord took a situation designed to be disruptive and turned it into a spiritual blessing that even today has a positive impact on many lives.

For I know the thoughts that I think toward you, says the Lord, thoughts of peace and not of evil, to give you a future and a hope. Jeremiah 29:11 NKJV

Marvin K. Mitchell is associate professor of teacher education at Pacific Union College in Angwin, California.

THE ELEVENTH MEETING

Norman K. Miles

Wolfgang Kunze

Lowell C. Hagele

Wendolin Pazitka-Munroe

John R. Jones

Kermit Netteburg

Gordon L. Retzer

Manuel Vasquez

Wil Clarke

Valerie N. Phillips

Come and hear, all ye that fear God,
and I will declare what He hath done for my soul.

Psalm 66:16

SEMINAR IN SERVICE *Norman K. Miles*

B etween 1972 and 1975 I was a graduate student at the University of Michigan in Ann Arbor. It was an exciting time for me. I discovered the joy of scholarly investigation in one of the most complete research centers of the world. It was also a time of tremendous culture shock.

I was not prepared for the campus radicalism of the time. Drug use was rampant, campus rallies supported the United Farm Workers, socialist newspapers cropped up on campus and classes often were dominated by spirited political discussion. At that time, it was chic to be a radical and anything religious generally was considered anti-intellectual, reactionary and ignorant. It was a constant challenge to maintain a positive Christian witness in such an atmosphere.

I was enrolled in a graduate seminar on African history taught by a world-famous scholar. The seminar met once a week for three hours for discussion of selected issues and reports on our research projects. I was researching the role of African Christian churches in developing nations.

One day in the middle of my report, a fellow classmate, Bill, jumped to his feet and began shouting at me. He was an African American graduate student who had played professional basketball in Europe for several years before returning to the United States. He was fluent in several languages and considered one of the brightest members of our class. He tore into me in an angry tirade. "I don't see how a black man who knows as much as you know about what white people did to our people in the name of Christianity could be a Christian."

I tried to explain that I was a follower of Christ, not other people, regardless of their profession. He rejected my response and left the room in anger.

One evening, two weeks later, I got a phone call from Bill. He was in the university clinic. He had not been feeling well and went in for a checkup. The doctors found that his blood pressure was so high he was a stroke waiting to happen. He was hospitalized immediately. He said he needed someone to get his car from campus and park it somewhere else, contact his wife and let his professors know about his illness.

I immediately went to the clinic, got his keys, moved his car, contacted his wife and professors, and for the next several days saw to it that the things he needed done were taken care of. The day he left the hospital, I asked him why, of all people, he had called me for help when he had disagreed with me so personally and violently in class.

"I've been watching you," he said. "I knew that I could depend on you to help me."

Live such good lives among the pagans that, though they accuse you of doing wrong, they may see your good deeds and glorify God on the day He visits us. 1 Peter 2:12

Norman Miles is president of the Lake Region Conference of Seventh-day Adventists in Chicago, Illinois.

LONG-RANGE ANSWERS *By Wolfgang Kunze*

After three exciting years of teaching German at Andrews University, I received a study leave to complete my doctoral degree. I had chosen UCLA because of my interest in a particular professor, a renowned scholar of early 20th-century German literature who was teaching there.

My plans had been carefully laid. With the small stipend from Andrews and a teaching assistantship promised by UCLA, I felt confident that my time could be directed wholeheartedly toward my study program. Shortly before leaving for California, I was shocked to learn that I could no longer count on the teaching assistantship. I had to find other work.

My wife and I both found part-time jobs at Lynwood Academy. This required a long morning commute that consumed valuable study time. Even more frustrating, the classes I most wanted to take were scheduled only during the morning hours. What a crushing disappointment! Finally, I had to give up my dream of studying with the renowned professor and choose another area of specialty in my program.

The second year, we were no longer able to continue teaching at Lynwood, so I submitted my name to the language tutorial center at UCLA. I was warned not to expect much because 15 names were ahead of mine on the list. But, that fall, I tutored five students and later learned that many tutors ahead of me hadn't received a single call. This work, along with a teaching assistantship my wife secured, helped us survive financially. At the very end of fall quarter, I learned that all my tutorial students were leaving. I wondered why God had provided me with these students in such a miraculous way for just the one quarter. Then, just one week later, my department chair called and offered me the teaching assistantship I had been denied earlier. God's timing became clear.

I returned to teaching at Andrews, completed my dissertation and branched out into some very rewarding research my new choice of specialty opened up for me. I felt very fulfilled, but occasionally I pondered why my original doctoral plans had seemed to be thwarted in such tangled ways.

In 1980, at a National Endowment for the Humanities seminar at the University of California at Berkeley, I chanced to meet my old department chair from UCLA. Our conversation turned to that renowned professor under whom I had wanted so much to study. I alluded to my disappointment in not having been able to work with him. Hearing my regret, the chair gasped and exclaimed: "Count your blessings!" Then he told me the sad stories of numerous doctoral students who had studied with that professor. Some gave up their doctoral studies altogether, others lost teaching positions for not finishing and one woman even had a nervous breakdown.

Perhaps this miracle of God's leading in my life might still be hidden from me if He, in His own good time, had not chosen to reveal it after so many years.

I have other questions close to my heart, but I'm patient. I know they will all be answered, perhaps not today, or even tomorrow—but someday.

He has made everything beautiful in its time. Ecclesiastes 3:11 NIV

Wolfgang Kunze is professor of German at Andrews University in Berrien Springs, Michigan.

MORE THAN MATH *By Lowell C. Hagele*

My wife, two preschool sons, and I had just returned to the States after completing four years of mission service on Guam where I had been a teacher and principal at Guam Mission Academy. I wanted to complete graduate school while my children were still young. My goal was to become a college mathematics teacher.

I chose a doctoral program in mathematics at the University of Northern Colorado. Returning to the classroom as a student can be very challenging and my first summer term kept me very busy. One of my courses that summer was topology, known as "rubber sheet" geometry. Since I hadn't taken the prerequisite course, I found the course very difficult. I did reasonably well up to the semester examination, but my final grade was not what is expected of doctoral students.

This was devastating. I wondered whether I should be in graduate school at all. I prayed, "Lord, why did I travel over 8,000 miles from Guam for this to happen? I thought You were leading me? I'm preparing to serve You and it looks like You don't care." The experience caused me to re-examine my goals and those of the program in which I was enrolled.

The Lord proved He cared for me by reminding me that my real interests were broader than just mathematics. I conferred with my professors and learned that the mathematics department also offered a doctoral degree in mathematics education that I had not previously considered. It focused on the teaching of mathematics at the college level and also provided the necessary background to lead in teacher education. After further prayer and study, I changed programs and continued studying mathematics along with a broad cross-section of courses geared toward preparing future elementary and secondary teachers.

Less than three years later, I successfully completed the program and simultaneously received an invitation to join the faculty of Japan Missionary College. While I had been intent on reaching my own goals, the Lord knew all along where He wished to use me in His work. In Japan, I used much of what I'd learned—including mathematics—and eventually chaired the college teacher-education program. At Union College, those studies continue to help me as I have taught mathematics and carried larger administrative responsibilities.

What happened to my classmates who remained in the program in which I originally enrolled? A number of philosophical differences and other problems within the university led to the termination of the program. My classmates enrolled there either didn't graduate or had to start over in the very program into which the Lord already had led me.

Those who know Your name will trust in You, for You, Lord, have never forsaken those who seek You. Psalm 9:10 NIV

Lowell C. Hagele is vice president for academic administration at Union College in Lincoln, Nebraska.

OUT OF THE WOODS *By Wendolin Pazitka-Munroe*

I t was an idyllic May morning in Denmark. I was touring Scandinavia as a member of the Newbold College choir. My boyfriend Donald and I decided to rise early and take a short walk together before our tour bus left for Copenhagen at 8 a.m.

We spent a wonderful time together following a spindly-legged fawn into a beautiful forest. Eventually we let the fawn slip away and decided it was time to head back to the Sanitarium where we were staying. That's when we discovered we were lost.

We randomly choose a direction and hoped for the best. We walked for an hour, seeing nothing that pointed the way. We began to panic. No signs of civilization appeared anywhere. We picked up the pace and walked on. Finally, we stumbled across an old, overgrown logging road. "Great! Surely, this will lead us out," exclaimed Donald, triumphantly. We ran as fast as we could until we came to a crossroads. Now, with hearts pounding and lungs aching, we had four ways to go, and not a clue. We just looked at each other hopelessly. The panic was back.

In twenty minutes, the choir would leave for Copenhagen. Donald turned to face me and, taking my hands in his, suggested that we pray.

We dropped to our knees right there, under the warming sun, and pleaded with our Heavenly Father to help us. Off our knees, we kept our initial course, going as fast as we could. A few minutes later we heard the promising sound of traffic and found a busy highway.

A woman approached on a bicycle. She had long, golden hair and was wearing a flowing skirt, a white blouse, bobby socks, and brown leather shoes. A brown wicker basket was attached to the handlebars of her bike.

"You're from the Newbold choir, aren't you!" she exclaimed.

"Yes, we are." The relief we felt was inexpressible. "Can you tell us how to get to the Sanitarium?"

She pulled a Bible from the wicker basket, held it up, and traced an imaginary map on the front cover. The Sanitarium was *eight kilometers* away (nearly five miles). It was now 7:50 a.m. Our cause was hopeless unless we got a ride.

Just then a white Morris Mini pulled over to the side of the road. The male driver rolled down the window, leaned across the seat and, to our utter astonishment, asked, "You're from the Newbold choir aren't you?"

"Why, yes! We need to get to the Sanitarium by eight o'clock. Can you help us?"

"I'm driving right by it. Hop in," he offered.

We pulled into the parking lot of the Sanitarium at precisely 8 a.m. Later that morning, during worship, Donald and I shared our experience with the choir. It was an experience that has remained indelibly etched in my memory. We know now that asking a caring Heavenly Father to guide us, not only in the difficult moments, but in all decisions we face every day, will make all the difference in the world.

Show me Your ways, O Lord, teach me Your paths; guide me in Your truth and teach me, for You are God my Savior, and my hope is in You all day long. Psalm 25:4,5 NIV

Wendolin Pazitka-Munroe is associate professor of music at Canadian University College in College Heights, Alberta.

ULTIMATE CONCERN *By John R. Jones*

As I drove the truckload of freshly harvested peas back to the processing plant, I wondered what my friend Les had been talking about a couple of days before. We had just begun summer jobs with a large harvesting operation. Les worked at the plant's vining machines where the trucks unloaded. He had more contact with other workers than I did. He often got acquainted with students from universities across the country who worked the summer harvests for the adventure and the good money. Sometimes the conversations got pretty deeply into philosophical issues.

Les had been telling me about a couple of fellows from the University of Chicago who had been students of Paul Tillich—a theologian of whom I'd heard, but knew almost nothing. "What's this business of ultimate concern they keep talking about?" Les asked me.

"I don't know; something about the convictions you're willing to pay an ultimate price for, I guess." Uncomfortable with my ignorance, I steered the conversation into less unfamiliar territory. Les had been offering to introduce me to his acquaintances, but I didn't think I wanted to meet them. All of a sudden my ministerial training at Walla Walla College began to feel parochial.

"The following drivers please report to the dispatch office," barked the loudspeaker back at the plant. "McDougal, Baker, Jones, ..." I recognized the names of my eight or nine fellow Adventists.

"Jones, we're letting you go. The management has decided you guys who can't be flexible about your weekly day off are too much trouble."

"But . . . But we agreed on this when we signed on for the summer." I stammered.

"So guess what? They changed their mind. So get outta here. Your final paycheck will be in the mail."

The dispatcher was belligerent and gruff.

"Are you proud of this?" I demanded.

"Sorry, man. I had nothing to do with it," he muttered, as he turned his back.

It was the longest summer of my life. The only work I could get at the end of June was in the college paint department—an opening so undesirable and poor-paying that no one had taken it. How could my faithfulness lead me into this? The Lord knew I needed that money for my training to serve Him. I could've landed other, better work and pay if I'd known this was to be the outcome. And all for the sake of Sabbath. I thought long thoughts about it all. Was it worth it? I knew that if I went back and agreed to work on occasional Sabbaths, I could have my truck-driving job again. A couple of my classmates had done so. One finds out what one's faith is made of in such a crisis.

The following school year was especially grueling. I had to work long hours to compensate for the good earnings I had missed the previous summer. Still, the debts built up. It was clear that the coming summer would have to be much more profitable if I was to recover.

When I picked up the ringing phone in April, I had been looking and praying for some serious summer work. It took me a moment to recognize the gruff voice of the dispatcher from my short-lived job the previous June.

"Jones, we're making up our crews for the coming season over here, and we wondered if you'd like us to hold a place open for you." In my silence, he must have caught my puzzlement and resentment. "Hey, man," he went on, "we've been talking. I explained to the owner and managers that several of you Advent guys were among our best drivers. I always knew that you put in an honest shift, worked hard in the field and didn't fool around on the road. We've figured out that we can work in three or four of you guys without too much problem. You're the first one I'm calling. What do you say?"

"I don't know . . .," my voice trailed off. He read my thoughts: *Would I get my summer messed up again?*

"It'll be okay, Jones. Trust me on this."

I did and was retained through the various harvests of the summer and beyond, even after the regular seasonal work was over. I worked long, well-paid days right up to my wedding in early September. Newly married and headed for seminary studies at Andrews University, I was thinking, "Now maybe I can learn about that "ultimate concern" business the theologians talk about."

Then it hit me: The Lord had already taught me that lesson in His own way.

And the world is passing away, and the lust of it; but he who does the will of God abides forever. 1 John 2:17

John R. Jones is dean of the School of Religion at La Sierra University in Riverside, California.

PASSING VALUES ON PASS INTERFERENCE *By Kermit Netteburg*

I was a sideline athlete during college. I loved sports and signed up for every intramural season. Flag football. Volleyball. Basketball. Softball. They were the four nine-week grading periods in my school year. However, because I was slow and weak and lacked hand-eye coordination, I seldom played. Hence, my status as a sideline athlete.

I particularly admired Kiff. He could jump high enough to spike the volleyball. His broad shoulders let him rebound in basketball; his speed made him an ace outfielder in softball. But it was during the football season that he taught me how to be a Christian athlete.

We made it to the championship game that season, Kiff and I. He ran precise routes over the middle or to the sideline. When the ball arrived, he caught it. That simple. So the ball was thrown in his direction often. And we won often.

The game was close through the fourth quarter. A touchdown would win for us, and we were driving toward that score. Kiff got open on a stop-and-go route. Ron launched the pass in Kiff's direction. It sailed directly toward me, as Kiff and the defender battled for position. I took my eye off the ball and watched the two players as both of them leaped to catch the ball. Kiff reached for the ball with both hands. The defender stretched one hand toward the ball, but shoved the other into Kiff's midsection. The nudge wasn't enough to knock Kiff down or attract the referee's attention, but it was enough to cause Kiff to pull his arms down just slightly.

The ball skittered off Kiff's fingertips. Incomplete pass.

Kiff looked at the ball, fallen to the turf. He looked at the defender quizzically. Then he walked back toward the huddle. No fight. No trash talking. No accusation of dirty play. Just a Christian athlete.

We lost that game, but I won two things: First, a sense of the importance of sports in life, that this was just a game and not nearly as important as keeping your Christian standards intact. Second, a newfound respect for the athlete I admired. He was great, not because he won but because he never lost his temper; never let the game overrule the important things in life.

A man of knowledge uses words with restraint, and a man of understanding is even-tempered. Proverbs 17:27 NIV

Kermit Netteburg is assistant to the president for communication of the North American Division of Seventh-day Adventists in Silver Spring, Maryland.

LOST AND FOUND By Gordon L. Retzer

Between my junior and senior years at Southern Missionary College (now Southern Adventist University), I spent the summer as a student literature evangelist in West Virginia. The publishing director gave me a large number of "leads" in a certain region and explained that they represented addresses that could not be found by the full-time literature evangelists. The director asked if I wanted to try these, assuring me that if I could find these interested customers I easily would make my scholarship.

Many of the "addresses" were actually imprecise paragraphs offering "directions" to the house: "Past the abandoned gas station . . .," etc. Because it was so difficult to find these places, the occupants usually were thrilled to see a salesperson. And they often had cash hidden away.

I developed a simple routine. In the morning, I laid out the lead cards I wanted to pursue and asked the Lord to help me find the people. It was a great partnership. Day after day I was successful in not only finding the addresses but in making the sales, and I knew God was leading.

Then one day, it seemed He wasn't. I hunted all day. I prayed several times. Backed up by the prayer, and all the experience I had gained in the artistry of finding these places, I still failed. I was lost. I stopped at a house and asked the lady if she recognized the "address." She just laughed and said I was "nowhere near." "But you might try the Baptist preacher next door," she said. My head was hanging, my faith in God's leading was about gone.

Unenthusiastically, I went over to the Baptist preacher's house, wondering where God was anyway. I was so discouraged that I probably did all the things that sales people (especially God's) are not to do.

The preacher quickly looked through every book, and then asked, "How much for everything you've got?"

"A lot!" was my faithless and surly answer.

He jumped up, went to his bedroom, and returned with cash for everything. "I've been looking for books like these and I also want my church to buy a set." I was shocked. And he wasn't finished.

"Can you come to prayer meeting tonight and I'll tell my members they should buy these books."

After the singing, preaching and an altar call, while the whole congregation was up front, the preacher introduced me by saying, "God has sent a young man to our town today." And then I watched as he persuasively explained the benefits to families who owned these books. It was a record day.

Whenever I wonder if God is really leading, I go back to the sights, sounds and smells of that little town in West Virginia where I was "lost" and where God opened my eyes to a much bigger picture.

I will lead the blind by ways they have not known, along unfamiliar paths I will guide them; I will turn the darkness into light before them and make the rough places smooth. These are the things I will do; I will not forsake them. Isaiah 42:16 NIV

Gordon L. Retzer is president of the Florida Conference of Seventh-day Adventists in Winter Park, Florida.

WITH MY FATHER'S BLESSING By *Manuel Vasquez*

I had a good job at a construction-form builder's company in Denver, Colorado. With several recent promotions and the company expanding, my future there seemed assured. Very active in my local church, I was happy and content with life. College was certainly not in my immediate plans.

Sixteen months earlier, while in the Navy, I had joined the Adventist Church, and through many wonderful witnessing experiences and a series of other events, I had felt a definite call to the ministry. But since coming home, I had almost forgotten about that calling.

One evening, I visited my friend John. He had been planning to go to Union College the next month. But he surprised me when he said his plans suddenly had changed. "Here," he said, thrusting his college application in my hands. "You take it. You're the one that should go to college."

I was stunned. My first reaction was, "This is God speaking to me."

Later that evening, as I drove home, I was overwhelmed and excited with the thought of going to college and studying for the ministry. But one thing stood in the way: my father.

Though he was a faithful member of the church, my father had let it be known that he didn't want any of his sons to become a minister. Ministers were "pansies." He considered them soft, always driving around in new cars and doing little more than preaching for 30 minutes on Sabbath morning. No, my father wanted a "real" profession for his boys.

Since very little time was left to get my application in, I stayed up late that night filling it out. I remember praying, "Lord, if you really want me to study for the ministry, please change my dad's mind so that I can have his blessing."

The next evening, at the supper table with everyone present, I nervously handed the college application to my father.

"Dad, this is my application to attend Union College. I want to study for the ministry." He looked at it, then put it down, and thought for a moment while the whole family waited in suspense to hear what he would say.

After a long pause, he said, "Okay, Manuel. You go to college and study for the ministry. Just promise me one thing: that you'll be a better pastor than the ones I've known."

The morning I left for college, my father got my mother and me out of bed at five o'clock. He took us into the living room and had me kneel before him while he put his hand on my head and prayed for God to be with me. Then, with tears streaming down his cheeks, he gave me his blessing. At that moment I had no doubt in my mind about God's will for my life.

I have not forgotten my promise to my father. I always try to live up to the expectations of my earthly father and my Heavenly One.

Honor your father and your mother, that your days may be long in the land which the Lord your God gives you. Exodus 20:12

Manuel Vasquez is vice president for special ministries of the North American Division of Seventh-day Adventists in Silver Spring, Maryland.

PENTECOSTAL WITNESS *By Wil Clarke*

He spoke with a pronounced Southern drawl. His grammar was abominable. He consistently dropped the final "t" or "d" from a word if it had such. I wondered, silently, if he had ever gotten through high school. He served in the United States Air Force at the base just south of Darmstadt, Germany. He was young, somewhat pudgy, and openly committed to Jesus Christ.

He attended the base chapel and claimed to speak freely in tongues as the Holy Spirit moved him. He prayed with a fervent eloquence and seemed to know the Lord on a personal basis.

I was at Seminar Marienhoehe, also just south of Darmstadt, to learn German. I didn't know a word of German on arrival. I lived a lonely life. For months, all I heard was a babble of talking around me and I couldn't even catch a single, isolated word. It peeved me that tiny children could speak so fluently, and, in spite of all my intelligence and effort, I couldn't.

I had come to Germany directly from Africa, where my parents had been missionaries for 26 years. I had been in boarding school since the tender age of twelve. At boarding school, well-meaning but misguided teachers had held up an impossible standard of purity and holiness. My young mind had been bombarded with the strictness of God. My teachers stressed that God would not forgive willful sin. Because I had indeed sinned willfully, I had come to accept unquestioningly the idea that God had doomed me to eternal damnation. I gave up on Christianity and decided to enjoy this life because I had no hope for a future one. This decision already had caused my expulsion from Helderberg College.

On Sundays, just to hear intelligible conversation, I joined the choir at the Air Force Base chapel. The young Pentecostal sensed my feeling of hopelessness. I became his personal missionary project. He warned me against the legalism that permeated Adventism.

I felt superior to him in every way. His poor English, my already superior education, and the fact that I knew "the Truth," steeled my whole being against his entreaties. Yet I was searching for hope.

One day he cornered me and read Romans 10:9 earnestly to me. He stressed that I didn't have to do all the things I thought I had to. All I had to do was confess and believe. This seemed too easy. The verse, however, would not leave my mind. It haunted me day and night. Finally, I accepted this new Jesus. My friend rejoiced in my conversion. Never once did he insist that I join his church or leave mine. He just wanted me to know Christ as he knew Him.

It has taken years of meditation and study to make that verse real to me. I have mountains of early misconceptions of God that keep resurfacing. I thank God for the free gift of His marvelous grace to me, a sinner.

If thou shalt confess with thy mouth the Lord Jesus, and shalt believe in thine heart that God hath raised Him from the dead, thou shalt be saved. Romans 10:9

Wil Clarke is professor of mathematics at La Sierra University in Riverside, California.

PUBLISH GLAD TIDINGS *By Valerie N. Phillips*

I t was the worst and best day of my entire semester. I was called to the office of an English professor I much admired and kindly but emphatically accused of plagiarizing my last paper. This was probably a task she also disliked, and I now suspect she accomplished it in as kindly a manner as possible. But, I was humiliated and deeply hurt to think that someone whom I so admired and who I thought had more faith in me would believe such a thing to be true.

I was embarrassed to admit that I'd been influenced by *nothing* I'd read in preparation for this paper, because I'd made *no preparations* at all for this paper. In fact, the day the outline was due, I'd forgotten we were scheduled for individual conferences about the progress of this paper which I had not yet even begun. So, as I awaited my turn in the "White House" lobby, I desperately selected a topic about which I felt strongly, and hastily constructed an outline, entirely out of my head. After the conference, I went back to my room and fleshed out the paper until I was really pleased with the results.

So, now, while I knew the beginnings of my paper indicated procrastination and poor planning, I knew for sure that copying was *not* a possibility. Although shaken, I kept quietly maintaining, "I do know what plagiarism is, but this paper is my own work."

After what seemed an eternity, she signaled that I was free to leave. Tears were very close, but I managed not to cry.

My next appointment was a conference with another professor about a religion paper, one which (thankfully) I had completed and polished. After reading that paper, he quietly asked if I'd given any thought to publishing it. What a different response from the meeting of that morning! He had faith in me, and he let me know it.

The tears I'd checked in sorrow now flowed as I told him how hurt, embarrassed and just plain awful I felt about the morning's encounter. Although I thanked him for restoring my faith in myself and others, I don't know if he realized what a difference his confidence in me made that day. I went to my room healed.

I've never forgotten the way Jim Londis' kind commendation, offered at just the right moment, changed my day, my attitude, my self-esteem and my modeling. I never did publish that paper, but I have invested myself in 17 years of ministry to an Adventist university campus. I enjoy it when I can call in a young person to share with them the talents and abilities I see in them which sometimes they have not yet noticed in themselves. And, besides everything else I do in the line of duty, sometimes I help proof my residents' papers. Who knows? Maybe they'll publish.

Like apples of gold in settings of silver, so is a word spoken at the right moment. Proverbs 25:11 Modern Language

Valerie N. Phillips is associate dean of women at Andrews University in Berrien Springs, Michigan.

THE TWELFTH MEETING

Clarence E. Hodges

Beverly Robinson Rumble

Harold Brown

Stephen L. McPherson

Janice Wood

Howard M. Shaw

Paul S. Ramalingam

Diane Pearson

George W. Reid

William Richardson

Come and hear, all ye that fear God,
and I will declare what He hath done for my soul.

Psalm 66:16

PRAYER AND THE ECONOMY *By Clarence E. Hodges*

I was a young freshman trying to master college and a full-time job. I wasn't in a Christian school, so the professors gave little or no thought to showing the kind of genuine personal interest in students we expect from Christian teachers.

At the beginning of the semester, my economics professor, a talented man of many years, instructed us to keep a record of certain economic trends. The financial section of the major newspapers contained this information daily. So for nearly a month, I kept careful records of economic movements, trends and ratio shifts.

The teacher moved on to other issues and made other demands which helped us to connect textbook concepts to experiences in life. After weeks of quizzes and tests, we finally reached the end of the term. It had been a good class. I had learned much about the economy and economics. With a high degree of intelligence, I could discuss money, banking, the Fed and key personalities in commerce and relevant federal agencies.

The final exam, however, did not require that kind of discussion. The teacher threw us a curve. He shocked that youthful freshman class into the reality that high school was over.

For the final exam, he directed us to prepare a chart in class, without advance notice, showing various economic trends for the semester. He said we should've brought that information to each class, including the final exam. If we had the newspaper reports and could compute the statistics, we should do well. This assignment would account for 50 percent of our final grade.

I was stunned. I had about one-fourth of the newspaper reports he required. Apparently, I hadn't understood his directions on that first day of class. Others apparently *had* understood or possibly he had reminded them sometime when I was not present. What could I do now? Pray. That is all I could do.

The teacher had made it clear that there was to be no checking with other students. We must work with our own materials. He didn't monitor the class very closely, so some students did take slow walks to the pencil sharpener, carefully observing the papers of those who appeared to be prepared. But I couldn't cheat.

I prayed. I confessed my failure of possibly not paying close attention. I vowed not to cheat even if the opportunity fell on my desk.

So, determinedly, I began charting those trends with the few clippings I had, making calculations and carefully drawing the lines up and down to indicate changes for each week. I guessed at what I didn't have, which was about three-fourths of what was necessary. I finished, prayed again, and placed the paper on his desk.

I can only say that an angel must have guided my hand straight to an A for the course. If not, then explain to me the likelihood of a college freshman correctly guessing the exact trends of a national economy for several successive weeks?

God does hear and answer prayers, even when we, through carelessness or inattention, are responsible for our own difficult situations.

When thou passest through the waters, I will be with thee; and through the rivers, they shall not overflow thee: when thou walkest through the fire, thou shalt not be burned; neither shall the flame kindle upon thee. Isaiah 43:2

Clarence E. Hodges is vice president and director of public affairs and religious liberty at the North American Division of Seventh-day Adventists in Silver Spring, Maryland.

GOD'S TRAVEL ARRANGEMENTS *By Beverly Robinson Rumble*

While attending Atlantic Union College, I decided to spend one home leave visiting a friend in New Jersey. Several other students were headed that way, so I arranged to ride with them. When we arrived, I enthusiastically greeted my friend's family while she ran to talk to my driver, a childhood classmate of hers. She promised to arrange with him where and when I should meet him for the return ride to college.

Several days later, I asked my friend about the arrangements for the return trip. Panic-stricken, she admitted that she had forgotten to discuss this with the driver. We tried repeatedly to contact him, but all our attempts were unsuccessful. Finally, it was noon on the last day of vacation, and I was many hours from South Lancaster. I had to be back in the dorm that night by 10 p.m. or I would be in trouble with the dean of women.

My friend apologetically drove me to the bus station, handing me a sack lunch, and what money she had. Even with her help, I had barely enough cash to buy a ticket to Worcester, Massachusetts. How would I get from Worcester back to college, an hour's drive through the snow from the bus station? I wasn't certain that I had enough money to call the dorm, and I was sure no one there would accept a collect call. (This was before the days of long-distance calling cards.) Furthermore, I had no idea who could pick me up, as few students had cars and most were on their way back to the college themselves.

Fighting back tears, I prayed much of the way to New York City, where I had to change buses and endure a long layover in a frightening New York Greyhound station. After much additional prayer about my predicament (as well as my safety in the big city), I boarded the bus for Worcester. Walking to the back, I spotted a fellow AUC student.

Seeing my tear-stained face, he asked what was wrong. After hearing my story, he reassured me. His roommate was expecting him to call from Worcester, he said; I could ride back to the college with them.

What a coincidence—or divine arrangement—that a fellow student, and one I knew well enough to recognize as such, happened to be at the very same station, on the very same bus, 200 miles from our ultimate destination. I can't help believing that this was God's direct answer to my prayer, and something He had to arrange well in advance—though ever since, I've made sure to check travel arrangements for myself.

Let Him have all your worries and cares, for He is always thinking about you and watching everything that concerns you. 1 Peter 5:7 The Living Bible

Beverly Robinson Rumble is editor of The Journal of Adventist Education *at the General Conference of Seventh-day Adventists in Silver Spring, Maryland.*

LAMBASTED *By Harold Brown*

S tunned and bewildered, I could feel the blood rushing through my body and the perspiration starting to flow. How could I respond to the man's sudden outburst. He had publicly lambasted me in the middle of the Revelation Seminar that I was conducting, and then he had angrily stomped out of the auditorium. All eyes were on me. What would I say?

It was the summer between my junior and senior years at Walla Walla College. I was a student pastor in Hood River, Oregon. The scenery along this stretch of the Columbia Gorge made this one of the most coveted areas to live. And why shouldn't I live here too, if only for the summer? My life had been fairly cushy. My parents had provided very well. I was one of the few lucky ones who didn't need to worry about how tuition would be paid. Most everything I needed had been handed to me—including my religion.

Religion to me was being able, intellectually and scripturally, to defend 27 points of doctrine. The doctrines all made sense to me. After all, I'd been exposed to them all of my life. And now I had been publicly confronted with a man who had been a Roman Catholic all of his life. The night of the Revelation Seminar when I presented the Papacy's role in prophecy, his anger erupted. "I've been a Catholic all of my life, and I'm going to die a Catholic!"

I don't remember what I said or how I managed to finish the seminar that evening, but I've never been able to forget that man's passion. His faith had passion; mine didn't. I somehow had managed to inherit a faith that gave me cognitive security, with little life behind it. When that man spoke, he was speaking from his heart—he was alive. That man had something that I wanted to have, too.

The next day I visited him at his home. I tried to explain my points from the night before. He was cordial but had no interest in any explanation or continuing the conversation. I felt I had failed. But I soothed my wounds by remembering how Christ must have felt when the Rich Young Ruler walked away. The difference that I neglected to see was that Christ could connect at the heart, not just at the head. I couldn't. I was stuck in my head—trying to pass on the same cerebral stuff that had not yet connected with my passion.

Someone has said, "If you ever have to choose between being right or being kind, choose kind." I wonder what would have transpired between this man and myself if I had only listened to him; if I could have felt where his passion was coming from; if I could have connected to what was important to him. I wonder what would have happened to *my* faith if I had allowed God to listen, feel and connect with all that is important to me, rather than restricting Him to my head.

O man, He has told you what is good; what does the Eternal ask from you but to be just and kind and live in quiet fellowship with your God? Micah 6:8 Moffatt

Harold Brown is dean of men at Loma Linda University in Loma Linda, California.

A LESSON FROM THE WALL *By Stephen L. McPherson*

Along the long, polished, black marble wall, I found Column 17-Line 43. The name leaped out at me. Here I was, alive and so blessed.

I was in Washington, D.C., for Annual Council meetings of the General Conference. One afternoon, I slipped away from the continuous meetings and discussions to visit the monument to those who died in the Viet Nam War. Memories of my first time away from home at an Adventist College during those troublous years began to overwhelm me.

I had plenty to handle during the first few weeks of my freshman year in college. I had to learn to set priorities for my time; to tend to business and to develop good study habits.

When I received my disappointing first-quarter grades, it was apparent that I hadn't yet learned these skills well enough. I was strongly tempted to quit or transfer to another college. However, my parents had taught me enough about life to know that nothing good comes easily. I realized it would take hard work, determination, and some serious self-discipline if I was going to succeed.

During those college years, I learned that the act of staying in school was, in the long view, of more value than the material I studied. It wasn't brilliance or good grades that helped me attain my goal. It was how I managed my emotions and the usual discouragements of life.

Of course, during my college years I didn't appreciate the full value of what my parents taught me about persistence in the face of setbacks. But that characteristic saw me through the challenges of college and the greater challenges of life.

One of my classmates at college somehow missed that lesson. He yielded to the temptation to quit. He dropped out of school and joined the United States Army.

Who can judge his decision? But I often wonder how things might have been different had he persisted in the face of discouragement and stayed in school. His name now appears in Column 17-Line 43 on that long, polished, black marble wall in Washington, D.C.

He who stands firm to the end will be saved. Matthew 24:13 NIV

Stephen L. McPherson is president of the Idaho Conference of Seventh-day Adventists in Boise, Idaho.

WITHOUT A CLUE By Janice Wood

From the first time anyone asked me, "What are you going to be when you grow up?" I knew I wanted to be a nurse. I pictured myself in a crisp white uniform, with white stockings and shoes and that cute nurse's cap on my head. Everyone told me they thought I would be a wonderful nurse and I just knew that's what I should be.

So why had I reached this crisis? I had taken almost all the required pre-nursing classes, including chemistry, anatomy and physiology, microbiology and nutrition. For the most part I had to force myself to attend these classes. I really didn't enjoy the subject matter and it definitely didn't come easily for me. But I had a dream, and no matter how difficult the journey, I was determined to become a nurse.

Now I sat in the office of the nursing adviser and listened to her advice that perhaps I didn't have an aptitude for nursing. The thought of breaking this news to my family and friends was almost as intimidating as dealing with the reality of an uncertain future. What now?

I had been so sure that the Lord wanted me to be a nurse. If He had something else in mind for me, the sign would have to be very obvious because I didn't have a clue.

My residence hall dean, Grace Sommerville, knew me well, since I worked for her. She said, "Jan, I think you have the ability to be a good teacher. Think about it."

With the encouragement of family, counselors, teachers, friends and lots of prayer, I changed my major to history and education. The obvious sign I was looking for was most apparent in the complete change in my attitude toward my classes. I *enjoyed* them. And the school work, although challenging, was interesting and often exciting.

As I look back at this time in my life, I'm grateful to Pacific Union College for providing the kind of environment where life-changing decisions can best be made. With the help of dedicated teachers and staff, God gave me the tools I needed to make a good decision. And today I find myself in the position of being one of those God uses to help others.

Call to Me and I will answer you and tell you great and unsearchable things you do not know. Jeremiah 33:3 NIV

Janice Wood is dean of women at Pacific Union College in Angwin, California.

A SIMPLE INVITATION *By Howard M. Shaw*

I was a graduate student at Vanderbilt University when I met Lorenzo Shepard. Lorenzo was a Vanderbilt seminary student by way of Oakwood College. One day while I was working as a cashier in the campus bookstore, Lorenzo walked in and we got acquainted.

Times were hard for me. I barely had money to buy food and was studying hard to earn good grades. I rarely knew where my next meal was coming from and I was hurting. Even though my Baptist parents had tried to raise their children in the fear of the Lord, I had not been to church in a long time. Things were not going very well in my life in spite of doing everything humanly possible to excel.

One day, while we were talking, Lorenzo asked me to go to church with him. I said, "Sure, when would you like to go?"

"How about this Saturday?"

"Saturday!" I said. "You go to church on Saturday?! Sorry!"

I was giving private tennis lessons on Saturdays to pay my tuition. Lorenzo said, "Fine, perhaps another time."

He wasn't pushy, but persistent. A week or so passed and he asked me again to attend church services with him on Saturday. Reluctantly, I accepted and canceled my tennis lessons for that day. We went to church and it was the most enjoyable, learning experience that I'd had in a long time.

Six months later, I was baptized into the Seventh-day Adventist Church.

All it took was a simple invitation.

Behold, a sower went forth to sow; and when he sowed, some seeds . . . fell into good ground, and brought forth fruit, some an hundredfold, some sixtyfold, some thirtyfold. Who hath ears to hear, let him hear. Matthew 13:3,4,8,9

Howard M. Shaw is associate professor of health and physical education at Oakwood College in Huntsville, Alabama.

THE LONG JOURNEY *By Paul S. Ramalingam*

The little Hindu boy ducked into a "Maatha koil" (Catholic church) to escape the torrential rain of the monsoon. It was a strange building. Through the murky darkness of the empty church, he saw with horror a statue of a dying man on a cross. Frightened, he ran out of the church into the rain.

That was my first experience with Jesus.

Back in my small village, we had no church and nothing there reminded me of the man on the cross. However, I achieved some minor celebrity status in the village when I subscribed to some lessons from a place called *The Voice of Prophecy* and thus began receiving the local marvel of regular mail. I had no idea at the time that the lessons were all about Jesus, but soon I learned more about Him. But for me the whole course was only an academic exercise to obtain the prized graduation certificate.

Several years later when I was a college student, a friend and I got caught in a monsoon rainstorm. We took shelter in a church. In this humble building there were no statues, no crosses, and nothing frightened me. But there were many friendly smiles. I thought it strange, but pleasant, to be accepted by those I didn't know and to be asked to participate in their vesper service. A few college students, like myself, were in that group and they made me promise that I would return the following week for a full Sabbath service. Within a year, my acquaintance with those students and the other members, and my growing knowledge of Christ, led me to become a Seventh-day Adventist.

That same year, I left India for the United States to further my studies at the University of Notre Dame. One Sabbath morning I got a ride to church with Mr. Halvorsen, a kind church member. After the service and a wonderful meal at the Halvorsens', we went for a short drive and ended up at Andrews University. What a surprise! I never thought there might be an Adventist university so near. An unusual emotional feeling rekindled and restrengthened my belief.

In South Bend, I met an Adventist student from Andrews University at a supper party intended for international students. She wondered why I, an Adventist, was studying at a Catholic university? Soon I married that Adventist woman on the Andrews campus.

What more did God have in store? When my visa came through, I moved to Canada. After working in two university positions, I was called to teach at Canadian University College.

Step by step, God brought me closer and closer to Him and to His service, even without my asking. He led me, a little Hindu boy from a small village in India, to His people, and to His schools. I have seen God's far-reaching power and I have learned to trust Him.

The Lord is my shepherd; I shall not want. Psalm 23:1

Paul S. Ramalingam is professor of biology at Canadian University College in College Heights, Alberta.

THESE THINGS *By Diane Pearson*

There it was. Every time I walked through the lobby of Conard Hall at Walla Walla College, I saw the tapestry. I don't know who made it, or the name of the dean who hung it on the wall close to the lobby entrance. But it included our residence hall scripture text. *"Whatsoever things are true . . . ."*

It didn't seem to matter if I was having a good day or a bad day. I could always rely on that tapestry to turn my thoughts toward my Strength.

"Whatsoever things are honest . . . ." Some days my conscience was needled by what I read on the tapestry. It gave me time for reevaluation of what my goals and ambitions were and how I was playing the game of life. Was I totally honest on every quiz and test?

"Whatsoever things are pure . . . ." Returning from a date with a special friend or a night on the town with my roommate, I was reminded that purity comes from thinking pure thoughts. Actions follow thoughts. I was given courage by beholding this tapestry and knowing that God was in control.

During my college years I attended both a secular and a Christian school. Nowhere on the secular campus was there anything that could compare to the tapestry. In fact, I could probably have used words opposite of true, honest, just and pure to describe my idea of what was happening there. True, I found Christian friends, but we were in the minority and few shared my Seventh-day Adventist beliefs. I was happy to return to a Christian college, for I was able to choose friends who could help me in my spiritual growth.

Would my life have been different in college without the tapestry? I think so. At Sabbath School and as a Pathfinder, I had memorized Philippians 4:8. I knew the content. But as a young, energetic, prank-playing college freshman, independent of home and parents, I had to establish my own spiritual values. I needed the reminder that the tapestry provided. I needed to think before doing things. I needed the reminder that good things happen when I have my thoughts in the proper place. And I needed the reminder that if I was about to engage in activities that were less than any of "these things," I needed to spend more time with the One who is the embodiment of all "these things."

Finally, brethren, whatsoever things are true, whatsoever things are honest, whatsoever things are just, whatsoever things are pure, whatsoever things are lovely, whatsoever things are of good report; if there be any virtue, and if there be any praise, think on these things. Philippians 4:8

Diane Pearson is dean of women at Walla Walla College in College Place, Washington.

More College Faith

A LEGACY THAT SHINES LIKE THE STARS *By George W. Reid*

Time had traced marks in her face and the brutality of real life left her wounded with a limp that put a cane in her hand. But you would never notice it, distracted as you would be by the simple, striking way she handled hordes of greenish freshmen with prime interests more focused on what's for lunch and who's going with whom than the challenges of real learning.

Strange how someone like her could engrave indelible impressions on passing youth. You really wouldn't expect it. What did she have? Certainly not generational identity, for already a full 40 years lay between her and the twittering freshmen filing through her classroom. Nor was it charm, that engaging personality so in demand in today's overstimulated, hyper-entertained crowd. As one of those freshmen, I never thought then about what it was, but from today's perspective so much falls into place.

There was a dignity about Miss Hyatt. She held no post of power, and was no extraordinary writer or speaker possessing a gift for eloquence. As noted, she had been robbed of attractive physical appearance. But something commanding was there. I could just sense it.

I was not that "typical" freshman—presuming there is such a species. I came from a country town, and was the product of a home fractured by my mother's death in my early childhood. Loving relatives gave me care, but growing up left its distortions. Like so many youth, I was trying desperately to sort out the meaning in life. Was I more than a biological event? What reason is there to be in a world such as ours? In high school, someone gave me David Hume's skeptical writings. Was Hume really right?

Enter Helen Hyatt. How she coped with being assigned to care about dozens of milling youth I now wonder. But her trademark was a genuine interest in each of us, in me as much as any, but not more so. Earlier, I called it dignity, but that's not enough. Miss Hyatt carried integrity with her dignity, and wrapped around it all was genuine affection. All these traits she gathered from her Lord. Without ostentation, she set before me the ideal of what it means to follow Christ. Today I relish the character gifts she slipped into my pocket when I wasn't even watching.

I suppose there is little of a factual nature she taught me that has survived the passage of time, but another legacy is ever so much more important. It is that certainty that through it all—whatever—we walk within the understanding, gentle watchcare of a heavenly Father. Beyond what even sermons could do, the ministry of Helen Hyatt laid a hand on the confused mind of a bewildered youth to introduce him to what he could become by the grace of God. As we plodded through the batteries of tests connected with her course in Personal Adjustment, piece by piece it came together, not in bare scientific format, but set in a matrix of God's purpose for our lives.

And I was not alone. One after another, hundreds of beginning college students came under the touch of her hand to emerge as maturing persons, but even more, maturing Christians. And all this was not lost. Before long, a new elementary school rose from foundations on the windswept Nebraska prairie to bear proudly the name, Helen Hyatt Elementary. And the name bears testimony to the legacy of a woman who led many to God.

And those who are wise shall shine like the brightness of the firmament; and those who turn many to righteousness, like the stars for ever and ever. Daniel 12:3 RSV

George W. Reid is director of the Biblical Research Institute at the General Conference of Seventh-day Adventists in Silver Spring, Maryland.

THE BRIGHT SIDE OF A DORM   *By William Richardson*

In the mid 1950s, Emmanuel Missionary College (now Andrews University) meant choices—lots of choices. To this small-town Ohio boy, the move to Berrien Springs, Michigan, seemed like non-stop adventure. Unknown to me, one reason my folks rejoiced when I chose EMC was because of the perceived *lack* of adventure available in that area. Any school surrounded by orchards, cows and a village of 1,200 was likely to have very dim fireworks.

Once my parents had me in Berrien Springs, they quite understandably wanted me to stay. So telling them I wanted to be off campus for the summer after my first school year didn't please them.

"Why do you want to quit your job at college? I thought you said running the linotype at the press was one of the best jobs on campus?"

"Well it is, but my roommate sold books last summer and he thinks I should give it a try."

"But the linotype is a sure thing. You know what you'll earn if you stay with the press. But who knows what you'll make if you sell books? And besides, who is this roommate who is so smart?"

It was that last question that decided the matter for me. That roommate was one of a rapidly expanding circle of friends whose many ideas fascinated me.

Parents often fear the "bad influences" that college dormitories seem to represent. Positive influences rarely get much press. But I concluded early on that the many choices and influences I encountered in dormitory living were not all on the dark side. The Spirit of God was also at work in those rooms and hallways. My college roommate was no angel in disguise. He was just a committed young Adventist whose influence on me was very positive and whose suggestions about summer employment were providential.

I never went back to the linotype. By God's grace, each summer's book sales increased until my last summer when my commission provided a year's tuition for both myself and my new wife.

Yes, that big school in Michigan meant choices, options, more friends and all kinds of counsel—sometimes thrown in my face by a revved-up roommate. But experience and observation have hammered home a truth: in college dorm rooms, then and now, God's Spirit counsels, guides and nudges young lives in one direction with one goal in mind—that "afterward thou wilt receive me to glory."

Thou shalt guide me with Thy counsel, and afterward receive me to glory. Psalm 73:24.

William Richardson is professor of religion at Andrews University in Berrien Springs, Michigan.

THE THIRTEENTH MEETING

Agniel Samson

Steve Daily

Dorothy Minchin Comm

R. Dean Davis

Fred Bennett

Woodrow Whidden II

Gail Perry Rittenbach

Malcolm Russell

Tom Shepherd

Ed Wright

Come and hear, all ye that fear God,
and I will declare what He hath done for my soul.

Psalm 66:16

15 KILOMETERS, 15 BAPTISMS By *Agniel Samson*

While studying at River Plate College in Argentina, I had the privilege of pastoring three small congregations in the middle of the pampas, some 200 kilometers from the school.

One Friday evening, when my train stopped at my destination, Brother Muller was not there to pick me up. So I started walking to his house, 15 kilometers away. It was raining, and the mud stuck heavily to my shoes, making progress difficult.

Because of the rain, the night was very dark. Out in the country, there was no light of any kind. I couldn't see anything except my phosphorescent watch. I was fearful of getting lost; fearful of falling into the huge road wash-out some 3 kilometers to my destination; and fearful of not being able to find the Muller's house at all, alone as it was in the middle of nothing but great darkness.

During that night, God performed four miracles. First, I was able to make the critical left turn that would lead me in the correct direction without seeing anything at all. In great faith, I had asked the Lord to bring me to that turn, wherever it was, at exactly 10 p.m. At exactly that moment, I made that turn.

The second miracle was that the only lighting of the night happened to be in a place that allowed me to make out the huge wash-out in the road and avoid a terrible fall.

The third miracle, after five hours of walking in the dark and rain, was that I saw a light coming under what seemed to be a door. "Certainly it's the

Muller's house," I thought. And it was.

I thanked Brother Muller for leaving the light on. He insisted that no light had been left on. After a few exchanges of "yes, there was," "no there wasn't," he said: "Brother Samson, you tell me the light was on; I know there was no light on. If you saw any light, it was an angel showing you the way."

The fourth miracle was the one I discovered while returning home the following Sunday afternoon. Brother Muller was driving me to the train stop. Suddenly he halted in the middle of the road and said: "Wait a minute, Brother Samson! Do you see those footprints all along the road?"

"Yes, I do," I replied.

"Don't you understand?"

"What?" I asked.

"Don't you realize that during the whole night you walked at the very edge of the steep embankment without ever falling in the brook? Certainly the angels of the Lord were walking in the brook bearing you up."

Less than a year after that eventful night, Werner Vyhmeister, then chairman of the theology department at River Plate College, went with me to that same area and baptized 15 of the people I had been studying with.

All during that baptismal celebration, I kept saying: "Thank you, Lord, for giving me one soul for every kilometer I walked during the darkest, most glorious night of my life."

I will bring the blind by a way they did not know; I will lead them in paths they have not known. I will make darkness light before them, and crooked places straight. Isaiah 42:16 NKJV

Agniel Samson is professor of New Testament and biblical languages at Oakwood College in Huntsville, Alabama.

LIBRARY BLUES By Steve Daily

One of my most vivid memories from college is of one of my most humbling failures. I was a freshman theology student trying to take a full class load and work 15 to 20 hours a week to help pay for my college expenses (which was my agreement with my parents). My roommate and I got jobs in the library, cleaning the seven floors of the building each night from 11 p.m. to 2 a.m. We were the only ones working in the building during those hours. We each covered three and one-half floors each night before falling exhausted into our beds after work.

Pushing a vacuum cleaner and emptying trash cans wasn't hard work, but it was extremely boring, especially after a long day of classes and study. After a couple of months of this routine, the boredom of the job began to get to us and the pressures of an approaching test week were mounting. We solved both of these problems with a single idea: Why couldn't we hustle through our three-hour job, finish it in two hours, and then spend the last hour, still clocked in, studying in the library for our tests?

We didn't know that our meticulous and conscientious supervisor randomly would stay up until 2 a.m. with a pair of binoculars to see if his workers were putting in their full hours. That is, we didn't know until the day we got fired.

The news came like a wrecking ball. It devastated me. What would I do for a job? What would my parents say? Would I have to drop out of college? I can still remember breaking down and crying as I apologized to the supervisor and custodial chief. I hoped I'd be forgiven and given a second chance, but I was only forgiven.

A few weeks later a dorm dean gave me a job as a monitor. I don't think I ever worked a job more conscientiously in my life. But, I learned a few good lessons from that experience.

1. Accept your failures for the opportunities they are.

2. Don't blame others for your own failures.

3. Rationalization is worse than rigidity.

4. We need some people in our lives who will forgive us but not give us another chance.

5. Even more, we need people in our lives who will forgive us and give us another chance.

Confess your faults to one another . . . that ye may be healed. James 5:16

Steve Daily is chaplain at La Sierra University in Riverside, California.

BEYOND OUR UNDERSTANDING *By Dorothy Minchin Comm*

Higher education? Well, I could have missed it. The spring that I was 16, my father finished up a year's teaching in England, and our family prepared to return to the United States. I faced a choice. Would I simply walk off with my high school credits from Newbold College, or would I try for the elusive but highly desirable London Senior Matriculation examination.

I'm not even sure why this decision suddenly became so important to me. I'd spent the entire school year like the proverbial grasshopper—thoroughly enjoying England and my friends and studying whenever I got around to it. Six of my classmates decided to try for Matric. It made little difference to us that only the top third passed the exam. At the time, going up to London together seemed a romantic adventure. In this rather reckless mood, we sent in our applications.

My father gave me the required two guineas for the application fee. Somehow between home and the post office at the old "Shoulder of Mutton" pub, I lost the money. Chastened, I returned to tell Dad the sad tale. Saying little, he replaced his contribution, and I trudged back to the post-office for the money order. That time, at least, I got it right.

Because our whole family skimped for want of enough money, I now began serious self-examination. My carnival spirit died away, and I became deadly in earnest over my plans. What if I failed? Thousands did, automatically, every year. Having spent the entire school-year in "fun and games," did I have any *right* to expect that I could pass Senior Matric?

I spent that night quietly in my room. I'd always known about praying in critical times, but I wrestled with the suspicion that I wasn't "good enough" to pray for success. Nonetheless, I did. I wanted to pass that exam. Above all, I didn't want to disgrace my family with failure or with wasting Dad's money. And I promised to study—hard. Suddenly, an almost physical presence enveloped me and a virtually audible voice said, "Study and you'll make it." I fell asleep almost instantly.

For the next six weeks I did study with the intensity and commitment of someone many years more mature. But I always slept well at night, secure in my promise.

Then, when the time came, I passed—the only one, as it turned out—of we seven Newboldians who went up for Senior Matric that year. Properly grateful, I nevertheless thought I had simply finished high school—with a little extra flourish perhaps. After all, I'd be going to college back in the United States, where the exam credential would mean little.

More than 20 years later, however, when I applied to enter doctoral studies at a Canadian university, I fully comprehended the pattern of my prayer story. I would not have been accepted at that university without having passed that British university matriculation many years before. All the "American" things I'd done in between didn't count.

Prayer? Guidance? Even when you scarcely know what you're asking for? It works. It produced my personal package-plan for higher education. Nothing quite like it has happened to me since.

God's voice thunders in marvelous ways; He does great things beyond our understanding. Job 37:5 NIV

Dorothy Minchin Comm is professor of English at La Sierra University in Riverside, California.

TO BLUFF OR NOT TO BLUFF *By R. Dean Davis*

While in college and graduate school, I noticed a marked difference among teachers in how they handled questions raised by students. Some tried to bluff their way through and provide some sort of answer even when it was clear they didn't have one. Others immediately and frankly said that they didn't know the answer. Ultimately, I concluded that it would be dishonest for me to try to pose as one who knew all the answers when, in reality, I often didn't know them. I resolved early on that I would frankly admit that I didn't know the answer when it was beyond my present scope of knowledge.

This lesson in my own education stayed with me in my professional life. While teaching theology in one of our overseas colleges, I regularly taught a Sabbath School class composed of some faculty, staff and community members.

One Sabbath an incident occurred that made no impression upon me until five or six years later when I received a letter from an individual I didn't even know.

The letter was from a woman who had a Jewish background. She wrote that she reluctantly had come to Sabbath services one day at the insistence of an Adventist minister who accompanied her to my Sabbath School class. At that time, she hadn't joined the Adventist church because she had no respect for Adventist ministers. In her view, they acted as if they knew it all. She wrote that in my class that day, someone had asked a question and I had frankly acknowledged that I didn't know the answer but would try to find an answer and would report back the following Sabbath with whatever I had found in my research. At that moment, she wrote, she resolved to join the church and commit her life to Christ.

This woman's letter showed me how an ethical decision I made in response to the example set by my teachers many years before helped influence another person in a life-changing way. When we have committed our lives to God's service, He uses us at odd times and in strange ways to accomplish His purposes and win souls to Him.

Therefore, as God's chosen people, holy and dearly loved, clothe yourselves with compassion, kindness, humility, gentleness and patience. Colossians 3:12 NIV

R. Dean Davis is professor of religion and theology at Atlantic Union College in South Lancaster, Massachusetts.

WHEN TIME RAN OUT *By Fred Bennett*

On graduation day, President Bowers gave me a genuinely personal and warm, "Congratulations, Fred," as he handed me my diploma. After seven seemingly interminable years of hard, physical labor and many long, exhausting nights of study, I had reached my goal of graduating from Walla Walla College with an engineering degree. It was a moment to be savored. I felt I was on top of the world. How soon I learned that I was only at the top of a professional roller coaster.

My immediate goal was to get my Engineer-in-Training certificate from the state of Washington so I could get my professional license four years later. The State Board of Engineering Examiners refused my application to take the test because Walla Walla's School of Engineering was not yet accredited. That meant another year of waiting. The next fall, I reapplied and was accepted. I reported for the test on a dismal Friday morning in November.

Around 3 p.m., buried in the details of the test, I glanced at my watch to see how much time I had left to finish. In one dreadful moment, it dawned on me that sundown, and the beginning of the Sabbath, would arrive more than an hour before the examination period ended.

My heart raced and my face flushed. What a dilemma! After a very sincere prayer, I picked up my books and my test booklet and went to the proctor. He said, "What are you doing? You did so well this morning. Don't quit now."

I tried to explain. Then he said, "Surely your pastor will understand this one time for something this important to your future as an engineer."

Having made up my mind, I left the test site and caught the ferry to cross Puget Sound for home. I stood at the rail in the cold rain and added my own warm teardrops, *"O Lord, why?"*

I prayed again and truly thanked Him for the Sabbath. As I opened my eyes and looked over the stormy salt sea, I saw a beautiful break in the clouds in the western sky as the setting sun introduced me to another Sabbath. It seemed at that moment, as it still seems to me now, that God was saying, "Bless you, my son."

Weeks passed and I had resigned myself to failure. The letter came. I couldn't bear to open it, so my wife did. I really wasn't surprised to see her start to cry.

"Oh, Fred, you passed! You got 72, two points more than required."

If thou turn away thy foot from the Sabbath, from doing thy pleasure on My holy day; and call the Sabbath a delight, the holy of the Lord, honourable; and shalt honor Him, not doing thine own ways, nor finding thine own pleasure, nor speaking thine own words; then shalt thou delight thyself in the Lord; and I will cause thee to ride upon the high places of the earth, . . . for the mouth of the Lord hath spoken it. Isaiah 58:13,14

Fred Bennett is professor of civil engineering at Walla Walla College in College Place, Washington.

PINK NOTES AND DOGGED FAITH *By Woodrow Whidden II*

I'm glad they do things differently at most Adventist colleges these days. When I was in school, students whose accounts were in arrears received a note to appear at the student finance office for a little huddle with the director. One problem with this was that everybody knew, by the infamous pink color of the note, that the subject was financial failure. And the really bad thing was that this awful communique was delivered, not at the dorm or through the mail, but personally to the hapless debtor in class. When I was the recipient of such a subpoena, I was mortified beyond words at the public exposure of my financial status with the college.

My well-meaning mother had been warning my brother and me for quite a while that the financial picture on the home front was a bit precarious. Her depressing reports arrived regularly by mail and did nothing for our courage. Our parents wanted to help, and they knew we were responsible, but our college years happened to be the most trying financial times in our family history.

Victory came through faith and prayer. First, we firmly told my well-meaning mother that we had gotten the message and that we were doing our best; we assured her that we knew that she and Dad were doing theirs—but please stop sending the doleful letters.

The next thing I had to do was to confront my embarrassment and go for the requisite chat with the director of student finance. He was kind and firm. I was firm, too, arguing that God would provide and that if the school didn't want me to stay, they were going to have to bodily carry me out of class and off the campus. He caved in, I returned to class and kept praying, trusting and working. A few days later my Uncle George advanced me the money to finish the school year.

I give God the glory and thank Him for this test of my faith. Through the years I've been able to encourage scores of friends (especially students) to doggedly pursue their educational dreams without allowing money to become the wall that blocks their most dearly held aspirations.

Rejoice in your hope, be patient in tribulation, be constant in prayer. Romans 12:12 RSV

Woodrow Whidden II is professor of religion at Andrews University in Berrien Springs, Michigan.

FENCED IN AND NOT THROWN OUT *By Gail Perry Rittenbach*

I don't know why I did it. It was a stupid thing to do. After being in the dorm four years at Milo and Laurelwood academies, the second year in a dorm in the late 1960s at Walla Walla College seemed at bit stifling. In at 10 p.m. with a sign-in-sign-out after-dark policy made me want to stay out.

I HAD to get out of the dorm, if just for a weekend. My roommate joined me and we worked out a simple scheme. She called her home in Portland, Oregon, and had her housekeeper call the dean to say that both of us would be home that weekend. The weekend-leave slip was signed and we were on our own.

We bought groceries—spaghetti, sauce, and breakfast cereal; put the groceries on the counter in a sparsely furnished relative's apartment and wondered what to do for the weekend. We were three blocks from the dorm so we couldn't go very far from the apartment. Certainly, we couldn't go to church—the deans would see us. We had to stay away from the town of Walla Walla; it was so small, we'd probably be spotted. We spent the weekend in hiding.

By the time Sunday morning dawned, responsibility kicked in. I was the secretary for the dean of men, Mike Loewen, and was responsible for recording the worship attendance. I guess I figured that Sunday was a quiet enough day that I could work all day in his office with nobody noticing. So I did. Then I checked into my dorm, supposedly having returned from my trip to Portland. An hour later, the women's dean called me into her office.

On Monday, when word came back from Dean's Council that I was on probation instead of being expelled from the college, I knew that Dean Loewen had interceded for me. It wasn't a long speech he greeted me with that afternoon, and it contained some gentle irony: "I can always count on you to be at work. Thank you." He believed in me.

Therefore submit yourselves to every ordinance of man for the Lord's sake, whether to the king as supreme, or to governors, as to those who are sent by him for the punishment of evildoers and for the praise of those who do good. For this is the will of God, that by doing good you may put to silence the ignorance of foolish men—as free, yet not using your liberty as a cloak for vice, but as bondservants of God. Honor all people. Love the brotherhood. Fear God. Honor the king. 1 Peter 2:13-17

Gail Perry Rittenbach is professor of education and psychology at Walla Walla College in College Place, Washington.

SAFETY IN NUMBERS *By Malcolm Russell*

Graduation from college provided me with very little immediate gratification after shaking hands with a very inspiring college president—Dr. Winton Beaven—on Saturday night.

The next morning I moved out of the dorm and started working at the only job I could find immediately: cleaning up construction sites with a crew whose specialized vocabulary made one word serve as verb, subject and adjective.

Soon, however, notification of my acceptance into graduate school for the fall term suggested that the rough hands and mental boredom would only be temporary. A few days later my alma mater's misfortune became my opportunity. Columbia Hall, the graceful administration building at Columbia Union College, had burned down a few months before, and Dr. Gordon Madgwick, the dean of students, needed help in organizing records that had escaped the flames but suffered water damage.

This being a task far more suited to my recently completed history major than picking up trash around new condominiums, I eagerly applied for the position and was hired. That summer taught me much about life, both from my fellow workers and from odd bits of information in the files themselves.

However, the most vivid lesson that summer came from Dr. Madgwick himself. He stopped to chat one day while I was recording some data, a task that required only modest attention, and he soon addressed the topic of life in graduate school and the professional world.

The discussion began about a recent sermon that had inspired us; then the conversation drifted to sermons and church services that left no discernable effect. Despite the quarter-century since then, Dr. Madgwick's chat seems clearer in my mind than this morning's lecture.

Education and graduate school might change me, he said, and very possibly my local pastor's sermons might fail to interest me spiritually or intellectually. But beyond any arrogance that such a conclusion might suggest, it was simply too dangerous to cultivate the idea that as an intellectual I would benefit more by staying home from services to commune with God privately through study and prayer. The slope, he said, very quickly became treacherously steep, and soon the Sabbath and other vital aspects of the church would seem insignificant.

Simply put, he made it plain that someone who stayed away from church too often strayed from church. By contrast, even if the sermon was boring, the music was flat, and the Sabbath School lesson amounted to reading helps from the *Quarterly*, attendance brought a vital renewal in the truth.

To this day, I cherish that advice from Dr. Madgwick. Living in areas quite densely populated with church members, my family and I have been fortunate both in the pastors we have heard and the convenience of an alternate congregation.

On occasion, I have missed church, particularly while traveling. But Dr. Madgwick's advice to a young graduate student has been a guiding light in my life, and one I am obligated to share with others.

Not forsaking the assembling of ourselves together, as is the manner of some, but exhorting one another, and so much the more as you see the Day approaching. Hebrews 10:25 NKJV

Malcolm Russell is professor of economics and history at Andrews University in Berrien Springs, Michigan.

VISITING WIDOWS By Tom Shepherd

When I was a student in the School of Public Health at Loma Linda University, I managed two blocks of apartments near the campus. I had to collect rents, arrange repairs and keep the units rented—all the usual things an apartment manager does. Several senior citizens lived there, including Mrs. Harris, who occupied the apartment next to mine. She was about 85 years old, a widow. Her husband had worked for a number of years for the Adventist church, it seems, but now she was alone. She was troubled by dizzy spells and usually responded with, "Terrible, terrible," when asked how she was.

One hot, early fall day, I had the windows and door of my non-air-conditioned apartment open, trying to catch a little breeze. I noticed a young woman walk past my open door. She knocked on the door of Mrs. Harris' apartment. Apparently, she had come to visit the widow. I was curious, and found this happened more than once; quite often in fact. Sometimes the young woman took Mrs. Harris for rides to the mountains in her car. Sometimes she took my next-door neighbor to evangelistic meetings.

On one of those occasions, when the young woman was taking Mrs. Harris out to her car, I saw my chance. I came out of my apartment at the appropriate time, just as Mrs. Harris and the stranger were getting into the car. I walked over and said to the dear widow, "Well, Mrs. Harris, when are you going to introduce me to your friend?"

She became a little flustered and tried to say something, when the young woman introduced herself.

"I'm Sherry Bom."

This gave me the opportunity I had counted on to introduce myself. And now I knew her name. I looked her up in the relevant publications. She was a medical student; not someone I would normally have had much contact with since the students of our two schools didn't have very many classes in common. Eventually, I invited her to go with me to a Social Action Corps clinic program, then roller skating, the symphony, etc.

I've known this young woman now for 23 years and I'm never ashamed to tell the way I met my wife. She was working for God, thinking of others, not herself, helping a poor widow. She put God first and He "opened a door." It just so happened that it was my door He opened. I saw the precious gem and have cherished it to this day.

Religion that God our Father accepts as pure and faultless is this: to look after orphans and widows in their distress and to keep oneself from being polluted by the world. James 1:27 NIV

Tom Shepherd is professor of religion at Union College in Lincoln, Nebraska.

SOMETHING FOR ME TO DO *By Ed Wright*

It took a VW bug loaded with friends, shovels and ropes to get the Jeep CJ-4 back on the road. My roommate Mark and I, out for a jaunt in his Jeep, had gotten ourselves mired. Some friends had come from the college to get us out. By now it was nearing midnight, well past room check. We'd have to smooth things over with the monitor on desk in Grainger Hall when we got there.

"Mark, let me drive it back!" John pled as we loaded up.

"Well," countered my roommate, "only because you helped us out." They had been lifelong friends. John had organized our rescue. How could Mark say no? "Be careful, now," Mark cautioned. "Let's go."

With Mark and me sharing the single passenger seat, John buckled up and turned down the Pope Valley road on our way back to Pacific Union College. As he moved through the gears, mud began to spatter against the wheel wells and fly past the windows. It had been raining all weekend; we were taking home an obvious souvenir of our Sunday-night excursion.

John was still accelerating as we neared a gentle left turn. I waited for him to turn the wheel. He didn't. Sitting closest to the canvas door, knuckles white on the sissy bar, I watched with widening eyes as both right wheels left the pavement.

Soon we were drifting off the shoulder. Now the Jeep was beginning to tip. Winter weed stalks from the far side of the ditch began to slap the windshield, and still John accelerated without noticeable correction. We were history.

"You fool!" I screamed at the top of my lungs (and immediately regretted such "last words").

With the sound of shattering glass, everything suddenly shifted into slow motion. The cartwheeling Jeep shot me through the canvas top, barely clearing the windshield without hitting the roll bar. Then I was floating, turning slow somersaults in the air. And yes, my life passed before me. Strangely, I felt no fear. I bounced, rolled, lay still. It was quiet. I was alive.

The next day I stood with my parents beside the crumpled Jeep. We walked along the stretch of road, kicking at the fresh tracks, pacing off the 60 feet of mangled fence. I looked into the field and wondered, *How did I miss all those rocks and trees and land in the mud?*

Walking back to the car with his hand on my shoulder, Dad spoke the obvious: "Ed, you could have been killed here last night. God must have a reason for sparing your life. He's got something for you to do."

How could I ever forget those words?

The Lord will fulfill His purpose for me; Your love, O Lord, endures forever—do not abandon the works of Your hands. Psalm 138:8 NIV

Ed Wright is senior pastor of the Collegedale Seventh-day Adventist Church in Collegedale, Tennessee.

THE FOURTEENTH MEETING

William C. Scales, Jr.

Lela Gooding

Mark Regazzi

Elmar P. Sakala

George P. Babcock

Neal C. Wilson

Carolyn S. Kearbey

Douglas A. Jones

Bill Wohlers

Richard Rice

Come and hear, all ye that fear God,
and I will declare what He hath done for my soul.

Psalm 66:16

FOUR FOOLISH/FAITHFUL FELLOWS *By William C. Scales, Jr.*

I was a proud member of The Oakwood College Quartet, along with Wayne Shepperd, Benjamin Reaves and James Edgecombe. One day while we were on a concert tour during my sophomore year, my voice completely left me. We had a concert scheduled at 8 p.m. that night in Shreveport, Louisiana. Twelve hundred people were supposed to attend, and I was without a voice.

A throat specialist examined me and said, "You might as well forget it. You won't be able to make a sound." All I could do was whisper. But I started praying and asked the other members of the quartet to pray with me. I went into my room and prayed earnestly. When I got up from my knees at 12 noon and tried to sing, nothing came out at all. So I prayed again at one o'clock. Still—no voice.

I was a little disappointed, but I kept on praying every hour on the hour with the same results. Exercising my faith in God, I put on my suit and bow tie. The other men saw me getting ready and joked among themselves: "Scales hasn't said a word to us all day. We know why he isn't talking to us. His voice has probably been coming back gradually, but he doesn't want to use it now. He is saving up his voice for the big program tonight."

We went over to the auditorium where those 1,200 people were waiting to hear us sing. Dr. E. E. Rogers, an Oakwood College professor who had accompanied us, said, "Let's go backstage and have a little season of prayer before we go out in front of all these people."

We went behind the stage, knelt down and all prayed audibly—except for me, of course. When we got up off our knees, it was five minutes before 8 o'clock. I opened my mouth, expecting the miracle. Nothing happened.

"If you men are willing to walk out on the stage with me," I whispered, "I'm willing to go." I turned and started out. To my surprise, three faithful (or foolish) fellows followed. All of us were going out on a limb of faith.

When Timothy Dennison, our pianist, struck the opening chord, I opened my mouth and *my voice was there*. We went through 16 songs that night with no sign of weakness or hoarseness in my voice. Dr. Rogers was on the side of the stage, standing like a track star on the starting blocks. He could hardly wait to race onto the stage to tell everybody that they had just witnessed a miracle. We listened to the tape recordings and couldn't believe our ears. God had truly worked a miracle.

But without faith it is impossible to please Him; for he that cometh to God must believe that He is, and that He is a rewarder of them that diligently seek Him. Hebrews 11:6.

William C. Scales, Jr., is secretary of the ministerial association of the North American Division of Seventh-day Adventists in Silver Spring, Maryland.

BECOMING FOOLISH TO BE WISE *By Lela Gooding*

"Where are you going?"

Dad knew very well where I was going. He'd known for weeks. But on the eve of my departure, as I tried to say goodbye, he continued to let me feel his displeasure at my decision to attend Caribbean Union College (CUC) on the neighboring island of Trinidad.

From the first, his disapproval had been insistent: "What will you do there? It's only a junior college and you're already beyond that. What can you get there that you don't already have?"

From a purely academic standpoint, I had no rebuttal to my father's argument. I had passed final examinations in a British secondary school which extended to junior-college level. My prized Higher School Certificate, representing the highest level of formal education offered in my Caribbean homeland, was my ticket to a respectable job at home or to university in Jamaica or England.

My parents would've been satisfied if their daughter had made either choice. But going to a junior college seemed distinctly a foolish move and a waste of time. That CUC was a Seventh-day Adventist college meant nothing. Back-slidden Adventists themselves, my parents nevertheless were believers who encouraged and supported my active involvement in church; but Adventist education was not a priority.

Like most Protestant girls on the island, after Methodist elementary I matriculated at Anglican High School. From age 10 to 17 I received a thorough, Christian, slightly Anglican-slanted education; but a variety of healthy, nurturing church activities helped to keep my focus on Adventism. After high school, a caring network of church mentors perceived that CUC would be best for me. Despite my dad's disgust, to CUC I went.

CUC changed my intellectual vision. Far from slowing down my academic advancement, it speeded up—many times over—the process of my gaining a true education. O brave new world!—Morning and evening dormitory worship with lusty song services; glorious Friday and Sabbath evening vespers with organ chimes hastening our footsteps from the dormitory; chapel periods, Bible classes, principles of Christian education and perspectives of Ellen G. White as a wise prophet, not a wet blanket. With the transfer credits of my Higher School Certificate, I completed in one year the requirements for an Associate of Arts diploma in Secondary Education. After graduation I was retained to teach full-time in the secondary school there.

And CUC changed the course of my life. During my first summer, I met an illustrious alumnus who had recently been called to the Oakwood College faculty. The next summer he flew to Grenada to seek my parents' approval before I would consent to marry him, and my father liked him at first sight. But this was only the icing on the cake. Dad's irritation about my going to CUC had evaporated long before, undoubtedly because he saw that the college was making me a better person. Without comment, we both knew that CUC had been the right choice; three siblings followed my footsteps there and another came to Oakwood—all with Dad's blessing.

If any man among you seemeth to be wise in this world, let him become a fool, that he may be wise. For the wisdom of this world is foolishness with God. 1 Corinthians 3:18,19

Lela Gooding is professor of English at Oakwood College in Huntsville, Alabama.

SABBATH DINNER *By Mark Regazzi*

I raced from my freshman comp class at the University of Notre Dame to drop off my books and grab a taxi. That Saturday morning, I was going to visit the South Bend Seventh-day Adventist Church for the first time. As a Catholic, I didn't want to explain to the cabby why I was going to an Adventist church, so I told him to drop me off in the 1300 block of E. Altgeld, even though the church was several blocks away.

I signed the guest book and sat in a Sabbath School class taught by the pastor's wife. On the way out of church a woman asked me, "Where are you from?"

"The university," I replied.

She offered to drive me back since she was going to see her sister anyway. I told her, "No thank you, I'll take the bus back." Only later did I discover that her sister lived near Andrews University, 25 miles from South Bend. Adventists in South Bend apparently assumed that a college student from "the university" had come from Andrews. When I realized the generosity of her offer, I was truly impressed. I attended church there two more weeks, each time signing the guest book with my Notre Dame address.

Apparently, someone eventually read the guest register and was mortified at missing a great opportunity to reach out to a Notre Dame student. When I returned to the church three Sabbaths later, I had not walked ten feet into the church before Ardis Meyer almost knocked me over, rushing to inform me that I would have lunch at her house that day.

From then until I left Notre Dame, I always had an invitation to Sabbath dinner. Members so much expected the Nelsons or Behners to take care of me that anyone wanting to have me to dinner called and asked *their* permission and then *told* me where I was eating that Sabbath.

A year later I was hospitalized in South Bend. My mother came from New Jersey to stay with me. After meeting many of the people from the church who came to see me in the hospital, my mother said, "Now I know why you became an Adventist. It's because those people loved you."

My mother was right.

Practice hospitality. Romans 12:13 NIV

Mark Regazzi is assistant professor of religion at Andrews University in Berrien Springs, Michigan.

A BATTLE OVER FIGHTING *By Elmar P. Sakala*

The wheat fields of the Pacific Northwest were a universe away from the killing fields of Vietnam. Yet in the late 1960s, when I was a graduate student in education and psychology at Walla Walla College, the war could be as close as the next day's draft notice. The military was not a voluntary organization as it is today. All young men of appropriate age and health had to register for the military draft and a lottery decided who would actually serve.

In my view, serving one's country in a just war was one thing, but being sent to a distant Asian jungle to fight in a futile war that could not be won was quite another. My male classmates were faced with deciding what classification they would request for their military draft status: combatant, conscientious cooperator, or conscientious objector. This was not a trivial matter, since American boys were being brought home from Vietnam in body bags. This choice could literally mean the difference between life and death.

As a Canadian citizen, I didn't have to register for the draft, but my heart ached as I put myself into my buddies' position and agonized with them over the many questions that begged for answers. How does one convince the local draft board of the sincerity of one's choice? How about the morality of the war? What about bearing arms? Is there any fundamental ethical difference between a rifle-carrying combatant (who pulls the trigger killing an "enemy" soldier) and a non-combatant medic (who carries no weapon but helps restore to health the soldier who pulls the trigger)? Maybe the best choice was to refuse any participation in the military, and seek alternative service in a hospital in the United States? Or is that merely a coward's way out?

My friends spent countless hours working through these very personal decisions, agonizing over the merits and weaknesses of the various options. I agonized right along with them. Myriads of prayers ascended to heaven seeking guidance and direction. Yet often the issues still remained hazy.

So we turned to a truly valued resource—Walla Walla College faculty members from many disciplines: English literature, history, physics, biology, theology, psychology, business, fine arts, engineering and sociology. What those late 1960s Walla Walla College teachers had in common—as demonstrated clearly in their classrooms and in their personal lives—was both a solid spiritual grounding and a willingness to be challenged to the very basic assumptions of their beliefs.

Those Friday evenings in my apartment, when we fellows would bare our souls and voice our fears to trusted faculty, were times of inestimable support. While not imposing their personal positions on us, they provided the accepting environment that allowed my collegiate contemporaries to come to grips with some of the most serious decisions they would ever make. I suppose those professors were only faintly aware of the invaluable contribution they were making in our lives.

**Plans fail for lack of counsel, but with many advisers they succeed.
Proverbs 15:22 NIV**

*Elmar P. Sakala is professor of gynecology and obstetrics at Loma Linda University School of
Medicine in Loma Linda, California.*

BORROWED FAITH By George P. Babcock

The job prospect in hospital x-ray looked attractive. As a senior education major at Columbia Union College, I knew the hospital job would pay considerably more than what I could expect to earn as a teacher. It was something to think about as I eagerly anticipated graduation.

Then, I contracted hepatitis. The doctors despaired of my life. They explained that my only hope lay in massive doses of steroids—doses so massive, in fact, that while the last young man who'd received such treatment had lived, he had become totally blind. With death as my only alternative, I signed the forms allowing the treatment.

As my condition began to stabilize, the doctors told me that now an intestinal blockage and a staph infection complicated my condition. They predicted I'd be in the hospital at least another month. I lost all hope of completing my work and graduating on schedule, so I asked my wife to drop me from college classes.

She filled out the usual drop forms and took them to the academic dean, Winton Beaven, for his signature. He refused to sign them. "Don't be in such a hurry," he said. "We're praying for George, and we'll work with him when he recovers. We want him to graduate."

My wife reported Beaven's response, but I still felt hopeless. One of my classes was entirely lectures. How could I possibly handle that in my condition? But a classmate, Noel Shanko, solved the problem. He taped the lectures for me. In the evenings, my wife sat in my hospital room, typing out the lectures on an old manual Underwood. Yet, even with that help, I was too sick to do much serious studying.

One day, while still in the hospital, I received a call to become a school principal when I graduated. I thought about that lucrative job prospect in the medical field, but while my life hung in the balance, I promised God that if He would spare me, I'd teach for Him regardless of salary.

Again, in the third week, I asked my wife to go and fill out drop forms for me. She did and again Dr. Beaven refused to sign them. "George is a good student," he said. "Once he's on his feet, he can catch up. Tell him to put his faith in God. We're all praying for him." I knew that was so. Several college staff members had come to me in person and prayed for me.

I tried one more time to drop out, with the same results. So, I quit trying to drop out and began studying in my hospital bed. At the end of the sixth week, I was released from the hospital, but my eyesight was failing. During the next few months, my eye glass prescription had to be changed four times. How could I teach if I were blind? With my own weak faith, I clung to Dr. Beaven's certainty. He was so sure God would heal me and I would graduate.

Finally I did make it back to classes; I studied hard, and with encouragement from all my teachers, I graduated in May. Dr. Beaven beamed as he shook my hands at commencement. "Well, George, you made it with the Lord's help. I knew you would."

For more than 35 years now, I've served as an Adventist educator all over the world. How often I've thanked God for sparing my life and for giving me a Christian teacher who shared his sure faith with an unsure student.

And the prayer of faith shall save the sick, and the Lord shall raise him up. James 5:15

George P. Babcock is vice president for academic administration at Southern Adventist University in Collegedale, Tennessee.

HUMBLED INTO HAPPINESS *By Neal C. Wilson*

As a senior at Pacific Union College, I was eager to graduate. But I was even more concerned about finding the right life companion. It wasn't a matter of having no social opportunities or lovely girl friends. My question was: Which one truly loved the Lord and would provide what I desperately needed as a companion wherever He might invite us to serve?

Since I had considerable experience in accounting, I had applied at the St. Helena Health Center in California for a job as a cashier, an accountant or some junior management position. Instead, I was assigned to the cafeteria to make salads, set up the food deck, and check meal tickets. I talked with the Lord about that.

I said, "This isn't fair. Why am I being penalized? Are You trying to test me?" I felt I was over-qualified for the job they had assigned me. In my youthful arrogance, I even said, "Lord, I have been the acting treasurer of the Oriental Watchman Publishing House. Besides, my father is the Division president. Why are You doing this to me?" I felt humiliated.

Somehow, the Lord led me to search my heart, to review His promises in the Bible, and to comfort myself in the encouraging writings of Ellen White. My faith was restored. I felt assured that God had something good for me if I was willing to follow His leading. He has satisfying surprises for us often when we least expect them.

My prayer about a special someone was still, "Lord, please show me who it should be." The answer came, clear and positive. It seemed almost as though I was on a phone call to the throne room of Heaven. I heard God say, "You've been looking at her almost every day." Of course! I had seen her the first time I checked meal tickets in that humiliating job in the cafeteria. She was blond, had blue eyes, was physically appealing and well proportioned. She was innocent, vivacious and charming. She carried herself with lady-like grace and elegance. She loved life. And, most of my bachelor friends thought she was a desirable prize. She, however, seemed to be very selective and choosey about special friends.

After a while, I became the assistant patient finance officer of the Health Center. Still, my big concern was whether or not I could measure up to that young lady's expectations. And, another thing, if she became my life companion, would she be willing to go overseas in response to missionary challenges?

Time, it seemed, was running out. The school year was almost over. Yet I was confident that Jesus would work things out for me just as He had promised. "Those who decide to do nothing in any line that will displease God will know after presenting their case before Him, just what course to pursue" (*Desire of Ages*, p.668).

What peace came to my soul when she said "yes!" What a marvelous wife and precious mother Elinor has been for more than 55 years.

Trust in the Lord with all your heart and lean not on your own understanding; in all your ways acknowledge Him and He shall direct your paths. Proverbs 3:5,6 NJKV

Neal C. Wilson is immediate past president of the General Conference of Seventh-day Adventists in Silver Spring, Maryland.

PLAYING WITH PAIN, TRUSTING WITH JOY   *By Carolyn S. Kearbey*

When I started school at Union College, one fact about which I was absolutely certain was that I didn't, in any way, want to be a teacher.

My parents were teachers. I knew first hand what a frustrating life a teaching career could be. I wanted a job that would allow me a life of my own outside of work.

I decided to major in piano performance, simply because music had been a large part of most of my life. Yet, in that, I was keeping an important secret. Arthritis had started settling into my fingers ever since I was sixteen. Although rheumatoid arthritis ran in my mother's family, I was afraid to admit to anyone how often my fingers would ache or that my hands could no longer reach an octave. I tried to play the best I could, but the pain was horrendous and some days the sound seemed even worse.

During my sophomore year, I was required to take a child-development class taught by Virginia Simmons, a new professor in the education department. Under her tutelage, children came to life in our classroom—from newborn infants up to adolescents. The more I heard, the more excited I became about the idea of working with children and affecting their lives in a positive manner.

I also felt a bit haunted. In high school, the only way I had been able to escape study hall was to join the Future Teachers of America club, spending one hour a day assisting in a primary classroom working with special-needs children. Now I began having dreams about these children every night.

About this same time, my piano teacher found out the secret of my hurting hands. Watching closely as I played a Beethoven piece one day, he suddenly stopped me and asked me to play an octave for him. Valiantly I tried and failed. Upset, he pointed out that I was not doing my hands any favors by continuing to ask them to perform what they so clearly could not.

That was the night I prayed to the Lord to help me evaluate the direction my life was going and to help me see where He needed me. Once again, I dreamed of the children I had taught. By the time I awoke the next morning, I knew the answer. Like Jonah, I'd been running away from the life God had intended for me, and now it was time to stop running.

I told my music adviser and Dr. Simmons that I was changing my major that day to elementary education. The music adviser nodded calmly, but Dr. Simmons literally jumped up and down with glee that she had helped guide another teacher to God's true pathway.

And your ears shall hear a word behind you, saying, "This is the way, walk in it," when you turn to the right or when you turn to the left. Isaiah 30:21 RSV

Carolyn S. Kearbey is associate professor of education at Atlantic Union College in South Lancaster, Massachusetts.

GOING HOME   *By Douglas A. Jones*

ven more exciting than studying English literature and history with a Walla Walla College study group for eight weeks at Newbold College was the prospect of seeing the Continent afterward. I had a Eurail pass, a little money and a sense of reckless abandon, all prerequisites for a month of travel with a few friends.

But one by one, my friends' travel plans changed, and I was pretty much striking off for Calais by myself. No problem. Max would meet me in Amsterdam and it would just be the two of us—easier to travel that way, anyway. But then his plans changed. At the American Express office, I read his wire: "Have to be at Bogenhofen earlier than I thought. Hope this doesn't foul you up."

Back at my room in the Fly Inn (no kidding, that's where I was staying) in one of Amsterdam's seedier neighborhoods, I considered my circumstances. Nixon had just devalued the dollar, I was losing weight and Janell's letter to me reminded me of where I'd rather be. Back home.

I thought about praying, but it was easier to brood over thwarted plans. Sometime, though, very early in the morning, I did pray. I knew I'd need God's leading over the next couple of days.

But I didn't know how much I'd need His help. Not only would I have a difficult time getting back to London, but I had to grapple with the nagging fact that I wasn't going to see Rome or Paris or anything. And that my friends would know I'd wimped out.

Back in London, I found a room (actually about 300 Americans found the same room). It was a warehouse full of cots. Seventy-five pence a night that included breakfast at a vending machine. I found that it's not easy switching tickets for charter flights back to the United States. Travel agent after travel agent reminded me of this fact.

I was tired, hungry and discouraged. Somewhere along Regent Street I prayed silently, asking for God's leading. At the next travel agent's counter, the clerk explained, "It's not easy, but we can probably help you. Just hand over your return ticket."

All my better judgment said "NO!", but I gave it to her, wondering if God was leading yet. "What you'll have to do is fill out these forms and deliver them to our adjunct agent in Crickelwood. At his flat." I took the tube, then a bus. And I walked, praying a prayer of apprehension.

I found the flat. A rumpled-looking fellow, not much older than I, answered the door. "Oh, you're the chap. Come in. Would you like some orange juice?" He made a call and assured me a ticket would be waiting at the airport.

That night, sitting on the cold Gatwick Airport floor, I prayed again. With assurance.

I lay my requests before You and wait in expectation. Psalm 5:3 NIV

Douglas A. Jones is director of public relations at Andrews University in Berrien Springs, Michigan.

WINNING BY LOSING *By Bill Wohlers*

L earning to accept the benefits of unrealized ambition was a lesson God taught me more than once.

My instruction actually began a couple of years before college while I was still attending the neighboring academy. When I lost my first student association election, the event allowed God to show me He always has better ideas for us than we do for ourselves.

Not to be denied, however, I didn't wait long before planning further political adventures. I was convinced that my high-schoolish disappointment had to presage collegiate success. In my college sophomore year I again decided to become a campus politician. This effort looked like it would be easy since there appeared to be no opposition. But the student association election commission took care of that by nominating a good friend of mine. He won by four votes.

One year later I was back, seeking votes again from my fellow students. By this time hubris was certainly clouding my judgment, since I, a village student, decided to challenge the exceedingly successful and popular dorm club president. My temerity lasted long enough to withstand the extended ovation for my opponent's speech from the overflow audience in the college chapel. I went ahead and spoke anyway; I also went ahead and lost—by a landslide.

Whether God wanted me to lose all those elections, I really can't be sure. I'm positive, however, that He helped me to grow because of them. One simple lesson was to accept that some defeats can be expected as a part of life. More immediate, if not more gratifying, were those unsought after opportunities to contribute to my college community even without occupying some lofty elected position. Many of those post-election responsibilities prepared me much more for my current vocation, (which in college I could only imagine *not doing*), than any victory ever could have.

Because of my own experience, I'm able to tell students today that losing can build more character than winning. And that's not simply a cliche.

O Lord, my heart is not lifted up, my eyes are not raised too high; I do not occupy myself with things too great and too marvelous for me. Psalm 131:1 RSV

Bill Wohlers is vice president for student services at Southern Adventist University in Collegedale, Tennessee.

SEMINAR IN EXCELLENCE *By Richard Rice*

Starting graduate school was a traumatic experience for me. One of the major reasons was a teacher named Samuel Olson.*

A renowned scholar and dynamic lecturer, Professor Olson was also a ruthless critic of others' work, no matter who they were—authorities in the field, faculty colleagues or lowly students like me. If he didn't like what he heard or read, he told the world in no uncertain terms.

I took a seminar in philosophy from Professor Olson during my first year at the University of Chicago. To begin each class, one student presented a paper and the others asked questions about it. The advanced students asked questions I couldn't understand and engaged Dr. Olson in discussions I couldn't follow. Each class meeting left me bewildered.

As the weeks went by, I grew more apprehensive about my up-coming presentation. I pored over the material I was supposed to explain, but each reading left me more confused than before. When I finally put words on paper, I could hardly make sense of what I'd written.

The dreaded day finally arrived, and Professor Olson called on me. I was the picture of insecurity. Above the pounding of my heart, I heard a thin, quivering voice—my own—tentatively reading the essay I had put together. I reached the end and looked up to see Dr. Olson staring at the ceiling with a strange expression on his face. I had a terrible time answering the questions. When someone offered a mild criticism of something I had said, I readily conceded that my point didn't make any sense.

This jolted Dr. Olson into action. "You can't do that," he said sharply. "When you take a position, you have to defend it. Don't abandon it just because somebody asks you to explain it."

"Okay," I said feebly. "I support the point."

And things went downhill from there. I had heard about students who walked out of class one day and were never heard of again. I knew exactly why. Somehow I survived that day and went on to finish the course, but I couldn't get over my fear of Dr. Olson.

I knew I would have to face this man again when I took my major exams, and if I repeated my earlier performance in his seminar, I was doomed. To steel myself, I took another class from him the following year. It was a tutorial, actually. Each week he met with three of us in his office for a couple of hours to discuss the books we were reading. To my surprise, my perspective on him changed. He was just as demanding as ever, but I began to understand why. It had nothing to do with pride or prestige or arrogance. It was all about scholarship. Dr. Olson demanded the best of himself. And he wanted his students to be the best they could be, too.

In time, I no longer feared his criticism; I welcomed it. I knew I was a better scholar because of it. Dr. Olson left Chicago at the end of the year for another university. And when they asked a student to speak at a farewell reception for him, of all people they picked me.

God's gifts to students come in many forms. But one of them is teachers who expect a lot from us and drive us to reach for the heights.

name has been changed

For whom the Lord loves He chastens. Hebrews 12:6 NKJV

Richard Rice is professor of theology at La Sierra University in Riverside, California.

THE FIFTEENTH MEETING

Elizabeth Sterndale

Ron Schafer

L. Melvin Roberts, Jr.

Lucille C. Lacy

Karl J. Hinkle

David Smith

Ed Wines

Sylvia Rasi Gregorutti

William Davidson

Morris Venden

Come and hear, all ye that fear God,
and I will declare what He hath done for my soul.

Psalm 66:16

CHARLES SHELDON AND "D AND R" *By Elizabeth Sterndale*

I was just beginning college and my first experience in a Christian school. I had been assigned a "big sister," Elizabeth (Liz) Hudak who was just finishing college. She had already impressed me with her helpfulness, her Christianity and her ability to make everything fun. Then I learned that we were to have small group meetings. I don't know how or why the groups got started. I only remember that Liz asked me to join a group that would meet in her room each week.

When a half-dozen or so crowded into her room, Liz told us that we would read portions of the book *In His Steps,* followed, each time we met, by a prayer session. Why *In His Steps?* I wondered. I hadn't heard of it before. Why not the Bible?

Actually, *In His Steps* by Charles Sheldon is a Christian classic, but I didn't know that. At the same time, I was feeling an overdose of another book, *Thoughts on Daniel and the Revelation,* in a course with a similar name. Not having attended a church school before, the class and the book in my first year of college almost did me in. My straight A's of public high school did not help when I encountered "D and R."

So amid all the other activities of college, our group faithfully met to read *In His Steps* and to pray our personal prayer requests.

And read that whole book we did. And absorb it we did. At last, Christianity was made practical. What a classic! What an impression! What a question it constantly asked! "What would Jesus do?" That question guided me through college and into the workplace.

Yes, "D and R" did a number on my grades; and, yes, "D and R" is important to my knowledge base of history, religion and prophecy. But the question "What would Jesus do?" keeps coming into my hearing—sometimes quietly, sometimes with force. It changes my course most when I answer the question honestly.

"What would Jesus do?"

To this you were called, because Christ suffered for you, leaving you an example, that you should follow in His steps. 1 Peter 2:21 NIV

Elizabeth Sterndale retired in 1996 as the director of the Office of Women's Ministries at the North American Division of Seventh-day Adventists in Silver Spring, Maryland.

KEYS OF FAITH *By Ron Schafer*

As a P.E. major at Andrews University, I joined the other department majors for our annual fall camp out in northern Michigan. At our campsite, we discovered that if we wanted our traditional campfire that night, we'd have to do some serious searching for wood. We jumped in the back of Doc Klein's truck and headed out. Doc said he knew of several locations that promised a good supply, but it seemed that previous campers had known of these areas, too. We drove from place to place, collecting more dead grass and weeds than wood, but finally the truck was full. We returned to camp to enjoy the evening around the fire.

After the Sabbath morning activities, one of the members of our group announced that he needed to return to the school for a function that night. He reached for his car keys and discovered his pockets were empty. Nervous, but not yet panicked, he solicited the help of his friends and together we turned the camp upside down. No keys. The level of anxiety was now significantly higher.

There was only one other possible place the keys could be, but the chance of finding them out in the bush was as probable as finding the proverbial needle in the haystack. In our search for wood, we had stopped at three or four places, miles apart, and had covered acres. Most of us felt that a search was a ridiculous waste of time and energy, but we went along to be polite.

We scoured each location and came up empty-handed. When we finished the last one, we decided that, indeed, we had wasted our time, and it was now time to send our friend home via his thumb or tell him to wait until Sunday morning. Maybe next time he'd be more careful or at least carry a second set of keys. It was a tough way to learn the lesson.

We gathered around the truck to announce our decision to call off the search and return to our campsite. Just then, Doc Klein's youngest son suggested that we pray about the keys. The boy obviously didn't or couldn't appreciate the complexity of this problem. But, just to be "kind," we gathered around and someone prayed that God would help us out of this predicament and find those keys. "Amen," we all said in unison.

As most of us turned to get into the truck, someone whose faith was greater than the rest of ours began kicking the grass with his feet. He hadn't moved more than ten paces when his foot caught something that flew up in the air. Sure enough, it was a set of keys.

Does God answer prayers? Not always as we'd like or expect. But once, when He needed to strengthen the faith of some P.E. majors who thought they could "go it alone," He answered loud and clear.

Therefore I tell you, whatever you ask for in prayer, believe that you have received it, and it will be yours. Mark 11:24 NIV

Ron Schafer is associate professor of physical education at Canadian University College in College Heights, Alberta.

A TEST OF FAITH *By L. Melvin Roberts, Jr.*

Six months had passed since I had entered the chemistry graduate program at Texas A&M University. Until then I believed that God was leading me into a career in chemical education. However, in those first six months of graduate school, I had very few successes to confirm that belief. My research was barely moving, and I knew that I was in the lower half of my classes. I began to doubt that God really was guiding me down this path. I wondered if I had simply convinced myself to do this.

My greatest worry was the cumulative exams the chemistry department gave every month. Graduates were required to pass six out of sixteen exams within the first two years. These exams were given on the first Saturday of each month and prepared each time by a different faculty member. Each exam included questions about general knowledge of chemical principles; more detailed questions on a particular chemical subject; and questions over the current literature.

Because I was a Seventh-day Adventist, the department allowed me to take the exams on Friday, the day before the other students took the exam. I was required to go to my adviser's office and pick up the exam in a large manila envelope. Then I'd find a quiet, isolated place and spend the next hour answering questions.

After six months, I had taken and failed four exams. It seemed to me that if I failed another—the fifth—there would be little chance of me passing six out of the next eleven.

Typically, I did well in the general knowledge sections but quite poorly in the specialized and literature questions. In preparation for the fifth exam, I studied ahead in my inorganic textbook, wanting to learn about any topic that hadn't been covered in my classes. After scanning several subjects, I randomly decided to study in more detail a class of compounds called boranes.

The days slipped by quickly and the time for my fifth exam arrived. With much apprehension, I sat down at a cubicle just outside the chemistry library. I stared at the unopened manila envelope for awhile, dolefully acknowledging that this one exam could well make or break my graduate school career.

Before opening the envelope, I asked God to direct my paths. If I was where He wanted me to be, He must help me pass. If I should be somewhere else, He must allow me to fail. I opened the envelope slowly and examined the contents.

The general and literature sections contained no surprises. The advanced section, however, provided an immediate answer to my prayer. For in that section I was asked to describe the structure and theory for a particular borane compound, exactly the subject I randomly had chosen to study in preparation for the exam.

For the next hour, as I successfully passed my first exam, I praised God for His assurance that He was, indeed, guiding me through graduate school.

For your Father knows what you need before you ask Him. Matthew 6:8 NIV

L. Melvin Roberts, Jr., is assistant professor of chemistry at Columbia Union College in Takoma Park, Maryland.

PROFESSOR "X" AND THE LIBRARY BOOK DROP *By Lucile Lacy*

When I was a teenager, a high-school teacher told me that I would never be a success in my life and that I'd be a detriment to society. It was the first time anyone had made such a sweeping negative evaluation of my potential, and I was devastated.

After completing a master's degree in music teacher education from George Peabody College for Teachers, I taught college for several years. Then I prayed, "Lord, if it is Your will for me to pursue the doctorate degree, prepare the way." Unexpectedly, I was awarded a United Negro College Fund Teaching Grant for $10,000, renewable annually. This to me seemed a notable honor for one who had been told by a professional educator that I had no future.

I wanted to get my doctoral degree from Ohio State University. From a pool of 400 applicants, I was one of the ten accepted into the program. Soon I met Professor "X" who told me that, as a Seventh-day Adventist, I had no chance of succeeding as a doctoral student at OSU. The graduate music program was impossible to complete while missing the Friday night and Saturday sessions. He said I should either attend the classes as required or withdraw from the program. I left his office determined to complete the program *and* keep the Sabbath.

One Friday afternoon at the end of one semester, Professor "X" gave the class an almost impossible "take home" final examination. It was due the following Monday and would require exhaustive research in the library all weekend.

Two hours before sunset on Friday, I closed up all my studies and prepared for the Sabbath. Saturday evening some of my classmates called to wish me success. They had spent all Friday evening and all day Saturday in the library and were far from finished.

By Sunday evening, after ten hours of research, I had answered three of the exam's ten questions. I stopped and communed with God for one hour. Then, one hour before the library closed, I was impressed to walk down the stacks. Praying silently, with tears running down my cheeks, I felt nothing but despair when suddenly, in front of me, a book dropped from the shelf and fell open to a page of information I needed. I quickly picked up the book and continued to walk down the aisle when another book fell from the shelf. Books began falling from high and low, faster and faster. Each book was opened to an exact answer.

I grabbed a cart and moved quickly down the aisle picking up books. The library assistants heard the sounds of the books falling from the shelves and asked if I knew who was throwing the books? I just smiled through my tears, rejoiced in the Lord, and kept on picking up those books.

I was the only student in the class who completed the entire exam. Professor "X" was shocked.

I have found that people cannot set limits for us when we pray and completely depend on a loving God Who honors those who trust in Him.

Thou hast commanded Thy precepts to be kept diligently. O that my ways may be steadfast in keeping Thy statutes! Then I shall not be put to shame, having my eyes fixed on all Thy commandments. Psalm 119:4-6 RSV

Lucile C. Lacy is associate professor of music at Oakwood College in Huntsville, Alabama.

GUARDING THE FOOLISH By *Karl J. Hinkle*

I helped pay my way through Pacific Union College by working for the college's security department. There were a number of times when I'm sure that my guardian angel was challenged and tested—challenged when I had no control of the events and tested when I acted foolishly.

The main street into the campus had planter boxes dividing the lanes at the approach to the street that ran between the business office and Newton Hall. The planter boxes were there to keep vehicles from turning left onto the main street from the drive behind the business office. I soon found just the right spot to park the security patrol car so it couldn't be seen while I watched for vehicles making an illegal left.

One evening, I saw a motorcycle turn left and come the wrong way down the street. As the motorcycle approached my hiding spot, I turned on my red overhead lights to have the driver stop and get his $5 ticket. The motorcycle didn't stop and the chase was on.

By the time I reached the bottom of the up-hill climb through the pass out of the valley, my ex-Highway Patrol police cruiser, with its 440 magnum engine, was already passing 85 m.p.h. By now, the Honda Electra-Glide was nearly to the top of the pass.

By the time I reached the "S" curve just after the pass I was traveling more than 105 m.p.h. As I started into the curve to the left, the Honda was starting to turn to the right. Instinctively, I knew I should not brake for the curve or I would lose control of the vehicle. There was only one thing to do: ACCELERATE!

I made the first half of the "S" curve in fine shape, but now I was going almost 115 m.p.h. and the old engine was pushed to the limit. I realized, too late, that I was not going to keep in my half of the road way and still make the last half of the blind curve. I was sure some innocent person and I were seconds away from the end.

Straining every bolt, the patrol car edged inexorably over into the other lane as I wrestled to keep it under control. There wasn't much time to pray, but I know my thoughts were heard. "LORD! Just get me out of this ALIVE! and I'll never . . . ."

As I came through the turn I took my foot off the gas pedal and edged back to my own lane. Up ahead, the motorcycle turned off the road onto a street that went sharply up a hill. He drifted gently to a stop and I rolled up behind him. I turned off the red lights; we looked at each other, smiled, and after awhile drove off.

I don't know how many angels it took to keep the old patrol car on the road or keep some other car from coming the other way. And I never bothered to find out who the motorcyclist was. But I did learn an important lesson. Even when I do something foolish, my Heavenly Father is strong to save and can send His angels to rescue me.

For He will give His angels charge over you to guard you in all your ways. Psalm 91:11 RSV

Karl J. Hinkle is director of security at Loma Linda University and Medical Center in Loma Linda, California.

A CHURCH SERVICE TO REMEMBER *By David Smith*

During my first two years as an undergraduate at Andrews University, I didn't consider spiritual matters as important as my social life, classes, work and sports. This was evident my sophomore year when a journalism teacher invited me to join a Bible study/prayer group. I declined, feeling that my life was hectic enough without adding Bible study time to it. Besides, the meetings might conflict with intramural sports.

In the spring of my junior year, something remarkable happened. My fiancee and I attended a Sabbath service at Pioneer Memorial Church. I don't remember who spoke that day, and I don't remember what he said. But I do remember that at the end of the sermon, the Spirit of God was so evident that no one wanted to leave. This is the only instance I have witnessed when no one would leave a church service once it had ended. The congregation remained and sang songs, prayed and shared testimonies. We ended by creating a human chain as hundreds sang "Side by Side" and clasped each other's hands. It was late afternoon before we finally left.

For weeks after that service, students on fire for the Lord, my fiancee and I among them, traveled from Andrews University to their home towns to witness of their new-found love for Christ. I remember standing before my home church congregation and sharing my experience with them.

Although the "high" of this revival did not last, it profoundly affected many of us students. For the first time, I had experienced directly the power and the presence of God. I had discovered peace, joy and hope. Like an Olympic torch, the spiritual flame from that experience still burns in my heart.

Perhaps no one is busier than college students whose lives are filled with assignments, tests, recreation, work, dating, career choices and so many other things. But when the power of God comes into a life, the work of true education begins as God takes His proper place in the heart of His child. In the midst of the chaos, He brings peace, joy and hope, and His children are never the same again.

May the God of hope fill you with all joy and peace in believing, so that by the power of the Holy Spirit you may abound in hope. Romans 15:13 RSV

David Smith is professor of English at Southern Adventist University in Collegedale, Tennessee.

FLYING ON FAITH *By Ed Wines*

As a kid, I had always loved airplanes. I yearned to be free, to fly effortlessly as a hawk. As a boarding academy student, I watched the construction of a private airport a half mile from the campus and wished with all my heart that I could fly. When at last I was a college freshman my opportunity arrived. A beginning course in aviation was offered and I signed up.

Near the completion of that course, I enrolled in flight lessons with an instructor. Three months later I acquired my private license. On a limited college-student income I still found some money to continue flying.

In my junior year, however, a much larger opportunity became a reality. At the suggestion and with the help of a minister-pilot friend, I launched a privately owned flying club for students and faculty at the college. I purchased a two-year-old plane, actively solicited members, and encouraged flying. I also began pursuing a commercial license and a flight instructor rating that would help in the business.

For me, a business major, this flying club proved to be a real-world opportunity to put into practice some of the skills I was learning in the classroom. I had not anticipated, however, that this business venture would also provide a real-life opportunity to test my faith in the Lord's provision for my needs.

Just a few months after I had purchased the plane, my insurance agent called to advise me that the premium was due in a few days. When I checked my bank account, I didn't have enough money available for this major expenditure. I didn't know what to do. I distinctly remember folding my hands at the desk where I usually studied and praying: "Lord, You know about this business of mine. You know what I'm trying to accomplish in providing this opportunity to students. You know that as a college student, I do need this business to go well to help me in pay for my college expenses. Please help me."

Taking God at His word that He would indeed "supply my need," I wrote out a check to the insurance company for the premium that was due and dropped it in the mail. Then I went to work over the next few days to collect the amounts that were owed by the members for aircraft rental as well as encouraging new members to join and pay their membership fees. By the time the insurance check cleared the bank, adequate funds were in my checking account.

My God had met my need, and in the process, this junior business major had personally experienced God's power at work in the everyday world of my chosen profession.

My God will supply every need of yours according to His riches in glory in Christ Jesus. Philippians 4:19 RSV

Ed Wines is vice president for financial administration at Andrews University in Berrien Springs, Michigan.

JUST START WITH THE BASICS *By Sylvia Rasi Gregorutti*

As I prepared to begin my graduate work at Georgetown University, the questions came: Would my 16-year Adventist education be up to par? What would it be like to attend a Catholic university with non-Adventists and many non-Christians? Was "going straight through" the right thing to do?

Fortunately, God saw to it that these large questions were answered early on: Yes, my Adventist education had equipped me formidably, and yes, this seemed to be where God wanted me to be.

As the semester progressed, I began to relax and enjoy my courses in linguistics. I became friends with classmates like Karen. We rode out on the same bus—she to her downtown apartment and I to outer suburbia. We discussed classwork, held animated gripe sessions, shared experiences, and inevitably, one night, we talked about our spiritual lives. Karen's family had been nominal Christians. She had experimented with drugs and had experience with a variety of non-Christian religions. After sharing this with me in the course of a couple of city blocks, she smiled and asked, "So, what do

Adventists believe?" I gulped. This should've been an easy one. I remember telling her about the Sabbath, diet, education and health care. But after eight city blocks, I felt that I hadn't gotten to the essentials. After talking for a few minutes about the value of meditation, we parted company. It was hard to concentrate on the reading I had planned to do during the remainder of my commute.

At home, I told my mother what had happened. She listened carefully, then recommended, "Next time, just start with the basics. The Sabbath is important, but tell her about God. Talk to her about Jesus."

"Makes sense," I thought, "but will there be a next time?"

The next time Karen and I rode on the bus together, we talked about personal problems. She was sorting out various things in her life, and I was attempting to maintain a long-distance relationship while adjusting to living at home again.

"You know, Karen," I said, "I believe what the Bible says in Romans 8:28. All things work together for good for people who love God."

She nodded. "Yeah. I think everything does work out in the end."

Karen and I still keep in touch. After that experience, I was given many "next times"—opportunities to share my faith with classmates, co-workers and teachers. And many times as I shared, I remembered my mother's advice: "Just start with the basics. They're what really count."

Yet for us there is but one God, the Father, from Whom all things came and for Whom we live; and there is but one Lord, Jesus Christ, through Whom all things came and through Whom we live. 1 Corinthians 8:6 NIV

Sylvia Rasi Gregorutti is assistant professor of modern language at Pacific Union College in Angwin, California.

A LORD WHO KNOWS ELASTICITY By *William Davidson*

My major professor and adviser for my doctoral studies at Penn State, Dr. Brielmaier, was a very able German structural engineer not readily given to compromise.

Two concerns from our first program-planning meeting stand out in my memory. First, Dr. Brielmaier stated that I must plan to take a course in "elasticity" as well as a number of other courses in engineering mechanics. I tried to explain that my interests lay in other areas, but to no avail. Second, as a matter of personal admonition, he counseled that my Ph.D. program must now become the most important thing in my life. As best I could, I explained that this priority was one to which I couldn't agree: God was first, my family second and my "job" third. After a lively exchange of ideas, we agreed on a "cease fire" and began a four-year relationship of mutual respect and a friendship which continued until Dr. Brielmaier's death years later. But—I still had to take the elasticity course.

Every term I scanned the class schedule for the 400-level elasticity course intended for the undergraduate engineering mechanics seniors and non-engineering mechanics graduate students. Each time the course was offered, it was scheduled for Tuesday, Thursday, and Saturday. Term after term the years slipped by. Finally, in the third summer of my stay at Penn State, I noticed in the class schedule an elasticity course that didn't meet on Saturday. However, I soon dismissed it as a possibility. It was an advanced course, "The Mathematical Theory of Elasticity," and the more basic 400-level course I needed was listed as a prerequisite for this one.

At summer registration another graduate student whom I had known from another course asked if I needed to take a course in elasticity. He could take classes only in the summer, and suggested that we take the advanced elasticity course "together." We talked with the teacher, requesting that he permit us to take the course without the prerequisite. He agreed, we registered and started classes. I knew immediately that I was in trouble.

After about three class periods, my "friend" came to my office and asked if I'd like to buy his textbook at half price (I didn't have one yet); he was dropping the course. To my plea that we were "taking it together," he replied that he hadn't slept since the first class. I bought the book. I haven't seen him since.

I was in a tight spot and knew it. As soon as he was gone, I shut my door, got down on my knees and told the Lord, "Now it's up to You. I'm not going to go to school on Sabbath (when the 400-level class is offered) and I must take an elasticity course. But I can't do it. You must, if You want me to finish this program. It's up to You. Thank You."

For ten weeks, the term went by in a blur, twelve hours a day, six days a week. Go to class, study, get stuck, kneel down and pray, study, study and do problems. After the term ended, I went to the professor's office to pick up some problems that hadn't been returned in class. He gave me my homework and then asked if I wanted to know my grade for the course. I wasn't sure. He asked if I'd ever taken another course in elasticity. I hadn't. He said, "I'm surprised. You've done better than some students who've taken work before in elasticity. I'm giving you an A in the course."

Praise the Lord! He knows the mathematical theory of elasticity and is willing and able to do for us what is necessary to accomplish His goals for our lives.

O taste and see that the Lord is good: blessed is the man that trusteth in Him. Psalm 34:8

William Davidson is professor of engineering, emeritus, at Andrews University in Berrien Springs, Michigan.

ALWAYS TALKING ABOUT JESUS By Morris Venden

As a new freshman at La Sierra College, I was awed by the upperclassmen and did everything they suggested. One of them said to me, "Why don't you put a blade in the razor next time?" And another one, that same week, said, "You could stand a little closer to the razor."

So I put a blade in and stood a little closer and was ready for their next bit of advice. It was to enroll in a particular Bible class by a particular professor. I said, "Why? Is it required?"

They said, "No,—but do it!"

So I did as I was told and then hurried to my first class period armed with plenty of paper and ball-point pens so that I could take notes to feed back to the professor at the end of the semester.

But nobody took notes in the class. The professor didn't ask us to memorize verses or draw maps or trace journeys. All he did was talk about Jesus. I didn't know there was that much to say about Jesus. He talked about what Jesus was like, what He said, and especially how He treated people. It was obvious that the professor was on speaking terms with this Friend of his. Our hearts were strangely warmed as our pens dropped out of our hands and the paper remained blank.

After those class periods, we didn't run to dinner or retreat to the gym to shoot baskets. We wandered across the campus to find a quiet place where we could sit and think about Jesus. "Could it be that Jesus treats us the same today?"

This was the high point in my Christian education, thanks to Dr. Tom Blincoe.

I finished college, including important classes like U.S. Constitution and Greek I and II. Then, one year, I found myself wandering in the lobby of the giant auditorium where the General Conference world session was being held in San Francisco. There were 10,000 people in the meeting and 10,000 people wandering around in the lobby. Suddenly, in all that crowd, I was face to face with my professor from that Bible class. We greeted each other. And then—it wasn't thirty seconds—he was talking about Jesus again.

As the flood of memories came rushing back, it was more than I could handle. I escaped to a place underneath a stairwell where I could weep and remember. My heart was warmed again as I recalled that everything slopes down from Jesus.

For I determined not to know anything among you except Jesus Christ and Him crucified. 1 Corinthians 2:2 NKJV

Morris Venden is associate speaker of The Voice of Prophecy *radio broadcast.*

INDEX OF PERSONAL NAMES